Suspicious Minds

WHY WE BELIEVE
CONSPIRACY THEORIES

Rob Brotherton

BLOOMSBURY
sigma

Bloomsbury Sigma
An imprint of Bloomsbury Publishing Plc

1385 Broadway   50 Bedford Square
New York   London
NY 10018   WC1B 3DP
USA   UK

www.bloomsbury.com

BLOOMSBURY and the Diana logo are trademarks of
Bloomsbury Publishing Plc

First published 2015, Paperback edition 2016

© Rob Brotherton 2015

Rob Brotherton has asserted his right under the Copyright,
Design and Patents Act, 1988, to be identified as Author of this work.

British Library Cataloguing-in-Publication Data
A catalogue record for this book is available from the British Library.

Library of Congress Cataloging-in-Publication Data has been applied for.

ISBN (paperback) 978-1-4729-1563-4
ISBN (ebook) 978-1-4729-1564-1

2 4 6 8 10 9 7 5 3 1

Typeset in Bembo Std by Deanta Global Publishing Services, Chennai, India

Printed and bound by CPI Group (UK) Ltd, Croydon, CR0 4YY

Bloomsbury Sigma, Book Eight

MIX
Paper from
responsible sources
FSC® C020471

To find out more about our authors and books visit www.bloomsbury.com.
Here you will find extracts, author interviews, details of
forthcoming events and the option to sign up for our newsletters.

For Lindsay

Contents

Introduction: Down the Rabbit Hole

All is not as it seems. There is a hidden side to reality, a secret realm buzzing with clandestine activity and covert operations. This invisible network constantly screens, sifts, and manipulates information. It conjures up comforting lies to hide the real, bewildering truth. It steers what we think and believe, even shapes the decisions we make, molding our perception to its own agenda. Our understanding of the world, in short, is an illusion.

Who is behind this incredible scheme? Some sinister secret society? Psychopathic bureaucrats in smoke-filled boardrooms? The Queen of England? The intergalactic shape-shifting lizards who she works for? All of the above?

No. This is an inside job. It's not *them*—it's *us*. More specifically, it's you. More specifically, it's your brain.

Everything Is a Conspiracy

There's a conspiracy theory for everything. Ancient Atlanteans built the pyramids. Abraham Lincoln was assassinated on the orders of his vice president, Andrew Johnson. The Apollo moon landings were filmed on a sound stage in Arizona. Area 51 is home to advanced technology of alien origin. Alex Jones, a conspiracy-minded radio host based out of Austin, Texas, is actually the alter-ego of comedian Bill Hicks (who faked his death in the early 1990s to pursue a career in conspiracism). And then there's Big Pharma, black helicopters, the Bilderberg Group, Bohemian Grove . . .

The rabbit hole runs deep. The conspiracy allegedly extends to the air we breathe (tainted by chem-trails), the food we eat (monkeyed with by Monsanto), the medicine we take (filled with deadly toxins), and the water we drink (spiked with mind-warping fluoride). Elections are rigged, politics is a sham, and President Obama is a communist Muslim from Kenya.

These are a few of the *theories*, but who are the *theorists*? According to cliché, conspiracy theorists are a rare breed—a small but dedicated lunatic fringe of basement-dwelling, middle-aged men, intelligent outsiders with an idiosyncratic approach to research (and, often, a stockpile of Reynolds Wrap).

Most elements of the stereotype, however, don't hold up. On the whole, women are just as conspiracy-minded as men. Education and income don't make much difference either. The ranks of conspiracy theorists include slightly more high school dropouts than college graduates, but even professors, presidents, and Nobel Prize winners can succumb to conspiracism. And conspiracy theories appeal to all ages. Senior citizens are no more or less conspiracy-minded than Millennials, on average. At the low end of the age bracket, legions of American teens suspect that Louis Tomlinson and Harry Styles of the inordinately popular boy band One Direction are secretly an item, and that the band's corporate overlords invented a fake girlfriend for Louis as part of the cover-up.

As for the idea that conspiracy theories are a fringe affair, nothing could be farther from the truth. All told, huge numbers of people are conspiracy theorists when it comes to one issue or another. According to polls conducted over the last decade or so, around half of Americans think their government is probably hiding the truth about the 9/11 attacks. Almost four in ten suspect that climate change is a scientific fraud. Something like a third believe the government is likely hiding evidence of aliens. More than a quarter are worried about the New World Order. In a 2013 survey, 4 percent of the people polled (which, extended to the entire population of the United States, would mean twelve *million* people) said they think "shape-shifting reptilian people control our world by taking on human form and gaining political power to manipulate our societies." A further 7 percent said they just weren't sure.

These sorts of public opinion polls, it's worth bearing in mind, only provide a rough indication of any particular theory's popularity. Estimates vary depending on exactly who you ask, how you ask them, and when. But this much is crystal clear: There are more conspiracy theorists out there than you might expect. Chances are you know some. Chances are you are one.

It's not just Americans. People in the United Kingdom and Europe are similarly suspicious. And it's not just Westerners. Conspiracism is a global phenomenon. According to a 2011 Pew Research Center survey, between half and three quarters of people in various Middle Eastern countries doubt that Arab hijackers pulled off the 9/11 attacks. In many parts of the world, vaccines and other Western medicines are viewed with suspicion. Four out of ten Russians think that America faked the moon landings, according to a 2011 poll. In India, shortly after the country's prime minister, Indira Gandhi, was assassinated in 1984, her successor told an audience of a hundred thousand people gathered in New Delhi, "the assassination of Indira Gandhi is the doing of a vast conspiracy whose object is to weaken and divide India." And in Brazil, a popular conspiracy theory asserts that the American military is planning to invade the Amazon rain forest and take control of its rich natural resources. As part of the propaganda campaign to prepare American citizens for the impending invasion, the theory goes, maps of South America in American junior high school textbooks show a huge swath of the Amazon under the control of the United Nations.

So, *was* there a gunman on the Grassy Knoll? Is Elvis alive, relaxing by the pool with Jim Morrison, Marilyn Monroe, and Princess Diana in some secret resort for aggressively reclusive stars? Who really rules the world, and what did they do with flight MH370?

If you're looking for answers to these questions, then I'm afraid you've picked up the wrong book. The truth might be out there, but it's not in here. If there really are sinister schemes taking shape behind closed doors at this very moment, if the real perpetrators of atrocities have not yet been brought to justice, if everything we think we know is a lie—it'd be nice to know. But there are plenty of other books dedicated to compiling evidence of some alleged conspiracy, and almost as many books that purport to tear the theories to shreds. That's not what this one is about. In fact, this book isn't really about conspiracy theories at all (though we'll encounter plenty of theories along the way). It's about conspiracy *thinking*—about what psychology can reveal about how we decide what is reasonable and what is ridiculous, and why some people believe things that, to other people, seem completely unbelievable.

Of course, if you ask someone why they believe—or why they *don't* believe—some theory or other, they'll probably tell you it's simple: They've made up their mind based on the evidence. But psychology tells a different story. It turns out that we're not always the best judge of why we believe what we believe.

Tidy Desk, Tidy Mind (or: The Unexpected Virtue of Neatness)

In a recent experiment, psychologists at the University of Amsterdam had students think about something that they felt ambivalent about—any topic about which they had both positive and negative feelings. Imagine, for instance, eating an entire tub of ice cream. It would be a nice way to spend twenty minutes, but it'd also be pretty bad for you in the long run. You know there are pros and cons. That's ambivalence.

Each student sat at a computer, thought about whatever it was that made him or her feel ambivalent, and typed up a few of the pros and cons. At that point, an error message appeared on the screen. Fear not—it was all part of the psychologists' devious plan. The researcher monitoring the experiment feigned surprise, and told the participant that they would have to complete the next (ostensibly unrelated) questionnaire at a different desk. The unwitting subject was led to a cubicle across the room, where they encountered a desk in disarray, strewn with pens, books, magazines, and crumpled pieces of paper. Then, nestled comfortably amid the detritus, the participant was shown a series of pictures.

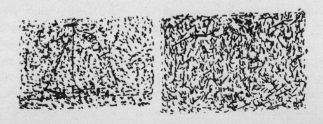

Some pictures, like the one on the left, had a faintly discernible image—in this case, a sailboat. Others, like the one on the right, consisted of nothing but random splotches. The students weren't told which were which; they simply had to say whether they saw a pattern in the static. Pretty much everyone spotted the boat and all the other real pictures. More interestingly, a lot of the time people said they saw images where, in reality, there was only randomness. There were twelve pictures that contained nothing but random blobs. On average, the students saw imaginary images in nine of them.

At least, that's how the experiment went for one group of students. For another group, things started out pretty much the same. They had to think about something that made them ambivalent, they saw an error message, they were led to the messy cubicle. Then there was one crucial difference. Before carrying on with the experiment, the experimenter asked each student to help tidy up the mess. Once the desk was straightened up, the students saw those same pictures. Compared to students who had worked amid the clutter, these students consistently saw fewer phantom images. They saw imaginary patterns in just five of the twelve meaningless pictures, on average—which was about the same number as people who hadn't been made to feel ambivalent at the start of the experiment.

Feeling conflicting emotions about something is unpleasant, the researchers explained. We habitually seek order and consistency, and to be ambivalent is to experience disorder and conflict. When that happens, we might try to change our beliefs, or simply ignore the issue. Or we can use more roundabout strategies to deal with our unwanted emotions. Ambivalence threatens our sense of order, so, to compensate, we can seek order elsewhere. This is why the first group of students saw so many imaginary images. Seeing meaning in the ambiguous splotches—connecting the dots—allowed them to satisfy the craving for order that had been triggered by their sense of ambivalence. And it also explains why the second group of students saw fewer imaginary images. The simple act of tidying the desk—transforming the chaos into order—had already satisfied their craving. They were no longer on the lookout for patterns in the static. They didn't need the dots to be connected.

What does this have to do with conspiracy theories? In another experiment, the researchers again made people feel ambivalent. This time, instead of looking at strange pictures, the students were asked to imagine they had been passed over for a promotion at work. What are the chances, the researchers asked, that a conniving co-worker had a hand in the boss's decision? Compared to a group of people who hadn't been made to feel ambivalent, the ambivalent students were more likely to suspect that a conspiracy was afoot. Sometimes, it would seem, buying into a conspiracy is the cognitive equivalent of seeing meaning in randomness.

A bit of clutter isn't the only thing that can subtly influence our beliefs. In another recent study, almost two hundred students at a college in London were asked simply to rate how plausible they found a handful of popular conspiracy theories. For half of the students, the allegations were written in an easy-to-read font—regular old Arial, size twelve, like so:

A powerful and secretive group, known as the New World Order, are planning to eventually rule the world through an autonomous world government, which would replace sovereign government.

For the other half of the students, however, the allegations were written in a font that was a little harder to read, like so:

A powerful and secretive group, known as the New World Order, are planning to eventually rule the world through an autonomous world government, which would replace sovereign government.

The students who read the theories in the clear, legible font consistently rated them more likely to be true. The students who had the harder-to-read font found the claims harder to believe.

The remarkable thing is that if you were to ask the students who took part why they rated the conspiracy theories the way they did, they might have told you something like "I heard a rumor about the New World Order the other day," or "Conspiracies happen all the time," or "It just makes sense that people are up to no good." None of the Dutch students would have told you that feeling ambivalent about a bowl of ice cream had influenced their judgment. None of the Londoners thought to themselves, "This is an attractive font, so I suppose the New World Order really is planning to take over." They didn't consciously choose to see the theories as more or less plausible. Their brains did most of the work behind the scenes.

Who Is Pulling the Strings?

As neuroscientist David Eagleman points out in *Incognito: The Secret Lives of the Brain*, there is a complicated network of machinery hidden just beneath your skin. Your body is chock-full of organs, each with its own special job to do, all working together to keep you alive and healthy, and they manage it without any conscious input from you. Whether you're paying attention or not, your heart keeps on beating, your blood vessels expand and contract, and your spleen does whatever *it* does. Our detailed scientific understanding of how the body works is a relatively recent development, and yet, for some reason, the idea that our organs can go about their business without us telling them to do it, or even being aware of what they're up to, doesn't strike us as particularly hard to believe.

Your *brain* seems different, though. The brain is the most complicated organ of them all. It is made up of billions of specialized cells, each one in direct communication with thousands of others, all ceaselessly firing off electrical signals in cascading flurries of activity. Somehow—it's still largely a mystery—out of this chaos arises *consciousness*: our experience of being *us*, of being a thinking, feeling, deciding person, residing just behind our eyes, looking out on the world, making important decisions like when to cross the road and where to go for lunch. Consciousness is all we know about what's going on inside our head, and it feels like it's all there *is* to know. Masses of psychological studies, however, lead to a surprising conclusion. Consciousness is not the whole story. We are not privy to everything—or even most—of what our brain is up to. The brain, like its fellow organs, is primarily in the business of keeping us alive, and, also like its less mysterious colleagues, the brain doesn't need much input from us to get the job done. All sorts of activity goes on behind the scenes, outside of our conscious awareness and entirely beyond our control.

But just because our brain doesn't let us in on all of its antics doesn't mean its subconscious processes are unimportant or inconsequential. On the contrary, our perception, thoughts, beliefs, and decisions are all shaped by our brain's secret shenanigans. Imaginative psychologists have come up with various metaphors for our mistaken intuition that we're aware of—and in control of—everything that happens in our brain. As David Eagleman put it, "Your consciousness is like a tiny stowaway on a transatlantic steamship, taking credit for the journey without acknowledging the massive engineering underfoot." Social scientist Jonathan Haidt likened consciousness to a rider on the back of an elephant: The rider can coax and cajole the elephant to go one direction or another by pulling on the reins, but at the end of the day, the elephant has whims of its own, and it's bigger than we are. Daniel Kahneman, one of the pioneers of the psychology of our brain's hidden biases and shortcuts, described the division of labor between our conscious and unconscious mental processes in cinematic terms. "In the unlikely event" of a movie being made in which our brain's two modes of activity were the main characters, consciousness "would be a supporting character who believes herself to be the hero," Kahneman wrote.

I'd like to propose a similar metaphor, one more in keeping with our theme. We imagine ourselves to be puppet masters, in full control of our mental faculties. In reality, however, we're the puppet, tethered to our silent subconscious by invisible strings, dancing to its whims and then taking credit for the choreography ourselves.

Suspicious Minds

Does this mean that conspiracy theories are inherently irrational, nutty, harebrained, confused, crackpot, or pathological? Some pundits enthusiastically heap this kind of scorn and ridicule on conspiracy theories, painting them as the product of faulty thinking, which disbelievers are presumably immune to. Because of this dim view, tensions between conspiracy theorists and their critics can run high. As far as some conspiracy theorists are concerned, looking for psychological reasons for believing conspiracy theories is worse than simply challenging them on their facts. It can seem like an attempt to smear believers' credibility, or even to write conspiracy theorists off as mentally unbalanced.

That's not my goal. This book isn't about listing conspiracy theories like some catalog of bizarre beliefs. It's not about singling out conspiracy theorists as a kind of alien species, or as a cautionary tale about how not to think. The scientific findings we've amassed over the last few years tell a much more interesting story—one that has implications for us all. Michael Billig, an early trailblazer of research into conspiracy thinking, warned that when it comes to conspiracism, "it is easy to overemphasise its eccentricities at the expense of noticing what is psychologically commonplace." Conspiracy theories might be a result of some of our brain's quirks and foibles, but, as we'll see, they are by no means unique in that regard. Most of our quirks simply slide by unnoticed. Psychology can tell us a lot—not only about why people believe theories about grand conspiracies, but about how everyone's mind works, and about why we believe anything at all.

So here's my theory. We are each at the mercy of a hundred billion tiny conspirators, a cabal of conspiring neurons. Throughout this book, we'll be pulling back the curtain, shining a light into the shadowy recesses of our mind, and revealing how our brain's secret shenanigans can shape the way we think about conspiracy theories—and a whole lot else besides. Whether conspiracy theories reflect what's really going on in the world or not, they tell us a lot about our secret selves. Conspiracy theories resonate with some of our brain's built-in biases and shortcuts, and tap into some of our deepest desires, fears, and assumptions about the world and the people in it. We have innately suspicious minds. We are all natural-born conspiracy theorists.

CHAPTER ONE
The Age of Conspiracy

"This is the age of conspiracy," a character in Don DeLillo's *Running Dog* intones, ominously—"the age of connections, links, secret relationships." The quote has featured in countless books and essays on contemporary conspiracism, reflecting a belief, widely held among laypeople and scholars alike, that conspiracy theories have never been more popular than they are right now. As one scholar put it, "other centuries have only dabbled in conspiracy like amateurs. It is our century which has established conspiracy as a system of thought and a method of action."

There's no shortage of guesses about what ushered in this alleged golden age of conspiracism. The prime suspect, as far as many twenty-first-century pundits are concerned, is the rise of the Internet. Political scientist Jodi Dean began an article published in the year 2000 by asserting that "as the global networks of the information age become increasingly entangled, many of us are overwhelmed and undermined by an all-pervasive uncertainty." Presumably things have only gotten worse since then; a 2015 study of the spread of conspiracy theories on social media dubbed this the "Age of Misinformation."

Other pundits point to tangible events. For journalist Jonathan Kay, the collapse of the Twin Towers opened up "nothing less than a countercultural rift," a sort of intellectual black hole that has sucked in "a wide range of political paranoiacs." Others trace the rise of conspiracism back farther. Maybe it started in the 1970s, with a crisis of faith in government that followed the unraveling of Richard Nixon's paranoia-tinged presidency. Or maybe the sixties, and the collective loss of innocence that came with the death of John F. Kennedy and the escalating debacle of Vietnam. Or maybe it began with the creeping Cold War paranoia of the fifties.

Until recently, this kind of hand-waving guesswork was all we had to go on. But in 2014, two political scientists, Joe Uscinski and Joseph Parent, undertook an inventive and ambitious project to find some solid answers.

It's not immediately obvious how to go about measuring the rise and fall of conspiracy thinking over a long stretch of time. In our digital age, getting an idea of what people are talking about is as easy as checking which hashtags are trending or how many "likes" a Facebook page gets. It's less obvious how we might figure out how much people were talking about conspiracies a century ago. But Uscinski and Parent realized that our analog ancestors left behind a rich trove of data: letters to the editor. The letters page of the newspaper, it's fair to say, is often overlooked, and is sometimes seen as a repository for the emotional outbursts of cranks. Yet social analysts have shown that letters to the editor are a good barometer of public opinion writ large, and therefore an invaluable research tool.

And so Uscinski and Parent set about analyzing more than a century's worth of letters to the editor published in the *New York Times*. They gathered a sample of a thousand letters per year, from 1890 to 2010, amounting to more than a hundred thousand letters in total. Then a team of well-trained (and, hopefully, well-compensated) research assistants painstakingly combed through each letter, checking for conspiracy theories. It didn't matter if a letter was promoting or debunking a conspiracy theory; either way, Uscinski and Parent reasoned, reciting the theory shows that the writer deemed it a topic worthy of discussion, and that the editor deemed it important enough to everyone else to be worth publishing.

Out of the hundred thousand or so letters, 875 mentioned conspiracies. At less than 1 percent of the entire sample, that might seem like a tiny fraction—but, as Uscinski and Parent point out, the letters page is open to any subject under the sun. It's no surprise that singling out any particular niche, be it conspiracies or comedy or cooking, results in a relatively small slice of the pie.

In terms of the allegations that the letter writers were throwing around, the researchers discovered some real peaches. Among the accused conspirators there were all the usual suspects, such as presidents, big business, and the media, as well as a fascinating array of lesser-spotted culprits, including dairy farmers, post office workers, the Walt Disney Company. In the 1890s, people worried that England and Canada were conspiring to reclaim territory from the United States, or that Mormons were rigging elections in favor of Republicans. For the first few decades of the twentieth century, typical theories involved financial interests attempting to subvert democracy. From the thirties until the sixties, many of the alleged plots featured communists. For the last fifty years or so, suspicion has shifted toward the American government itself, particularly its various intelligence agencies.

So what about the questions at hand? Has talk of conspiracies increased since the Second World War? Did it gain traction with the Kennedy assassination, the Watergate scandal, or the 9/11 attacks? Has it skyrocketed since the advent of the Internet? "Despite popular hoopla," Uscinski and Parent report, the answer to all these questions was a resounding no.

There were a couple of bumper years for conspiracy theories, but they weren't the ones you might expect. The number of conspiracy-themed letters shot up in the mid-1890s, when fears about big business flourished, and in 1950, when the Red Scare hit fever pitch. But these spikes were short-lived, and the number of letters quickly fell back to baseline. There has been no exponential increase over the years. If anything, people are talking about conspiracies a little *less* than they used to. The researchers counted slightly fewer conspiracy-themed letters per year, on average, in the five decades since the Kennedy assassination compared to the seven decades before it. The overall trend, however, was long-term stability. The amount of conspiracy talk was, for the most part, a stable background hum, remarkably impervious to political events, the economy, or advances in communication technology.

"The data suggest one telling fact," Uscinski and Parent concluded. "We do not live in an age of conspiracy theories and have not for some time." So if our current fascination with conspiracies is not new, how far back does it go? Pretty far, it turns out.

While Rome Burned

July 19, C.E. 64, was a scorching summer's day in Rome, according to historian Stephen Dando-Collins. It was the eve of

the Ludi Victoriae Caesaris, the immensely popular annual
Roman Games. The Circus Maximus, a giant stadium with
capacity for a quarter of a million spectators, was already being
prepared, and visitors were flocking into the city. That evening
the fast-food joints that lined the narrow streets around the
stadium stoked their ovens, busily preparing to feed the dawn
crowds. It is impossible to say where exactly, but somewhere in
the vicinity of the stadium, a fire broke out. Fires were not
uncommon in Ancient Rome, but this one proved to be different.
Fanned by strong wind, the blaze quickly spread through the
narrow, winding streets, consuming the tightly packed buildings.
The inferno, which would become known as the Great Fire of
Rome, raged on for almost a week. Countless people died in the
flames, and half the city's population was made homeless. All
told, two thirds of the city was reduced to rubble and ash.

Even before the embers had cooled, conspiracy theories
began to spread. Suspicion immediately settled on the emperor,
Nero. According to the Roman historian Tacitus, who had
lived through the fire as a child, "nobody dared fight the flames.
Attempts to do so were prevented by menacing gangs. Torches,
too, were openly thrown in, by men crying that they acted
under orders." As for Nero, Tacitus reports that he had been
thirty-six miles away, in his hometown of Antium, when the
fire broke out. When he got back to the city, he quickly organized shelter and food for the homeless masses. Yet his relief
efforts earned him little gratitude from the public. Rumors were
already spreading that while the city was burning, the young,
immature, self-involved emperor had been in Antium giving a
singing recital.

Tacitus stayed on the fence about Nero's involvement in the
fire, reporting the rumors without explicitly endorsing them.
Others were less reserved. Suetonius, who was born five years
after the fire, had at one time been a respected historian with
unfettered access to Rome's official archives. After offending
Emperor Hadrian, possibly by having an affair with the empress,
his access to the archives was revoked. As a result, his biography
of Nero, written fifty years after the fire, was based largely on
gossip. "Pretending to be disgusted by the drab old buildings
and narrow, winding streets of Rome," Seutonius wrote, Nero
"brazenly set fire to the city. Although a party of ex-consuls

caught his attendants, armed with [kindling] and blazing torches, trespassing on their property, they dare not interfere." In a dramatic flourish, Suetonius adds that, after arriving back from Antium, "Nero watched the conflagration from the Tower of Maecenas, enraptured by what he called 'the beauty of the flames,' then put on his tragedian's costume and sang 'The Sack of Ilium' from beginning to end."

Cassius Dio, writing 165 years after the fire, went even farther, claiming that Nero had a team of well-organized lackeys torch the city out of sheer malice. Dio was clearly taken by the idea of Nero singing with demented glee while the city burned around him, too, and added embellishments of his own. His melodramatic retelling of the fire is worth quoting at length:

> Nero set his heart on accomplishing what had doubtless always been his desire, namely to make an end of the whole city and realm during his lifetime . . . Accordingly he secretly sent out men who pretended to be drunk or engaged in other kinds of mischief, and caused them to first set fire to one or two or even several buildings in different parts of the city, so that the people were at their wits' end, not being able to find any beginning of the trouble nor to put an end to it . . . While the whole population was in this state of mind and many, crazed by the disaster, were leaping into the very flames, Nero went up to the roof of the palace, from which there was the best general view of the greater part of the conflagration, and assuming the lyre-player's garb, he sang the *Capture of Troy*, as he styled the song himself, though to the eyes of the spectators it was the Capture of Rome.

Whether the fire was an inside job or not, and whether Nero really serenaded it with his lyre, we do know this: He was not happy to be the subject of conspiracy theories. In an effort to scotch the rumors, he came up with a conspiracy theory of his own. According to Tacitus, "Nero fastened the guilt and inflicted the most exquisite tortures on a class hated for their abominations, called Christians by the populace." False confessions were forced out of a few Christians, on the basis of which many more were rounded up. They were convicted, Tacitus reports, "not so much of the crime of firing the city, as of hatred against mankind." Nero's treatment of the scapegoats was ruthless. "Mockery of every sort was added to their deaths," Tacitus reports. "Covered with the skins of beasts, they were torn by dogs and perished, or were nailed to crosses, or were doomed to the flames and burnt, to serve as a nightly illumination, when daylight had expired."

The Great Fire was far from the only event in Roman history that gave rise to conspiracy theories. Rome's infatuation with conspiracy goes back to the very beginning of the empire. Romulus, one of the city's founders and its first king, supposedly disappeared under mysterious circumstances. It was rumored that his political advisers, the senators, had assassinated their leader in a bid to increase their own power. Cassius Dio described the deed in his signature lurid style, writing that the power-hungry senators had surrounded Romulus as he was giving a speech, and "rent him limb from limb" right there on the floor of the senate-house. Adding an ironic twist, Dio claimed that the deed had been concealed "by a violent wind storm and an eclipse of the sun—the same sort of phenomenon that had attended his birth. Such was the end of Romulus." As historian Victoria Pagán has cataloged, the entire history of ancient Rome is suffused with stories about suspected plots. Many of the stories were based on truth; assassinations and other nefarious schemes were par for the course in ancient Roman politics. But many—such as the sensational rumors of Nero's pyromania or Romulus's dramatic demise—were unquestionably embellished, or fabricated entirely.

It wasn't just Rome. The ancient world was teeming with conspiracies and conspiracy theories. Going back at least as far as the fifth century B.C.E., historian Joseph Roisman points out that the work of the famed orators and playwrights of ancient Athens was riddled with "tales of plotting that involve almost every facet of Athenian life. There are plots against people's lives, property, careers, or reputations, as well as against the public interest, the regime, and in foreign affairs." Just about everyone was on the receiving end of charges of conspiracy, from politicians and businessmen to immigrants and slaves, and both the establishment and the masses seem to have taken such stories seriously.

Fascination with conspiracy endured throughout the Middle Ages. As before, conspiracy theories were popular among the unwashed masses and the aristocratic establishment alike. Famine-struck peasants often saw their plight not as "simply the result of bad weather, or poor distribution methods, but of the nefarious actions of speculators," as historians Barry Coward and Julian Swann put it, while the ruling elite frequently blamed unwelcome change on "the plotting of courtiers, ministers, favourites, heretics or freemasons." Though the names and dates changed, the thread of conspiracism runs unbroken through the centuries. Coward and Swann point out that "English MPs in the early seventeenth century, for example, often drew on Tacitus and Roman history to interpret the politics of their own day."

The Great Fire of London, which ravaged the city for four days in the year 1666, offers a striking example of history repeating itself and conspiracism regurgitating itself. Even as the fire was still raging, Samuel Pepys noted in his diary that rumors had begun to flourish "that there is a plot in it." There were those who suspected it was an inside job, started on the orders of King Charles II himself—some even drew "an odious parallel between his Majesty and Nero," according to a contemporary report. Others suspected that the fire was a terrorist attack by Catholic conspirators or England's European enemies. A Frenchman, Robert Hubert, was soon arrested, and confessed to having started the fire acting in league with a cabal of French popish spies. His confession didn't quite stack up. For instance, he claimed at first to have started the fire in Westminster. When he was informed that the fire had actually started on Pudding Lane, and had never even reached Westminster, his story changed. Regardless, Londoners—and the authorities—seized the opportunity to lay blame for the fire at the feet of a willing scapegoat. With his questionable confession as the only evidence against him, Hubert was hanged on October 27, 1666, in front of a mob of delighted spectators.

As this potted history goes to show, the golden age of conspiracy theories goes back thousands of years, and shows no sign of letting up. Some of the theories of antiquity bear a remarkable resemblance to contemporary conspiracy theories. There are some noteworthy differences, however. For classical conspiracy theorists, alleged plots generally concerned local, isolated issues, and the motives behind the ostensible plots were fairly petty and personal. It's also worth noting that, even though many of the theories were unquestionably embellished, they weren't *all that* farfetched. When absolute power was invested in emperors or monarchs, taking up cloak and dagger against them was often the only way to effect any meaningful change.

Over time, people's conspiratorial concerns broadened. There was a shift from theories about local and petty conspiracies of self-interest, to altogether grander theories. The proposed plots became more mysterious, subversive, and universal. The conspirators were imagined to be working toward less tangible, and more sinister, ends.

The road from the trivial theories of old to the all-consuming theories of today was marked by two major milestones, the first of which came courtesy of a young German idealist named Adam Weishaupt.

Illuminati Panic

In 1772, following in the footsteps of both his father and godfather, Adam Weishaupt became a professor of law at the University of Ingolstadt in Bavaria. Law was never his real passion, though. At just twenty-four years of age, Weishaupt was restless and idealistic. Disillusioned with his strict, mechanical Jesuit education, and inspired by the blossoming Enlightenment, he had developed a headstrong ambition to improve society using the power of reason to dispel religious superstition. He was also a "cynical and unscrupulous careerist and liar," the historian John Roberts wrote; "All the evidence of this period of his career reveals him as a familiar hazard of academic and collegiate life: the clever, cantankerous, self-absorbed and self-deceiving bore."

According to Roberts, Weishaupt's true passion was for intrigue. From an early age, he had been fascinated by secret societies like the Pythagorean Brotherhood. He joined a Masonic lodge in 1774, but found himself disappointed by the Freemasons' lack of political aspirations or genuine secrecy, and by the high membership fees. He decided to start a secret society of his own. The inaugural meeting was held on May 1, 1776, with just Weishaupt and four of his students in attendance. He called it the Order of the Illuminati.

Weishaupt's dual personality was woven into the fabric of the Illuminati. Its philosophy was idealistic to the point of naïveté. The sole goal of the order, according to the statutes Weishaupt drew up, was "to render unto man the importance of the perfection of reason and his moral character . . . to oppose the wicked designs in the world, to assist against the injustice suffered by the unfortunate and the oppressed, to encourage men of merit, and in general to facilitate the means of knowing and science." On the other hand, being the supreme leader of his very own secret society allowed Weishaupt to indulge his taste for attention and subterfuge. He carefully curated an aura of mystery for his sect. Initiates were required to take false names, learn a secret vocabulary, go through an elaborate set of initiation rites, and were instructed to sever ties with family and friends. To recruit new initiates, Weishaupt had Illuminati members infiltrate Masonic lodges and pick off their members. Weishaupt developed an elaborate hierarchy, which was itself concealed from all but the most senior members. Advancement required complete, unquestioning obedience. The true political goals of the order—the peaceful transformation of society—were only gradually revealed as a member climbed up the many ranks.

By the early 1780s, the order had gained around three hundred members spread across Europe. But the expansion came at the cost of secrecy. Weishaupt's pedantic, domineering personality rubbed some recruits the wrong way. A few members spilled the beans about Illuminati activity to nonmembers, often with alarming exaggerations. By 1784, rumors about the order had caught the attention of the authorities. The Bavarian government issued an edict banning unauthorized associations, and Weishaupt suspended the Illuminati's meetings. Material continued to leak, and scurrilous rumors were increasingly published by journalists and repeated by preachers, accusing the Illuminati of "irreligion, disloyalty to the dynasty, political intrigue and moral corruption."

In a last-ditch effort to exonerate his order, Weishaupt personally approached Charles Theodore, Elector of Bavaria, and told him most of the Illuminati's secrets. It proved to be in vain. On March 2, 1785, Theodore issued another edict, specifically condemning the Illuminati. Weishaupt fled Bavaria. Investigations commenced, arrests were made, and masses of the

Illuminati's secret documents, including Weishaupt's personal letters, were published for all to see. The Illuminati was gone—but not forgotten.

The discovery of a very real secret society with very real political aspirations, combined with the many horribly embellished rumors about its sordid, subversive activity, was a recipe for confusion and alarm. Already it was rumored that Weishaupt's secret society continued to operate, and had simply gone underground. Freed from the hassle of actually existing, the Illuminati grew to mythic proportions in the fretful imaginations of its critics—not only in Bavaria, but across Europe and as far afield as the newly independent United States. The exposure of Weishaupt's Illuminati tarnished the reputation of the Freemasons, too. A few lodges really had been infiltrated, after all—and who was to say that all the Illuminati operatives had been ferreted out. The conspiratorial machinations of subversive secret societies increasingly looked like a viable explanation for troubling events. And then the French Revolution happened.

"It is very easy today to underrate the emotional shock of the French Revolution," Roberts notes. "Because it opened an era of revolution in which we still live, we are used to the idea of revolution in a way in which the men of the eighteenth century were not." Over the course of ten violent, chaotic years, between 1789 and 1799, the age-old ways of hereditary aristocratic privilege crumbled, to be replaced with a new, more egalitarian, secular society. The revolutionary ideas began to spread across Europe, and soon millions of people had been granted basic human rights that they had never before enjoyed, while the aristocracy suddenly found their power and wealth decimated. It was a profound and unprecedented transformation—the rapid emergence of an entirely new political reality. People understandably struggled to come to terms with it. "The scale and violence of the changes . . . seemed to exhaust all conventional and familiar categories of explanation," Roberts wrote. "Some new dimension of understanding was needed."

At the tail end of the Revolution, in 1797, two authors published, almost simultaneously, books that provided that new dimension of understanding. One was Augustin de Barruel. Barruel was a French nobleman, an ordained Jesuit priest, and a polemicist. He had already earned some literary success for his publications criticizing the Enlightenment philosophy, based on his staunch religious views. In 1789, the year the French Revolution broke out, Barruel had published a pamphlet blaming it on the corrupting ideology of the Enlightenment and the weakness of the French clergy. But by 1797, when he published the first two volumes of his *Memoirs Illustrating the History of Jacobinism*, Barruel had become convinced that the whole thing had actually been carefully engineered from behind the scenes. "Even the most horrid deeds perpetrated during the French Revolution, every thing was foreseen and resolved on, was premeditated and combined," he wrote; "they were the offspring of deep-thought villainy." The villains, he claimed, included the Enlightenment Philosophes, the Freemasons, and the Jacobins. But these groups, Barruel wrote, were only the "most obvious villains in a great plot whose authors and agents have been far longer at work and are far more widespread." Lurking behind them all, coordinating the whole scheme, Barruel said, was an even more powerful, sinister enemy: Adam Weishaupt's dreaded Illuminati, whose "aim is not merely the destruction of the French monarch but universal dissolution, the overthrow of society and religion itself."

Scotsman John Robison, a professor of natural philosophy at the University of Edinburgh, had the same idea. He published his book shortly after Barruel, under the snappy title *Proofs of a Conspiracy against all the Religions and Governments of Europe, carried on in the Secret Meetings of Free-Masons, Illuminati and Reading Societies, etc., Collected from good authorities*. Though Robison disagreed with Barruel over a few of the details, his premise was the same. The Illuminati was behind the French Revolution, he said, and it was only their first step toward inciting total, world-wide anarchy. According to Robison, the Illuminati leaders "disbelieved *every word* that they uttered, and every doctrine that they taught . . . Their real intention was to abolish *all* religion, overturn every government, and make the world a general plunder and a wreck." In case his readers weren't alarmed enough, Robison warned that the Illuminati "still exists, still works in secret . . . Its emissaries are endeavoring to propagate their detestable doctrines among us."

Nothing Barruel or Robison had to say was particularly original, Roberts notes. Even since the earliest years of the

Revolution, rumors had circulated that the Masons or some other secret sect had a hand in it. Robison and Barruel's genius was not for invention, but integration. They took all the existing plot theories and wove them together into a single grand theory. It not only explained the entire French Revolution, but had the potential to explain just about anything that had happened in the world, past, present, or future. The clear, comprehensive conspiracy theory Barruel and Robison articulated resonated perfectly with the fears and needs of the moment. Despite being riddled with factual errors and logical missteps, both books were quickly reprinted, translated, and exported around Europe and across the Atlantic to America.

The foundations of modern conspiracism had been laid. The petty plots of the eighteenth century and earlier could now blossom into an all-consuming political vision.

All things considered, though, the Illuminati panic was short-lived. Once thought to be the architects of revolutions, nowadays Weishaupt's order has been demoted to managing the careers of pop stars. Musicians like Jay Z, Lady Gaga, Kanye West, and Kesha have all been branded "Illuminati puppets," and accused of "poisoning the youth of the world with traumatic mind-control performances." To be fair, some musicians do seem to have a penchant for arcane symbolism. Jay Z's signature "Roc" hand gesture, for instance, echoes the Masonic pyramid and all-seeing eye. The trend may have jumped the shark in early 2015, however, when Madonna released a song called "Illuminati." Asked about the track in interviews, Madonna revealed, "I know who the real Illuminati are, and where that word came from." It essentially just means a group of smart people, she asserted; the message of the song is, "So, if you think I'm the Illuminati, then thank you very much, a compliment, because I would like very much to be part of that group, the real Illuminati."

Whatever: The reason the Illuminati panic died down fairly quickly, sociologists Seymour Lipset and Earl Raab speculated, is that a successful conspiracy theory needs two elements. One is the "mysterious cabal" thought to be pulling the strings. But it also needs "some less mysterious, more visible target group associated with the cabal." A conspiracy theory about some far-flung popish plot, for instance, will only really take off if you have a few Catholic immigrants who can act as ambassadors, personifying the threat, making it tangible. The real-life Illuminati scandal was still on people's minds when they were grasping for explanations for the French Revolution. Within a few years, however, the Illuminati was little more than a memory.

The second milestone in the evolution of the modern conspiracy theory came with the concoction of a new mysterious cabal. Unlike Weishaupt's Illuminati—which was guilty, at least, of having actually existed—this new cabal was entirely imaginary. Its unfortunate ambassadors, however, were all too real.

The Wise Men of Zion

The *Protocols of the Learned Elders of Zion* makes for a meager pamphlet, filling just eighty pages or so. But its diminutive size belies the monumental revelations inside. The *Protocols* outlines a conspiracy of apocalyptic scale, dating back eons and coming tantalizingly, terrifyingly close to completion. And this is no mere exposé, cobbled together by some outside party. It is a confession dictated by the conspirators themselves—the minutes of a secret meeting of the supreme council of worldwide Jewry, the eponymous Elders of Zion. The lecture notes were intended for Jewish eyes only, of course, but a copy somehow turned up in print in Russia shortly after the turn of the twentieth century. Apparently the lecture had been overheard by a Russian spy—or, depending on who you listen to, a transcript was confiscated from an attendee, pilfered from some secret Zionist archive, or even pinched by the mistress of a philandering Elder.

The "protocols" themselves are twenty-four short sermons, delivered by the Chief Elder to his attentive colleagues, in which he spells out, in appalling detail, their plan for total world domination. The first protocol outlines the moral principles on which the scheme is founded. The "Goyim"—non-Jews—are unthinking barbarians, the Elder argues, lacking the keen intellect, good judgment, and self-control of the Jews. As a result, letting people govern themselves is like the blind leading the blind. The only viable form of government, he argues, is a tyrannical world dictatorship headed by Jews.

The subsequent protocols provide a helpful guidebook on how to subvert democracy and hasten its demise. All around the world, the *Protocols* instructs, Jews should sow the seeds of discord, fostering antipathy among races, classes, and nations. They must control the media, manipulate politics, and undermine religion by replacing it with ruthless materialism (the theory of evolution was invented by the Elders, apparently). And that's on a good day. When more drastic measures are called for, they will spread plagues and famines, conjure up recessions, assassinate heads of state, and start futile wars. The populace must be instilled with helpless dread, terrorized into submission. The trick, the *Protocols* says, is to do all this while remaining hidden until it is too late for the gentiles to do anything about it. Once their grip on the reins of society is sufficiently loosened, the Jews will sweep in and take charge. Under the Elders' rule, loyal citizens will spy on one another. The tyrants will exercise absolute control over every aspect of citizen's lives and stamp out any dissent instantly and ruthlessly. Anyone who acts, speaks, or even thinks anything contrary to the Jewish regime will be summarily executed.

This diabolical manifesto caught people's attention. The *Protocols* itself is conveniently vague, outlining the Elders' general strategies for world conquest, but omitting any specific names, dates, or locations. This meant it has proved infinitely adaptable. As Richard Levy put it, the *Protocols* offered up a "veritable Rosetta stone of history, the single key that unlocks all the perplexing mysteries of the modern world." Anything that happened in the world could be explained as the result of the Elders' secret machinations. Observant readers needed only fill in the blanks with whatever societal ill they wish to pin on the Jews. The French and Russian revolutions? Orchestrated by the Elders. The First and Second World Wars? Ditto. The economic crash of 1929 and the ensuing Great Depression? You guessed it. The wars in Korea, Vietnam, Afghanistan, Lebanon, and the Gulf? Elders, Elders, Elders. And they aren't only behind such lofty endeavors as igniting wars and revolutions. According to some of the *Protocols*' proponents, the Elders have a penchant for micromanagement. They've been accused of everything from popularizing jazz (of particular concern was "the abandoned sensuousness of sliding notes" and the "indecent dancing" that it encouraged) and distributing chewing gum (in an effort to make women more promiscuous), to encouraging prostitution, alcoholism, and even, for some reason, dog exhibitions.

The shocking revelations contained in the *Protocols*, coupled with its ability to explain any and all ills and upheavals in the world, earned it a place in history. The *Protocols* has been printed and reprinted around the world, in books with titles ranging from the relatively benign *Secrets of the Wise Men of Zion*, to the somewhat alarmist *The International Jew: The World's Foremost Problem* (a commentary published in the United States by Henry Ford), to the outright apocalyptic *The Jewish Antichrist and the Protocols of the Elders of Zion* (the title of an edition published in Nazi Germany in 1938). Millions of copies have been sold or given away. One scholar estimated in 1939 that, in terms of distribution, the *Protocols* was second only the Bible.

There's just one small problem, of course. There are no Elders. The *Protocols* is a fake. And not even a good fake. To quote the historian Norman Cohn, the *Protocols* is an "atrociously written piece of reactionary balderdash." It is a shoddy, obvious, callous forgery, wantonly and lazily plagiarized from a handful of more obscure sources. The story of the *Protocols'* creation is a tale of conspiratorial intrigue in its own right. But the *Protocols* didn't single-handedly invent the myth of the Jewish world conspiracy. It was centuries in the making.

The History of a Lie

Superstition and prejudice toward Jews dates back to the earliest years of Christianity. Saint John Chrysostom, a fourth-century preacher widely admired for his eloquence, eloquently denounced Jews as baby-killing devil worshipers. In 1215, Pope Innocent III was concerned that Christians might find themselves unwittingly having relations with Jews. His solution was to make Jews wear distinguishing clothing, leading to the yellow "badge of shame" that many Jewish people around Europe were required to wear throughout the Dark Ages—and again under the Nazis. A couple of decades later, Pope Gregory IX established the Inquisition, a formalized effort to prosecute heresy against the Roman Catholic Church, which eventually led to mass executions of Jews, among other accused heretics, and mass burnings of their holy books.

According to the pious logic of some medieval theologians, the Jewish Talmud was both blasphemous and, paradoxically, a testament to the truth of Christian teaching. Just as the Devil knows the truth of Christianity but is determined to deny it and destroy those who believe it, so too, Christian scholars argued, do the Jews. People came to see Jews as being in league with Satan, possessing arcane knowledge and black magic, and harboring an unquenchable hatred for Christianity. Allegations that Jewish people were plotting against Christians became commonplace.

One popular theory had it that Jews were in the habit of poisoning Christian drinking wells. When the Black Plague ravaged fourteenth-century Europe, outbreaks were often blamed on the international Jewish well-poisoning conspiracy. In some cases, torturers coerced confessions from a handful of Jewish suspects, on the basis of which thousands more were burned alive. The worst of the pogroms was in Strasbourg. Fear-stricken locals, desperate to prevent the plague from reaching them, decided to preemptively slaughter the town's Jews. (Some of the town's nobility were also in debt to Jewish money-lenders, and may have seen an opportunity to clear their tab.) City authorities attempted to intervene but couldn't hold the mob at bay. All told, around nine hundred Jewish people were burned alive, and the rest were baptized or banished. The plague soon swept through town regardless, leaving sixteen thousand people dead in its wake.

There was also the "blood libel"—the allegation that Jewish people routinely murder Christians and drain them of their blood, which they allegedly used to make the Passover meal, to make medicine to heal their physical defects, or to perform unholy rituals. The myth was invented in the twelfth century, when a young Christian boy was found dead on the outskirts of Norwich, England, the day before Easter Sunday. Thomas of Monmouth, a Benedictine monk turned amateur detective, offered a convoluted explanation. Jewish teaching, he claimed, asserts that Jews must spill Christian blood in order to regain their homeland. Thus, a secret council of Jewish elites convenes once a year to select a sacrificial Christian child. Monmouth's idea caught on. For centuries thereafter, whenever a Christian child went missing or turned up dead, local Jews were often the first suspects.

These religiously motivated fears circulated for centuries. Meanwhile, Jews in many regions were denied citizenship and property rights, confined to ghettos, or banished from Christian society altogether. This began to change in the wake of the French Revolution, when many Jewish people were granted basic human rights and began to emerge from isolation. They naturally tended to favor liberal and democratic political policies that represented their best hope of increasing liberty. Still sidelined from traditional occupations, many migrated to the cities and pioneered inventive new ways of making a living. While most remained impoverished and out of sight, a few became extremely wealthy.

This all led to new social tensions. A lot of people weren't thrilled about the radical changes taking place around them. For some, the newly integrated Jews became a defining symbol of the modern world. The age-old prejudice that had given rise to the blood libel and well-poisoning myths was reinvigorated and updated to reflect modern anxieties and resentments. Jews were no longer enemies of God, but enemies of man. In 1879, a new word, antisemitism, was coined to reflect the fact that what was once a collection of primitive medieval superstitions had become a fully-fledged political ideology.

The *Protocols* tapped into this new political antisemitism perfectly. It wasn't an instant hit, though. It was first published, in abbreviated form, in the Russian newspaper *Znamia* ("The Banner"), in 1903. The paper's publisher, Pavel Krushevan, was a member of the Black Hundreds, whose slogan was "kill the Jews, save Russia." The *Protocols* surfaced again in 1905, as an appendix in the third edition of a book published by an eccentric religious fanatic, Sergei Nilus. Nilus reissued the book several times over the coming decade, giving the *Protocols* pride of place. Despite his best efforts, however, the *Protocols* lingered in relative obscurity. In 1913, he lamented to a friend, "I cannot get the public to treat the *Protocols* seriously, with the attention they deserve."

Things changed in the aftermath of the Russian Revolution and the First World War. Suddenly the *Protocols* appeared prophetic. The *Protocols* swept Russia, and then the world. In the United States, Henry Ford became one of the *Protocols'* biggest supporters. His self-published antisemitic literature was given away at Ford dealerships. "The only statement I care to make about the *Protocols*," Ford declared, "is that they fit in with what is going on. They are sixteen years old and they have fitted the world situation up to this time. They fit it now." In England, the (now-defunct) *Morning Post* gave the *Protocols* its full backing in a series of articles, later published as a book titled *The Cause of World Unrest*. More reputable publications were taken in, too. The London *Times* prevaricated, "Are they a forgery? If so, whence comes the uncanny note of prophecy?"

Then, almost as quickly as it swept the world, the *Protocols* was debunked. As early as 1920, a German scholar, Joseph Stanjek, had pointed out the uncanny similarity between the meeting described in the *Protocols* and a work of fiction published fifty years earlier. The author of the earlier work, a German named Hermann Goedsche, was a "scandal-mongering writer of trashy novels," as one scholar put it. In a chapter of his 1868 novel *Biarritz* titled "In the Jewish Cemetery in Prague," Goedsche (writing under the pen name Sir John Retcliffe) revived Thomas of Monmouth's myth of the secret Jewish council in sensational style. Once every hundred years, Goedsche's story goes, princes of the twelve tribes of Israel meet under cover of darkness, their ceremonial robes gliding soundlessly over grass and tombstones. One by one, they report on the progress of their ancient plan for world domination. In the words of Herman Bernstein, an American journalist, it is "a clumsy piece of blood-curdling fiction of the dime-novel variety." In 1921, Bernstein published a book detailing the similarity between the *Protocols* and *Biarritz*. It was a clear-cut case of forgery, he said. "Every substantive statement contained in the *Protocols* and elaborated in them is to be found in the Goedsche-Retcliffe novelette."

More damning revelations were to come. Whoever wrote the *Protocols* hadn't just ripped off someone else's idea, they had stolen someone's words. Philip Graves, correspondent for the London *Times* in Istanbul, began his exposé of the *Protocols*,

THE AGE OF CONSPIRACY

published over the course of three days in August 1921, with an air of intrigue. He had been approached by a Russian exile, he reports, a "landowner with English connexions," who wished to remain anonymous. Mr X., as Graves refers to the man, came bearing a mysterious book: "a small volume in French, lacking the title page, with dimensions of 5 ½ in. by 3 ¾ in. It had been cheaply rebound. On the leather back is printed in Latin capitals the word 'Joli.'" Mr X. had attached a note. "Read this book through," it said, "and you will find irrefutable proof that the 'Protocols of the Learned Elders of Sion' is a plagiarism."

There's irony in the fact that the Protocols was plagiarized from a book with nothing at all to do with Jews—which was, in fact, a scathing critique of totalitarianism. The premise of the mysterious book, Graves explained, is an encounter between two historical figures, the dastardly Machiavelli and the liberal French philosopher Montesquieu, set on a desolate beach in Hell. A series of twenty-five dialogs ensues, in which Machiavelli cynically outlines the need for political leaders to employ dirty tactics to dominate their subjects. The dialogs were a thinly veiled satirical critique of the reign of Napoleon III, France's despotic emperor during the 1850s and '60s, with Machiavelli playing the part of Napoleon.

Graves laid out some of the incriminating passages, side by side, for comparison. Whole sections of the Protocols had been copied verbatim from this earlier work. Others parts were thinly paraphrased. The plagiarists, Graves notes, had barely made any effort to cover their tracks. It was as if someone had simply thumbed through this book, page by page, hastily paraphrasing or copying whatever took their fancy. At the time, Graves couldn't know the author of the mysterious book. It was soon identified, however, as the work of a Frenchman named Maurice Joly. A lawyer by profession, Joly was also a keen observer of politics. Aware that he could be imprisoned (or worse) if he published an allegorical attack on the emperor in France under his own name, he attempted to smuggle it in via Belgium. He was found out. The book was seized, and Joly spent time in prison. His book was lost to obscurity—until, that is, it fell into the hands of the men who used it to fabricate the Protocols.

Mr X. could only tell Graves that he had acquired the incriminating book from a former officer of the Okhrana, the Russian secret police. The same year, Princess Katerina Radziwill, a Russian exile living in New York, provided more pieces of the puzzle. In the 1890s, she had been close friends with Okhrana operatives in Paris. One day, an agent named Golovinskii showed her an unfinished, handwritten manuscript. She didn't know it at the time, but he was showing her a work-in-progress *Protocols*. He boasted that it was a forgery he was concocting to implicate the Jews in a worldwide conspiracy. Radziwill thought little of the incident at the time. The Okhrana often used forgeries to achieve unsavory political goals, and nobody in her circle took such forgeries very seriously, she said. She only recalled it more than two decades later, when she realized that the very same forgery had taken the world by storm, and was considered by many to be authentic.

So by the autumn of 1921, the sordid origins of the *Protocols* had been revealed. It had been produced in Paris, hastily cobbled together from two earlier books, sometime before the turn of the century, by Russian Okhrana operatives hoping to foment hatred of Jews in their homeland. Herman Bernstein titled his exposé *The History of a Lie*. The London *Times* published Graves's revelations under a headline declaring the *Protocols* a "Historic 'fake.'" An editorial published alongside his damning articles hoped that myth of the Elders might "be allowed to pass into oblivion." "So much for the *Protocols*," Graves concluded.

Unfortunately, that was not to be the end of the *Protocols*.

CHAPTER TWO

What's the Harm?

Shortly before eleven o'clock on a sunny Saturday morning in June 1922, Walther Rathenau, the German minister for foreign affairs, set out from his home on the outskirts of Berlin to the Foreign Ministry in the heart of the city. As usual when the weather was nice, he rode in the back of his open-top coupe. A few minutes later, as his driver wound his way along the tree-lined Königsallee, a dark gray car peeled off a side street and swerved in front of them, blocking the road. Two young men outfitted in long leather coats leaned out of the car. One shot at Rathenau with a submachine gun, hitting him five times, while the other tossed a hand grenade. A third man, the getaway driver, sped the assassins away while the explosion lifted Rathenau's car off the ground. Rathenau bled to death at the scene.

The two assassins were tracked down three weeks later. The gunman, a twenty-three-year-old student named Erwin Kern, was killed in a shootout with the police. Hermann Fischer, the accomplice who had thrown the grenade, committed suicide rather than face capture. By then, the getaway driver, twenty-one-year-old Ernst Techow, was already in police custody. His family had turned him in a few days after the assassination. Techow soon stood trial as an accomplice to murder, and on the witness stand, he made an astonishing claim. The reason he and his accomplices had murdered Rathenau, he said, was because Rathenau was an Elder of Zion.

Rathenau had been appointed minister for foreign affairs just six months before his assassination. There was widespread dissatisfaction with the fragile new Weimar government at the time, but Rathenau wasn't only politically divisive—he was a Jew. He had quickly become a target of right-wing vitriol, antisemitic slurs, and death threats. The rumors of his involvement with the Jewish world conspiracy, however, stemmed from one sentence in an essay he had written years earlier.

"Three hundred men, all of whom know one another, guide the economic destinies of the Continent and seek their successors among their followers," Rathenau had written. He was criticizing the oligarchical business practices that were common at the time. But for some German publishers of the *Protocols*, when Rathenau said *men*, what he really meant was *Jews*. It wasn't an indictment of shady business practices, they said, but a coded reference to the dreaded Elders of Zion. And what's more, they reasoned, the only way Rathenau could know the precise number of Elders is if he was one of them himself. And so the reason Rathenau had to die, Techow explained at his trial, was that he "had himself confessed, and boasted, that he was one of the three hundred Elders of Zion, whose purpose and aim was to bring the whole world under Jewish influence."

Rathenau was not the first victim of the *Protocols*. In the two decades since its publication, it had already helped spark horrific pogroms in Russia, in which thousands of Jewish people had been brutally murdered. But Rathenau's execution at the hands of militant German nationalists was a harbinger of worse to come.

The Jewish Problem

Shortly after Adolf Hitler became chancellor of Germany in 1933, he had a monument to Rathenau's killers erected in the cemetery where they lay buried, a large stone bearing an inscription hailing the two assassins as "advance fighters" for the Nazi cause. At a memorial service held where the two had died, leading Nazis offered heartfelt eulogies. Ernst Röhm, the commander of the Storm Battalion, the Nazi Party paramilitary, praised the assassins' "glorious deed." Heinrich Himmler asserted that "without the deed of these two, Germany today would be living under a Bolshevist regime." Meanwhile, university students across Germany, assisted by brown-shirted storm troopers, staged mass book burnings, at which Rathenau's writings were among the many volumes tossed into the flames. In Berlin's Opera Square, forty thousand people gathered to hear Propaganda Minister Joseph Goebbels declare, "the era of extreme Jewish intellectualism is now at an end."

Hitler literally put his antisemitic credentials on his CV. In 1921, in a résumé sent to an unknown recipient, he bragged, "though I came from a fairly cosmopolitan family, the school of harsh reality turned me into an anti-Semite within barely a year." In the *Protocols*, "Hitler heard the call of a kindred spirit," the historian Norman Cohn wrote, "and he responded to it with all his being." The first German translation appeared in 1920, just as Hitler was embarking on his career in politics. He began citing the *Protocols* in speeches as early as 1921—the same year it had been so thoroughly debunked. In those early years, Cohn notes, Hitler kept a large photograph of Henry Ford, America's most famous supporter of the *Protocols*, by his desk, referring to him as the "heroic American, Heinrich Ford."

Hitler's 1924 manifesto, *Mein Kampf*, deals extensively with the reality of the Jewish conspiracy, and lavishes praise on the *Protocols*. "How far the entire existence of this people is based on a continuous lie is shown in an incomparable manner and certainty in the *Protocols of the Wise Men of Zion*," Hitler wrote. He dismissed the allegations that it was a forgery as mere Jewish propaganda—evidence, in fact, that the information in the *Protocols* is true after all. Echoing Henry Ford, and many other pundits of the day, he argued that "the best criticism applied to them is reality. He who examines the historical development of the past hundred years, from the points of view of this book, will also immediately understand the clamor of the Jewish press." It makes no odds "from what Jewish brain these disclosures originate," he went on; "the important thing is that with positively terrifying certainty they reveal the nature and activity of the Jewish people and expose their inner connection as well as their ultimate final aims." Once the German people are sufficiently familiar with the book's revelations, he concluded, "the Jewish menace can be regarded as already vanquished."

Less than a decade later, the Nazis had gained control of Germany, and they soon added the *Protocols* to the national school curriculum. An official Nazi Party edition, published in 1933, instructed readers, "it is the duty of every German to study the terrifying avowal of the Elders of Zion, and to compare them with the boundless misery of our people; and then to draw the necessary conclusions."

Throughout his rise to power and reign as Führer, Hitler repeatedly made it clear that "to restore Germany to freedom and power . . . the first thing to do is rescue it from the Jew who is ruining our country." He constantly referred to Jewish people in grotesque, dehumanizing terms, as an abscess, a fungus, a plague of rats, and an infection that needed to be eliminated for the health of the nation. Over the course of the 1930s, the Nazis progressively stripped Jewish citizens of their rights. Germany's Jews were "reduced to the status of outlaws" in their own country, as historian Robert Wistrich put it.

But, for all his talk of Jews as vermin and bacteria, Hitler didn't look down upon them as an inferior form of life that needed merely to be marginalized and banished. Inspired by the vast, demonic conspiracy codified in the *Protocols*, he saw the Jewish people as a powerful foe, the metaphysical opposite of the Aryan race. "Has it not struck you how the Jew is the exact opposite of the German in every single respect, and yet as closely akin to him as a blood brother?" he reportedly asked a confidant—"Two groups so closely allied and yet so utterly dissimilar." For Hitler, the battle between the Jews and Aryans could only end in an apocalyptic struggle. "It is in truth," he said, "the critical battle for the fate of the world!"

With the benefit of hindsight, Hitler's genocidal ambition is all too evident in one of the first speeches he gave after leaving Landsberg jail in 1925. "There are two possibilities," he explained; "either the enemy walks over our corpse or we over theirs." In January 1939, on the sixth anniversary of his ascension to power, Hitler offered an ominous, goading vision of things to come.

In the course of my life I have very often been a prophet, and have usually been ridiculed for it. During the time of my struggle for power it was in the first instance only the Jewish race that received my prophecies with laughter when I said that I would one day take over the leadership of the State, and with it that of the whole nation, and that I would then among other things settle the Jewish problem. Their laughter was uproarious, but I think that for some time now they have been laughing on the other side of their face. Today I will once more be a prophet: if the international Jewish financiers in and outside Europe should succeed in plunging the nations once more into a world war, then the result will not be the Bolshevizing of the earth, and thus the victory of Jewry, but the annihilation of the Jewish race in Europe.

His prophecy was self-fulfilling. Eight months later, Hitler invaded Poland, setting off the Second World War.

Throughout the war, even as millions of European Jews were being systematically rounded up and sent to gas chambers, Hitler and his Nazi propagandists defined the war as one waged by the world's Jews against Germany. Even at the end of it all, as Berlin was crumbling around him, Hitler maintained that he was blameless. "It is untrue that I or anyone else in Germany wanted the war in 1939," he claimed in his final political statement, dictated on the morning of April 29, 1945. "It was desired and instigated exclusively by those international statesmen who were either of Jewish descent or worked for Jewish interests." In the final sentence of the statement—his last words to posterity—Hitler urged his successors to keep up the fight against the Jewish conspiracy. "Above all I charge the leaders of the nation and those under them to scrupulous observance of the laws of race and to merciless opposition to the universal poisoner of all peoples, international Jewry."

By the time Hitler took his own life the next day, six million Jewish people—two thirds of Europe's Jewish population—had been killed in pursuit of his "endlösung der Judenfrage"—the final solution of the Jewish problem.

From his first political speeches to his last recorded words, Hitler's belief in the mythic Jewish conspiracy embodied in the *Protocols* was at the heart of his worldview and his actions. In the hands of the Nazis, Norman Cohn wrote, "a preposterous fabrication," expressly designed to "appeal to all the paranoid and destructive potentialities in human beings," became nothing less than "a warrant for genocide."

License to Kill

The scale of the devastation left behind by Hitler's Third Reich is incomparable, but it is not the only time an imaginary conspiracy may have inspired a real atrocity. There's Anders Breivik, the Norwegian who killed seventy-seven people in

2011, many of them teenagers attending a political summer camp. According to the fifteen-hundred-page manifesto he uploaded to the Internet shortly before launching his attack, Breivik imagined that there was an ongoing Islamic conspiracy to destroy Western civilization. There's Tamerlan Tsarnaev, the Boston Marathon bomber. According to *Boston Globe* reporter Sally Jacobs, Tsarnaev imagined that the U.S. government was conspiring against its citizens, and gave his landlord a copy of the *Protocols of Zion*, telling her, "this is a good book." There's Jared Loughner, who opened fire on Congresswoman Gabrielle Giffords and a crowd of people she was speaking to in January 2011, seriously injuring Giffords and killing six bystanders. According to a video he posted to YouTube, Loughner imagined that "the government is implying mind control and brainwash on the people by controlling grammar [*sic*]." There's James Wenneker von Brunn, a white supremacist who shot and killed a guard at the United States Holocaust Memorial Museum in Washington, D.C., in June 2009. According to a notebook found in von Brunn's car, he imagined that "the Holocaust is a lie. Obama was created by Jews. Obama does what his Jew owners tell him to do. Jews captured America's money. Jews control the mass media."

And there's Timothy McVeigh, a disillusioned veteran of the United States Army. On the morning of April 19, 1995, McVeigh parked a rented truck in front of the Alfred P. Murrah Federal Building in Oklahoma City. In the back was five thousand pounds of homemade explosives. McVeigh lit the fuse and made his getaway. The massive explosion reduced a third of the nine-story building to rubble, injuring hundreds of people and killing 168, including nineteen children. (In addition to the offices of fourteen federal agencies, the building was home to a daycare center on the second floor).

When he was arrested later that day, McVeigh was wearing a T-shirt with a picture of Abraham Lincoln and, below it, the Latin phrase that Lincoln's assassin, John Wilkes Booth, shouted as he pulled the trigger: "Sic semper tyrannis"—Thus ever to tyrants. According to journalists Lou Michel and Dan Herbeck, who interviewed McVeigh at length while he awaited execution, McVeigh had grown increasingly concerned about the federal government and the coming New World Order since leaving the military. He drifted into the patriot movement, where he heard rumors that the government was "planning a massive raid on gun owners and members of the Patriot community in the spring of 1995." Something had to be done, he thought. As the writer Gore Vidal put it, McVeigh "declared war on a government that he felt had declared war on its own people."

McVeigh's growing distrust of the federal government had been fueled in part, he said, by incidents like the siege at Waco, Texas. The date of the Oklahoma bombing, April 19, was the second anniversary of the violent ending of the siege, in which the FBI, imagining that a religious sect called the Branch Davidians was stockpiling illegal weapons and abusing children, had launched a military-style raid on their compound. A fire broke out, killing seventy-six of the group's members, including twenty-five children. Terrorists aren't the only ones with potentially dangerous imaginations.

What are we to make of all this? Incidents like these are undeniably unnerving and impossible to ignore, but are they the rule, or the exception? Is conspiracist thinking inherently tied to violence and destruction?

In 2010, Jamie Bartlett and Carl Miller, researchers at a British think tank called Demos, combed through the literature, statements, and propaganda of more than fifty extremist groups, running the gamut from far right to far left, and from radical religious groups and cults to eco-warriors and anarchists. Conspiracy theories formed a core component of many of the groups' beliefs. Sometimes, the researchers concluded, conspiracy theories push extremists in a more extreme, and potentially dangerous, direction by "pointing to forces beyond our control, articulating an enemy to hate, sharply dividing the group from the non-group and, sometimes, legitimizing violence." But it wasn't entirely clear cut. Bartlett and Miller also found that many groups believe conspiracy theories without resorting to violence (such as the 9/11 Truth movement), and many violent extremist groups didn't seem to believe conspiracy theories (such as the Real IRA, an Irish nationalist paramilitary).

So much for organized extremists. How about regular Joes? In 2012, Joe Uscinski and Joseph Parent had twelve hundred Americans take a survey designed to reveal whether people who believe conspiracy theories are harboring potentially violent tendencies. The results were similarly ambivalent. Disconcertingly, the more someone agreed with conspiracy theories, the more likely he or she was to favor less restrictive gun laws, and to agree with statements like "violence is sometimes an acceptable way to express disagreement with the government," and "violence as an acceptable way to stop politically extreme groups in our country from doing harm." More reassuringly, however, the majority of people—even among the most fervent conspiracists—said they opposed the use of political violence.

So when it comes to the link between conspiracy theories and violent extremism, there are some worrying possibilities, but few certainties. There's no denying that certain conspiracy theories, under certain circumstances, have the potential to inspire certain people to commit atrocities—especially, as journalist Chip Berlet pointed out, when they draw on existing prejudices, demonize and scapegoat vulnerable enemies, and assert that urgent action is required. However, it would be premature (not to mention a little paranoid) to imagine that there are legions of disgruntled conspiracists out to get us. Believing conspiracy theories is not always a recipe for violence. On the contrary, most conspiracy theorists say that political violence is not an acceptable tactic, and most of those who do say it is acceptable will never act on the sentiment. As Uscinski and Parent point out, "if only 1 percent of the population agreed with the statement strongly enough to take forceful action, there would be blood in the streets daily."

Tragic, headline-grabbing acts of violence and terrorism can't help but catch our attention. But the potential consequences of believing conspiracy theories need not be so spectacular to be concerning. Sometimes the effects are more insidious.

Deadly Choices

Stephanie Messenger is an Australian author of self-published educational books for children, such as *Don't Bully Billy* and *Sarah Visits a Naturopath*. In 2012, she published a book that, according to promotional materials, "takes children on a journey to learn about the ineffectiveness of vaccinations and to know they don't have to be scared of childhood illnesses, like measles and chicken pox." The blurb on the back of the book talks about how nowadays we're bombarded with messages urging us to fear diseases, from people who have "vested interests" in selling "some potion or vaccine."

Messenger called the book *Melanie's Marvelous Measles*. Perhaps she drew inspiration from the beloved British children's author Roald Dahl's *George's Marvellous Medicine*. Which would be ironic, given Dahl's own feelings about measles, which he wrote about in 1986.

> Olivia, my eldest daughter, caught measles when she was seven years old. As the illness took its usual course I can remember reading to her often in bed and not feeling particularly alarmed about it. Then one morning, when she was well on the road to recovery, I was sitting on her bed showing her how to fashion little animals out of coloured pipe-cleaners, and when it came to her turn to make one herself, I noticed that her fingers and her mind were not working together and she couldn't do anything.
>
> "Are you feeling alright?" I asked her.
>
> "I feel all sleepy," she said.
>
> In an hour she was unconscious. In twelve hours she was dead. The measles had turned into a terrible thing called measles encephalitis and there was nothing the doctors could do to save her.

In 1962, when the measles took Olivia's life, there was no vaccine. Practically everyone caught the measles at some point in childhood. Most recovered without any lasting damage, but it killed around a hundred children in the United Kingdom and more than four hundred in America every year, and put tens of thousands more in the hospital, leaving some blind or brain-damaged. When a vaccine was licensed in the United States a year later, in 1963, the number of people who caught measles plummeted by 98 percent. "In my opinion," Dahl concluded, "parents who now refuse to have their children immunised are putting the lives of those children at risk."

Fortunately, we now have a vaccine that protects not only against measles, but against mumps and rubella as well: the

combination MMR shot. The World Health Organization estimates that between the years 2000 and 2013, measles vaccination
saved more than fifteen million lives around the world.
Unfortunately, since the late 1990s, MMR has been the focus of
intense debate and fear, often with conspiratorial undertones.

The trouble with MMR started in the United Kingdom. When
the vaccine was introduced there, in 1988, it was an immediate
success. In the first year, a million children were vaccinated. For
the next ten years, uptake of the vaccine remained above 90
percent. Then, in 1998, a doctor called Andrew Wakefield,
along with a team of colleagues, published a study that ignited
controversy. In the paper, which was published by a highly
respected medical journal, *The Lancet*, Wakefield and colleagues
claimed to have found measles virus in the intestines of a handful
of autistic children. The paper speculated that the MMR shot
may have played a role in causing the children's autism, but
pointed out that the findings were not sufficient to prove the
relationship. Regardless, Wakefield took the findings directly to
the media. In a press conference held the day before the paper
was published, and that many of the paper's coauthors refused to
attend, Wakefield claimed that the danger posed by MMR was
so great that the vaccine ought to be immediately withdrawn,
and individual measles, mumps, and rubella shots, given a year
apart, ought to be used instead. (Wakefield himself, it is worth
noting, has never opposed vaccination across the board; in fact,
he has maintained that vaccines are an important part of
health—just not the combined MMR shot, which he continues
to argue is linked to autism.)

Concerned parents are understandably influenced by the
media, and there is no better illustration than the panic that
followed Wakefield's alarming announcement. Interest in the
story was modest at first. In 1998, the year of Wakefield's press
conference, a handful of news stories reported his claim, and
vaccine uptake began to fall slightly. It wasn't until 2001 that the
story began to take on a life of its own. For several years, the
idea that the MMR vaccine causes autism received more
coverage in the British media than any other science story. As
fear-mongering coverage peaked between 2001 and 2003,

uptake of the vaccine dipped to 80 percent. Some parts of the country, particularly parts of London, had drastically lower vaccination rates.

The falling vaccination rates prompted outbreaks of the diseases that the vaccine prevents—particularly, since it's so highly contagious, measles. The first outbreak was in Dublin in 2000, where vaccination rates were already lower than in the United Kingdom. Almost sixteen hundred cases of measles were reported. More than a hundred children were admitted to hospital with serious complications, and three died. A thirteen-year-old boy died in England in 2006, becoming the first person to die of measles in England since 1994. In 2008, measles was declared endemic in the United Kingdom for the first time in fourteen years. In 2012 there were more than two thousand cases of measles in England and Wales—mostly affecting children and teenagers whose parents had declined the MMR vaccine years earlier. In 2013, another outbreak in Wales infected more than a thousand people, hospitalizing eighty-eight, and killing a twenty-five-year-old man.

In 2004 it emerged that the entire MMR-autism debate was built on a lie. Investigative journalist Brian Deer uncovered evidence that, before beginning his research, Wakefield had been involved in a patent application for an allegedly safer alternative to the combined MMR vaccine. He had also received a payment in the region of half a million pounds from a personal-injury law firm to conduct the research, and the same law firm had referred parents who believed their children to be vaccine-damaged to Wakefield so he could use the children in his research. But failing to declare a conflict of interest was the least of Wakefield's wrongdoing. Deer discovered that the study, which involved conducting invasive medical procedures on developmentally challenged children, had not been granted ethical approval. Finally it emerged that Wakefield may have fudged elements of the children's medical histories to fit his MMR-autism theory, and a co-worker suggested that Wakefield had knowingly reported incorrect test results. Ultimately the paper was retracted, and Wakefield's license to practice medicine in the United Kingdom was withdrawn.

That all looks pretty bad, I think it's fair to say, but we shouldn't necessarily dismiss the hypothesis that MMR somehow causes autism on the basis of Wakefield's behavior alone. Since his paper was published, dozens of independent, large, well-conducted studies, involving hundreds of thousands of children across several continents, have found no association whatsoever between the MMR vaccine and autism. As Paul Offit, a pediatrician and immunologist, has pointed out, we still don't know for sure exactly what causes autism, but by now we can say with considerable certainty that vaccines can be crossed off the list of suspects.

Despite Wakefield's study being utterly discredited, and despite the weight of evidence against his claims, concerns about MMR continue to linger, in Britain and elsewhere. It didn't take long for the panic over MMR to cross the Atlantic, where the anti-vaccination cause was taken up by celebrities such as Jenny McCarthy and her then-boyfriend Jim Carrey. Along the way, the claims mutated and merged with other fears. A particular concern in the United States was the presence in various vaccines of a mercury-based preservative, thimerosal, which was held by some anti-vaccine activists to be responsible for the increasing prevalence of autism. (Studies have shown this claim to be mistaken, too.) For many concerned parents, the controversy has thrown suspicion on the entire vaccine schedule. According to a 2009 survey, more than one in ten American parents have refused at least one recommended vaccine for their child, and twice as many parents choose to delay certain shots, leaving their child unprotected for longer.

Wakefield remains a polarizing figure, a hero to some and a dangerous quack to others. A recent article, written in the wake of a measles outbreak that began at Disneyland in California in December 2014, described Wakefield as the "father of the anti-vaccine movement." Yet unfounded fears about vaccines predate Andrew Wakefield. In fact, this wasn't the first time a British doctor had gone to the media with trumped-up claims of vaccine-related harm. An uncannily similar episode had transpired a few decades earlier.

The most common symptom of pertussis is uncontrollable fits of coughing. Because of narrowing of the throat, the struggle to draw a breath sometimes produces a high-pitched whooping noise, hence the disease's colloquial name, whooping cough.

The coughing can be violent enough to result in bleeding eyeballs, broken ribs, and hernias. In extreme cases, the coughing can last up to four months, sometimes leading to malnourishment, loss of sight or hearing, or brain damage. But pertussis is most dangerous in infants. Infants don't whoop. Instead, unable to breathe, they sometimes quietly turn blue and die. The World Health Organization estimates that almost two hundred thousand people die each year from whooping cough around the world, most of them young children in developing countries.

Fortunately, we have a vaccine that protects not only against pertussis, but also against diphtheria and tetanus: the DTaP shot, formerly known as DPT. Unfortunately, in the 1970s and '80s, DPT became the subject of intense debate and fear, often with conspiratorial undertones.

In 1973, a British doctor called John Wilson gave a presentation at an academic conference in which he claimed that the pertussis component of DPT was causing seizures and brain damage in infants. The research was based on a small number of children, and it has since emerged that many of the children were misdiagnosed, and some hadn't even received the DPT vaccine. Regardless, Wilson took his findings to the media, appearing on prime-time television in a program that contained harrowing images of sick children and claimed that a hundred British children suffered brain damage every year as a result of the DPT vaccine. Uptake of the DPT vaccine fell from around 80 percent at the beginning of the decade to just 31 percent by 1978. This was followed by a pertussis epidemic during 1978 and '79, in which a hundred thousand cases of whooping cough were reported in England and Wales. It's estimated that around six hundred children died in the outbreak.

Despite flaws in Wilson's study, as well as a growing number of studies that found no evidence of the alleged link between DPT and brain damage, by the early eighties the fear had spread to America. In 1982 a documentary called *DPT: Vaccine Roulette* aired on U.S. television. Like its British precursor, it was full of emotive scenes of children who had allegedly been harmed by the DPT vaccine. The damage was being covered up or ignored by the government and medical establishment, the documentary argued. It stopped short of telling parents outright not to have their children vaccinated, but the implication was clear.

One parent, a woman named Barbara Loe Fisher, watched *Vaccine Roulette* and came to believe that her own son had been injured by the DPT vaccine. Together with other parents who believed their children had been hurt by vaccines, Fisher formed a group called Dissatisfied Parents Together (or DPT for short). The group still exists, now going by the name National Vaccine Information Center. The change of name reflected the fact that their distrust of vaccines had broadened beyond the DPT shot. Over the years, Fisher's group, and others like it, has questioned the safety and efficacy of practically every vaccine in use.

Which brings us back to where we started. The May 2, 1998, issue of *The Lancet* carried a letter to the editor penned by none other than Barbara Loe Fisher. She referred to a critique of Andrew Wakefield's research as a "pre-emptive strike by US vaccine policymakers." Hinting at nefarious motives, she wrote, "it is perhaps understandable that health officials are tempted to discredit innovative clinical research into the biological mechanism of vaccine-associated health problems when they have steadfastly refused to conduct this kind of basic science research themselves." Fisher's National Vaccine Information Center later bestowed upon Andrew Wakefield an award for "Courage in Science."

So the current epidemic of fear over the MMR vaccine is in many ways simply an extension of the vaccine anxiety that blossomed in the 1970s. But it didn't start there. In fact, people have been worried about the safety of vaccines—and the motives of the people who make and sell them—since the discovery of the very first vaccine.

A Pox on You

Common symptoms of smallpox included foul-smelling and excruciatingly painful pus-filled blisters all over the face and body. Open sores inside the mouth poured virus particles into the mouth and throat, meaning that the disease was highly contagious, spread by coughing, sneezing, and even talking. Around one in three infected adults died of the disease, and four out of five children. Those who survived were often left disfigured, or worse—many were blinded, pregnant women miscarried, and children's growth was stunted.

Smallpox killed more people than any other disease throughout history. As recently as 1967, smallpox killed an estimated two million people around the world in that year alone. The virus shaped the course of history. Battles and wars were won and lost because of outbreaks of smallpox. It killed monarchs and rulers in office. It helped clear the way for the colonization of North and South America by European settlers by killing off millions of the native inhabitants.

Fortunately, you're not going to catch smallpox. The virus has been eradicated from the wild, thanks to the discovery, two centuries ago, of the world's first vaccine. Unfortunately, the new practice of vaccination gave rise to the kind of vaccine anxiety and organized anti-vaccine movements that persist to this day.

The vaccine was discovered by Edward Jenner. Jenner was a classic mildly eccentric eighteenth-century English country gentleman. He dabbled in things like fossil collecting, hot air ballooning, and growing oversized vegetables. His interest in smallpox was piqued when, flirting with a milkmaid one afternoon, he learned the folk wisdom that catching cowpox, a disease that caused blisters on cows' udders, somehow seemed to protect milkmaids and other farm workers against smallpox. In humans, cowpox just caused a few harmless blisters on the hands, but it seemed to somehow offer lifelong immunity to smallpox. Jenner decided to put this folk wisdom to the test. He initially exposed fifteen farm workers who had previously suffered from cowpox to smallpox virus. None became infected. Then, in 1796, he undertook his boldest experiment to date. He deliberately infected a young boy with cowpox, and then exposed him to smallpox. The boy did not get sick. Jenner called the procedure vaccination, derived from the Latin *vaccinae* meaning "of the cow," and published his findings in 1798. By 1820, millions of people had been vaccinated in Britain, Europe, and the United States, and the number of people dying from smallpox was cut in half.

Not everyone was impressed. There immediately arose some sporadic opposition to the vaccine. Objections were occasionally raised on religious grounds—to vaccinate oneself, some argued, was to question God's divine plan. Others objected for economic reasons, or simply out of disgust at a vaccine derived from sick cows, coupled with distrust of the doctors who administered them. By 1800, Jenner was moved to defend his vaccine from detractors, writing "the feeble efforts of a few individuals to depreciate the new practice are sinking fast into contempt." His optimism was misplaced.

The first truly organized anti-vaccination movements have their origins in the Compulsory Vaccination Acts passed by British Parliament in the 1850s and '60s. The first law, introduced in 1853, threatened parents who failed to vaccinate their children with fines and imprisonment. The law was widely accepted at first, due in large part to a particularly bad smallpox epidemic that had swept through England the year before, but vaccination rates fell off again when people realized that the law simply wasn't enforced. Parliament passed a new tougher law in 1867. It was in reaction to these laws that the first dedicated and well-organized anti-vaccination leagues were formed. Critics claimed that the vaccine was at best useless, at worst a scam or a poison. By 1900 there were in the region of two hundred anti-vaccination groups across England. The United States quickly followed suit; American anti-vaccination societies began to spring up in the 1870s.

In 1898, the English critics of vaccination won. The British government gave in, passing a law that allowed so-called conscientious objectors to opt out of vaccinating their children. Objection certificates were made easier to obtain in 1907. Vaccination rates fell, and outbreaks of smallpox rose once again in parts of England. In neighboring Scotland and Ireland, where anti-vaccination movements had not gained as much traction, vaccination continued to be readily accepted, and smallpox continued to decline.

So vaccine anxiety was a side effect of the very first vaccine, and the symptoms have never quite cleared up. Perhaps the most remarkable thing about the long-standing unease about vaccines is how little the arguments have changed over the centuries. Jenner's critics created elaborate cartoons depicting doctors as unfeeling monsters, intent on sacrificing innocent, helpless children. Twenty-first-century anti-vaccinationists write blog posts with titles like "Doctors want power to kill disabled babies." Nineteenth-century activists claimed that the smallpox vaccine contained "poison of adders, the blood, entrails, and excretion of bats, toads and suckling whelps" and fought for their right to remain "pure and unpolluted." The modern-day "green our vaccines" movement doesn't go so far as to say vaccines contain entrails, but they still misconstrue vaccines as containing "toxins" including antifreeze, insect repellent, and spermicide. And, as Paul Offit has pointed out, the current concerns about MMR somehow causing autism are about as plausible, biologically speaking, as the claim, widely reported in the early 1800s, that the smallpox vaccine caused recipients to sprout horns, run about on all fours, and low and squint like cows.

And throughout it all, there have been theories alleging a vast international conspiracy to trump up the dangers of the diseases that vaccines, to hide the truth about vaccine side effects, and to ensure profits for Big Pharma and the government. One nineteenth-century British activist wrote of smallpox, "this infection scare is a sham, fostered, if not got up originally by doctors as a means of raising their own importance and tightening their grasp on the throat of the nation's common sense which has lain so long paralysed and inert in their clutches." More than a century later, Barbara Loe Fisher called the HPV vaccine "one of the biggest money making schemes in the history of medicine."

In some parts of the world, conspiracist fears about vaccines have provoked more drastic measures than simply opting out of vaccination. In parts of Pakistan, local religious leaders have denounced vaccination as an American ploy to sterilize Muslims. According to the BBC, more than sixty polio workers, or their drivers or guards, have been murdered in Pakistan since 2012. (The CIA, it's worth pointing out, inadvertently fanned the flames of distrust by setting up a fake vaccination program in Abbottabad in 2011, as part of an effort to confirm Osama Bin Laden's whereabouts by having vaccine workers surreptitiously collect DNA samples from Bin Laden's family members. When the stunningly misguided plan came to light, it put every vaccine worker in the country under suspicion.) Similar killings of polio workers have taken place in Nigeria. Pakistan and Nigeria, not coincidentally, are two of only three countries in the world where polio remains endemic.

Of course, not every parent of an unvaccinated child is a raving conspiracy theorist. Some unvaccinated children are too young to have received the vaccine. Others have medical conditions that make vaccination impossible. And many parents who fail to stick to the recommended vaccine schedule do so not out of fear of a Big Pharma conspiracy, but because they lack the time or money for doctor visits, and because they have fallen through the cracks in the health care system. These are the children who rely on "herd immunity"—the protection that comes from most of the people around us being immune to a disease. Parents who consciously choose to deny their children vaccines are putting not only their own child in harm's way, but other children, too.

And yet it would be a mistake to demonize parents who choose to reject vaccines. They are thoughtful, caring, well intentioned, and often well informed. Thanks to a small but vocal minority of dedicated anti-vaccinists, the Internet is rife with conspiracy-laced misinformation urging us not to trust vaccines. Making matters worse, the media often portrays the controversy with a false sense of balance. Most parents have heard the claims about autism and vaccines, and, according to a recent study, merely reading anti-vaccine conspiracy theories can reduce parents' willingness to have their children vaccinated. (We'll talk more about why it's so easy for concerned parents to believe vaccines might cause harm in Chapter 8.)

The science is clear: Vaccines do not cause autism. But conspiracy theories erode our trust in science, allowing controversy to linger long after the questions have been settled.

Tilting at Windmills

So some conspiracy theories come with a body count. In the case of violent extremism, conspiracy theories can tap into our darkest prejudices; in the case of vaccine anxiety, conspiracy theories can tap into our desire to protect the people we love the most. Before we run for the hills, however, it's worth pointing out that most conspiracy theories are made of less incendiary stuff. When people believe that Jewish people are engaging in an apocalyptic conspiracy, or that life-saving vaccines are poison, it's worrying. When they believe that Elvis is alive and well and living in Kalamazoo, Michigan, we probably don't need to lose too much sleep over it.

That said, even ideas that seem more innocuous might have unfortunate consequences. In 1995, a trio of Stanford University psychologists led by Lisa Butler interviewed people either just before or immediately after they had watched Oliver Stone's conspiracy-laden 1991 film *JFK*. As compared to people on their way into the movie theater, people walking out of the showing said they were less likely to vote in an upcoming election and to volunteer or donate to a political campaign. Merely watching the movie eroded, at least temporarily, a little of the viewer's sense of civic engagement.

More recently, Joe Uscinski and Joseph Parent surveyed Americans shortly after the 2012 presidential election. They found that the more someone believed conspiracy theories, the less likely he or she was to have voted in the election. He or she was also less inclined to put up political signs, attend meetings, volunteer for a candidate, donate money, or run for office. (Those who believed conspiracy theories were more likely, however, to believe that election results are rigged.)

As Uscinski and Parent point out, this political detachment is a doubly dismaying trend, because the more conspiracy theorists withdraw from mainstream politics, the less likely politicians are to pander to them. Political cynicism is self-perpetuating. And that's a real shame, because there's no denying that conspiracy theorists can be proactive, organized, and vocal. These virtues could be put to good use exposing and fighting genuine misdeeds. But the self-isolating logic of conspiracism means that, more often than not, conspiracy theories send us running down intellectual dead ends in pursuit of phantom conspirators.

I happened to be in New York on the tenth anniversary of the 9/11 attacks. Wandering around Lower Manhattan, I listened to the names of the people who had died in the attacks reverberating around the subdued streets of the financial district, read aloud by friends and loved ones at the newly completed memorial where the Twin Towers once stood. A couple of blocks east, however, the victims' names were drowned out by chants of "controlled demolition, nine-eleven," and "three buildings, two planes." Dozens of people were gathered, many of them wearing identical black T-shirts bearing the logo 9/11 WAS AN INSIDE JOB! and armed with placards, banners, fliers, and DVDs to hand to passing strangers. These street rallies remain an annual occurrence, an uninvited guest accompanying the official 9/11 memorial events each year, distracting from the real grief and pain still felt by many New Yorkers.

Moreover, the conspiracy theories distract attention from the very real problems that the attacks brought to light. While the U.S. government is probably not the perpetrator of an evil conspiracy, neither is it entirely blameless. There were things that could and should have been done differently leading up to 9/11. The CIA, for instance, was aware that two of the hijackers were living in the United States for months before the attacks. The FBI would have had the authority to investigate the men if they had known of their presence on U.S. soil. As Lawrence Wright reported in his book *The Looming Tower*, an agent assigned to the CIA's Osama Bin Laden unit repeatedly emailed his superiors requesting permission to pass key information on to the FBI. His emails went unanswered.

The problem was not conspiracy within the government, but incompetence. Endemic lack of inter-agency communication—failure to divulge information to those who most needed it—rendered everyone blind to the clear and present danger right in front of their eyes. Mistakes were made, and by calling attention to them we may be able to prevent the same mistakes from being made in the future. And yet the network of U.S. intelligence and counterterrorism agencies is now more convoluted than ever, with ever-increasing levels of bureaucracy and redundancy. Governments collect masses of information on potential threats (not to mention on millions of harmless civilians), and yet terrorists continue to slip through the cracks. These real issues tend to receive much less attention from the public and the media than do conspiracy theories.

Not everything can be explained as incompetence, of course. There are real conspiracies, too. Yet one of the ironies of conspiracism is that real wrongdoing is invariably revealed by whistleblowers, journalists, academics, and officials working inside the very system that is supposed to be irredeemably corrupt. "Conspiracy theorists are correct about one thing," journalist Chip Berlet wrote: "there are inequalities of power and privilege in the world—and threats to the world itself—that need to be rectified." And yet, he argues, conspiracism is nearly always a distraction from the hard work of investigative research and social change. "Conspiracy theories spotlight lots of fascinating questions—but they seldom illuminate meaningful answers."

The conspiracist worldview paints the world in black and white—a cartoonish portrait of valiant conspiracy theorists battling monolithic conspiracies. But reality is shades of gray. By making scapegoats of imagined conspirators, conspiracy theories distract attention from real and potentially rectifiable issues. You can't win when you're fighting a conspiracy that doesn't exist.

CHAPTER THREE

What Is a Conspiracy Theory?

On September 11, 2001, hijackers crashed airplanes into the World Trade Center towers in New York City, the Pentagon in Washinton, D.C., and a field in Pennsylvania, killing 2,996 people. The attack was secretly planned by members of al-Qaeda.

Or . . .

On September 11, 2001, hijackers crashed airplanes into the World Trade Center towers in New York City, the Pentagon in Washington, D.C., and a field in Pennsylvania, killing 2,996 people. The attack was secretly planned by members of the United States government.

It seems like everyone knows what a conspiracy theory is. The phrase peppers mainstream news websites and obscure Internet forums alike; trips off the tongues of politicians and pundits; graces the titles of books, films, and television shows; and has been appended to alternative explanations for just about everything. It's easy to reel off examples. The moon landing was faked, the CIA killed Kennedy, Princess Diana was murdered, the Freemasons are up to no good, the New World Order is taking over.

But simply listing conspiracy theories doesn't explain what a conspiracy theory *is*. Consider those two accounts of 9/11. Both offer an explanation for something that happened in the world. Both explain it as the result of a conspiracy. On paper, the claims are virtually identical. The only difference is in the organization cast as the conspirators. And yet only *one* of the statements is widely referred to as a conspiracy theory. Why is that? What's the difference? *Is* there a difference?

When in search of a definition, a good place to start is in a dictionary. The *Oxford English Dictionary* added an entry for conspiracy theory in 1997: "The theory that an event or phenomenon occurs as a result of a conspiracy between interested parties." *Merriam-Webster's Collegiate Dictionary* (Eleventh Edition) offers a similar interpretation, albeit with the addition of a vague hint that the perpetrators might be influential: "A theory that explains an event or set of circumstances as a result of a secret plot by usually powerful conspirators."

A conspiracy theory, according to these literal-minded definitions, is essentially just a theory about a conspiracy. But when people call something a conspiracy theory, they're usually not talking about just any old conspiracy. Conspiracies, after all, are a dime a dozen. From outlaws plotting bank heists to corporate executives planning to mislead their customers, and from drug smuggling and bribery to coups, kidnappings, assassinations, and terrorist attacks, plenty of things happen in the world are the result of conspiracy between interested parties or secret plots by powerful conspirators. There's nothing especially noteworthy about theorizing the existence of conspiracies like these. Our definition ought to reflect how people actually use the term, and in regular conversation not every theory about a conspiracy qualifies as a *conspiracy theory*. The term is more than the sum of its parts.

A common objection to studying conspiracy theories as a psychological phenomenon is that each theory is unique; they come in a staggering variety of shapes and sizes, and it makes no sense to lump them all together. While engaging each claim on its own unique evidential merits is undoubtedly the only way to get to the bottom of whether that particular theory is *true* or not, that's not the question that concerns us here. We're interested in conspiracy theories not as empirical hypotheses, but as *ideas* that people believe—or disbelieve, as the case may be. And the fact is, for all their outer differences, if we look below the surface, at the logic and structure and assumptions that form the foundation of the claims, conspiracy theories start to look a lot alike.

There's no one-size-fits-all definition. All definitions of complex ideas are fuzzy around the edges if you think about them for long enough. The difficulty of defining the term *conspiracy theory* has been likened to attempting to define pornography—a task that famously forced United States Supreme Court Justice Potter Stewart to conclude, simply, "I know it when I see it." But even if we can't hope to come up with a precise, succinct, universally agreeable definition of conspiracy theory, we can still put together a useful enough working definition. Richard Hofstadter, an influential scholar of conspiracism, talked about conspiracy theories as a "style" of explanation. Much as a historian of art might speak of the motifs that collectively constitute the baroque style, or a music critic might parse the subtle differences between dubstep and grime, our task in distinguishing *conspiracy theories* from regular old theories about conspiracies is to identify some of the most important rhetorical themes, tropes, and flourishes that collectively constitute the conspiracist style.

Unanswered Questions

Where better to begin than with the question that causes most of the animosity between conspiracy theorists and their critics: Are conspiracy theories simply *wrong*? There's no denying that the label has less-than-favorable connotations in some intellectual circles, at least. "If you're down at a bar in the slums, and you say something that people don't like, they'll punch you or shriek four-letter words," Noam Chomsky once said. "If you're in a faculty club or an editorial office, where you're more polite—there's a collection of phrases that can be used which are the intellectual equivalent of four-letter words and tantrums. One of them is 'conspiracy theory.'"

Plenty of journalists—or, at least, their headline-writing copy editors—are happy to write off conspiracy theories as self-evidently delusional, judging by the frequency with which the term *conspiracy theory* is accompanied by adjectives like *crazy*, *wacky*, and *debunked* in the click-baiting headlines of otherwise more demure authors. Politicians, too, generally sling the term around when they want to imply that unflattering allegations are entirely unfounded. George W. Bush provided a famous example when he urged his fellow Americans never to "tolerate outrageous conspiracy theories concerning the attacks on September 11, malicious lies that attempt to shift blame away from terrorists themselves, away from the guilty." Maybe scholars are more reserved? Going by the titles of some of the books dealing with belief in conspiracy theories, not so much. David Aaronovitch called his book on twentieth-century conspiracy theories *Voodoo Histories*. Francis Wheen is similarly damning in *How Mumbo-Jumbo Conquered the World*, while the subtitle of Damian Thompson's *Counterknowledge* lumps conspiracy theories together with "quack medicine, bogus science, and fake history."

How about people on the receiving end of the label? "To be sure, wacko conspiracy theories do exist," Michael Parenti acknowledged in *Dirty Truths*—but the idea that a conspiracy was behind JFK's assassination is an indisputable fact, he argues, and therefore doesn't belong in the category of "kooky fantasies." British journalist Robert Fisk made a similar disclaimer in a 2007 op-ed for the *Independent* on the subject of the 9/11 attacks. "I am not a conspiracy theorist. Spare me the ravers. Spare me the plots," he wrote, immediately after repeating classic 9/11 Truther canards, such as the apparent implausibility of World Trade Center Building 7's collapse. As psychologist Jovan Byford points out in *Conspiracy Theories: A Critical Introduction*, Parenti and Fisk aren't denying that conspiracy theories are bogus, they are just passing the buck. Conspiracy theories are not to be believed, the argument goes—but *this* ain't one. Only other people believe conspiracy theories, it seems.

So pretty much everyone seems to agree that there is a distinction to be made. *Conspiracy theories* are bogus; a claim of conspiracy that's *true* isn't really a conspiracy theory at all. Does that mean we can go ahead and define *conspiracy theory* as a false claim of conspiracy? Some scholars think so. According to historian Daniel Pipes's definition, "a conspiracy theory is the fear of a nonexistent conspiracy." Some conspiracies are real, he admits, but conspiracy theories "exist only in the imagination." Political scientists Cass Sunstein and Adrian Vermeule made the same point, though dressed up in slightly more restrained academic lingo, proposing to limit their study of conspiracy theories to claims that are "demonstrably false," ruling out "ones that are true or whose truth is undetermined."

The problem with going down this path is that it treats the distinction between true and false, real and imaginary as entirely uncomplicated—a matter of simply consulting the facts, or even, as David Aaronovitch suggests (quoting the historian Lewis Namier), employing an "intuitive understanding of how things do not happen." But intuition leads different people to very different conclusions. One person's conspiracy theory is the next person's conspiracy fact. Any attempt to draw a neat line between true and false conspiracies is doomed to endless debate about what evidence is compelling, who the real experts are, and whether they can be trusted. These are all good questions, but as far as our definition goes, blithely asserting that conspiracy theories are bullshit doesn't get us very far.

More importantly, getting hung up on determining whether a contested claim is true or false misses a crucial feature of the conspiracist style. Kathryn Olmsted said it most clearly when she wrote that "a conspiracy theory is a proposal about a conspiracy that may or may not be true; it has not yet been proven." At first glance, this might seem to simply invite more bickering about the definition of *proven*. For believers, a theory may be true beyond doubt; for doubters, it may be unquestionably false. But that's not the issue. I'm not saying conspiracy theories are unproven merely because they have failed to meet some evidential bar. I'm suggesting something deeper. Conspiracy theories are unproven *by design*.

By way of example, consider two potential explanations of the Watergate affair. According to one account, Nixon's reelection committee conspired to spy on his political rivals, and Nixon himself subsequently got involved in the conspiracy to cover up the fact. Despite alleging a conspiracy to subvert democracy extending all the way up to the Oval Office, nobody calls this a conspiracy *theory*. Why? Because it's describing a conspiracy that is over and done with. Nixon's lackeys were caught breaking into the Watergate Hotel, evidence of the cover-up was laid out, and Nixon eventually resigned the presidency. The beans have been spilled.

According to another account—this one put forward by Gary Allen, coauthor of the classic *None Dare Call It Conspiracy*—Nixon wasn't behind the Watergate conspiracy at all. It was a setup. The scandal, according to Allen, was carefully engineered to get Nixon out of the White House as part of a bigger, even more sinister conspiracy involving Nelson Rockefeller, Henry Kissinger, the Council on Foreign Relations, and the coming New World Order. *Now* we've got ourselves a conspiracy theory. Being as yet unproven is baked right into it. Even if you are convinced that it's *true*, the theory itself tells us that the cover-up is ongoing. Kissinger hasn't come clean, the public is still in the dark, the truth is yet to be fully revealed.

We can see the same dichotomy in our two competing versions of 9/11. According to the view that al-Qaeda did it, the conspiracy has come to an end, and we pretty much know all there is to know—not least because Osama Bin Laden owned up to it. According to the inside-job theory, however, the real perpetrators are still busily scheming to hide the incredible truth. The theory may or may not be true; either way, to endorse it is to assert that the conspiracy has not yet come undone. Same goes for any other conspiracy theory you care to mention. The deed may have been done, but the perpetrators have not fessed up or been caught. The masses are still in the dark, the cat remains in the bag, the beans have yet to be spilled.

As scholar Mark Fenster explained, conspiracy theories don't merely aim to *describe* something that has happened; they purport to *reveal* hitherto undiscovered plots in the hopes of persuading the as yet unalerted masses. They come with a tacit admission that the ultimate truth is just out of reach, behind the next curtain, able to be glimpsed but not yet grasped. The conspiracy is forever being unraveled, but the holy grail of incontrovertible proof—the undeniable evidence that will alert the masses and finally topple the house of cards—has not yet been produced. Whether they turn out to be true or not, conspiracy theories, deep down, are *unanswered questions*.

Nothing Is As It Appears

Most conspiracy theories of 9/11 assert that the attacks were a "false flag" operation. The term originally referred to ships literally hoisting a flag other than their true nationality, usually for the purposes of piracy or warfare. The meaning of the term has since expanded; it now encompasses any instance in which a country organizes an attack against its own citizens and makes it look like someone else did it, as a pretext for some nefarious goal like passing draconian laws or starting wars.

As precedent for the U.S. government's alleged willingness to orchestrate attacks against its own citizens, one might point to Operation Northwoods. The plan, drafted by military chiefs in the early 1960s, was for U.S. government operatives to arrange acts of terrorism against American military and civilian targets and pin them on the Cuban government. "We could blow up a U.S. ship in Guantanamo Bay and blame Cuba," one document reads; "Casualty lists in U.S. newspapers would cause a helpful wave of national indignation." Other ideas included sinking a boatload of incoming Cuban refugees, and staging terrorist attacks in Florida and Washington, D.C. Fortunately, however, even military chiefs have to run plans like that by their bosses, and the Kennedy administration immediately nixed the operation.

According to conspiracy theorists, however, other administrations have proved far more amenable. In the case of 9/11, the theories go, what appears to be the action of al-Qaeda was an inside job, a self-inflicted wound. In the years since 9/11, cries of "false flag" have followed just about every mass shooting and terrorist attack. Yet the current fashion for false-flag theories is a product of old habits. Our second crucial element of the conspiracist style is the idea that we're not merely being kept in the dark about something—we are being actively fooled. In the world according to conspiracy theories, appearances mislead, and nothing is quite as it seems.

This feature is most obvious when conspiracy theories rub up against *official stories*. We are told that the 9/11 attacks were pulled off by nineteen al-Qaeda hijackers, acting on plans devised by Osama Bin Laden, and that they succeeded thanks in large part to incompetence, bureaucratic inertia, and petty rivalries between the agencies in charge of national security. As for the Twin Towers and World Trade Center Building 7, they collapsed due to structural damage and fire. This general account is based on several investigations of huge proportions, amassing insights from thousands of individual experts with differing specialties and affiliations, and has been queried, substantiated, clarified, and extended by many more independent scholars.

As far as the conspiracy theories are concerned, however, George W. Bush—or whoever is *really* in charge of things— simply pulled the story out of his back pocket. When they balk at "official stories" or "government-sanctioned explanations," conspiracy theorists imply that mainstream understanding of the event is nothing more than one possible interpretation, cooked up by some self-professed authority. Worse, it is often thought to be handed down by the very people who are behind the alleged conspiracy. It's not merely a mistaken account, but a deliberate fabrication. The official story is, according to conspiracy theorists, just what the authorities *want* us to believe.

Of course, "official stories" don't deserve our unreserved acceptance. Both the Warren Commission report on JFK's assassination and the 9/11 Commission Report contained flaws and omissions. But that's not to say they are entirely useless, either. The best explanation is one that is backed up by multiple, independent, converging sources. Painting an explanation as the "official story" means it can be written off wholesale, even if it actually reflects the accumulated insights of a multitude of people, with differing affiliations and agendas, all arriving at a broadly consistent explanation. (Much as the term *conspiracy theory*, I might add, is sometimes used to dismiss inconvenient points of view with little consideration of the evidence.)

Opposing an official explanation isn't a prerequisite, however. Conspiracy theories can be conjured up in the immediate aftermath of an event, before an official story has had time to take shape. And sometimes a conspiracy theory *is* the official explanation. As Jesse Walker points out in *United States of Paranoia*, America was founded on conspiracist suspicions. The Declaration of Independence painstakingly lists a "long train of abuses and usurpations" the Colonies have suffered, adding up to "a design" to establish "absolute Tyranny over these States."

Distaste for official stories is just a symptom of the deeper logic of the conspiracist style. Mike Wood and Karen Douglas explain that conspiracy theories operate on the assumption that "there are two worlds: one real and (mostly) unseen, the other a sinister illusion meant to cover up the truth." As a result, conspiracy theories are contrarian by nature. They flip conventional wisdom on its head. In the world according to conspiracy theories, the obvious answer is never correct, and there is always more to things than meets the eye. Accidents are planned, democracy is a sham, all faces are masks, all flags are false. Taken to extremes, the conspiracist style casts doubt on absolutely everything, even our basic understanding of reality. Fact becomes fiction and fiction becomes fact: Universities are purveyors of state-sponsored lies, while conspiratorial plots in films and books are "predictive programming," designed to subconsciously prepare us for the coming New World Order.

"A virtuoso conspiracy theorist turns black into white and white into black," wrote Daniel Pipes. And there is no more skilled virtuoso than David Icke. "Just look at us," Icke implores readers of *The David Icke Guide to the Global Conspiracy* (quoting the alternative health practitioner Michael Ellner). "Everything is backwards; everything is upside down. Doctors destroy health, lawyers destroy justice, universities destroy knowledge, governments destroy freedom, the major media destroy information and religions destroy spirituality."

Everything Is Under Control

The plot among nineteen young al-Qaeda members to hijack commercial airplanes and fly them into American landmarks is credited with being the deadliest terrorist attack on American soil, and it shaped events around the world for years to come. Yet, as well orchestrated as the attacks were, the conspiracy didn't go entirely according to plan.

United Airlines Flight 93 took off from Newark Liberty Airport at 8:42 A.M., forty minutes after its scheduled departure time. It was the only hijacked plane that was significantly delayed. Forty-five minutes later, the four hijackers on board rushed the cockpit, killed the two pilots and a flight attendant, and diverted the plane to Washington, D.C. The plan was to fly the plane into the White House or the Capitol. Minutes later, at 9:32 A.M., an air traffic controller in Cleveland heard a transmission from the cockpit: "Ladies and Gentlemen: Here the captain, please sit down keep remaining sitting. We have a bomb on board. So, sit." The hijacker apparently thought he was talking to the plane's passengers, rather than Air Traffic Control. By that time, planes had already crashed into both World Trade Center towers. Passengers and crew on board Flight 93 began calling people on the ground from cell phones and the air phones on the plane, and quickly learned that America was under attack. Realizing the hijackers were on a suicide mission, a group of passengers decided to fight back. The last thing one passenger told his wife before hanging up was, "don't worry, we're going to do something." Minutes later, the plane crashed into an empty field in Pennsylvania.

But according to some conspiracy theories, this wasn't a hitch; everything went exactly according to plan. In fact, United 93 didn't crash at all. The wreck site in Shanksville was staged. The phone calls to loved ones from passengers on the plane were faked. The plane landed at Cleveland Hopkins Airport, where passengers were taken to a nearby NASA research facility and never heard from again. What's more, every element of what transpired on September 11 was carefully orchestrated by the United States government. What the 9/11 Commission Report described as failures "in imagination, policy, capabilities, and management" were all, in fact, part of the meticulously planned ruse.

The world is a complicated place with many interacting parts. As the fate of Flight 93, not to mention botched and blown conspiracies like Watergate or Iran-Contra, go to show, it's hard to put together a good conspiracy, and harder still to stop anyone from screwing it up or blabbing. That doesn't stop people from trying, but even when things go pretty much according to plan, there are often unforeseen and unintended consequences. The results achieved differ, as a general rule, from the results aimed at.

Things seem a whole lot simpler in the world according to conspiracy theories. As Daniel Pipes put it, conspiracy theorists seem to have "startling faith in the capabilities of their enemies." At the very least, they propose that when the conspirators set events in motion they are able to predict how things will unfold with seemingly clairvoyant foresight. The conspirators are apparently willing and able to pull together as a team in total obedience to the conspiracy, almost as if it were a singular organism rather than a collection of people, each with his or her own personal ambitions, scruples, families, hobbies.

At their most extreme, conspiracy theories propose that the conspirators are virtually omnipotent. Richard Hofstadter captured this element of the conspiracist style. "Unlike the rest of us," Hofstadter wrote, "the enemy is not caught in the toils of the vast mechanism of history, himself a victim of his past, his desires, his limitations." On the contrary, "he wills, indeed he manufactures, the mechanism of history, or tries to deflect the normal course of history." Often the conspiracy is said to exert total control over some effective source of power—it controls the media, the economy, science; it rigs the elections and tampers with our medicine and food. And the conspiracy is responsible for all the world's ills. It "makes crises, starts runs on banks, causes depressions, manufactures disasters, and then enjoys and profits from the misery" it has caused. This is a "distinctly personal" interpretation of history, Hofstadter concluded; "decisive events are not taken as part of the stream of history, but as the consequences of someone's will."

There is a caveat, however. The conspirators are staggeringly competent—except every now and then when they mess up just a little bit. Like many conspiracy theories, the idea that United 93 landed safely in Cleveland was spawned by a mistaken news report, hastily repeated in the midst of ongoing confusion, and quickly retracted when the error was spotted. As far as the conspiracy theory is concerned, however, the report was correct all along, and its retraction is proof of a cover-up. Portentous slipups like this are the basis of many conspiracy theories. If the conspiracy were absolutely perfect, after all, if the conspirators never let slip a single clue, then *nobody* would have any idea what they were up to. As Loren Collins bluntly explained, the conspiracy always seems to be "exactly as competent and powerful as the conspiracy theorist needs it to be."

Everything is Evil

"It is already possible to know beyond a reasonable doubt one very important thing: The destruction of the World Trade Center was an inside job, orchestrated by domestic terrorists," Professor David Ray Griffin told audiences during a 2005 tour to promote his wildly popular book *The New Pearl Harbor: Disturbing Questions About the Bush Administration and 9/11*. "The welfare of our republic and perhaps even the survival of our civilization depend on getting the truth about 9/11 exposed," Griffin concluded. He received a standing ovation.

Professor Griffin is the soft-spoken, academic face of the 9/11 Truth movement. Alex Jones, a gravel-voiced Texan with a nationally syndicated daily radio show, brings a little more bravado to the proceedings. Wielding a bullhorn at a 2006 Truther rally in downtown Chicago, Jones told passersby, "the government is carrying out terrorist attacks as a pretext to reengineer America into a police state. Why? To capture us to be their political slaves, to use us as an engine of global empire to invade the planet. Ladies and gentlemen, 9/11 is an inside job."

Jones and Griffin are not unusual in their apocalyptic alarmism. Sensational allegations have been a central motif of the conspiracist style, from the antisemitic blood libel to the first fully fledged conspiracy theories that emerged in the wake of the French Revolution. "AN ASSOCIATION HAS BEEN FORMED for the express purpose of ROOTING OUT ALL THE RELIGIOUS ESTABLISHMENTS, AND OVER-TURNING ALL THE EXISTING GOVERNMENTS OF EUROPE," wrote John Robison, author of one of the anti-Illuminati treatises we encountered in Chapter 1 (and whose liberal use of capitalization to drive home the scale of his reve-lations foreshadowed enraged Internet commenters' abuse of the caps-lock key centuries later).

Conspiracy can be necessary and benign. People conspire to throw surprise parties for their friends. Intelligence agencies conspire in the interests of national security (in theory, at least). That said, cruel and destructive conspiracies are not uncommon, from plots to bump off a spouse and cash in on the life insurance policy, to horrific terrorist atrocities. Secrecy is sometimes necessary precisely *because* the deed being concealed is morally suspect. But even these kinds of plots tend to be limited in ambition and scope. Conspiracy scholars Emma Jane and Chris Fleming aptly sum up the kind of conspiratorial activity we know about. "As far as we are aware, we do not live in a world with one or two powerful conspiracies in operation—but in one in which millions of minor ones—and perhaps a few medium ones—are grinding away all the time." The majority of real conspiracies, they add, are "so banal . . . it's hardly worth theorizing them."

The conspiracist style has no time for such trifles. Conspiracy theories generally feature an altogether more sinister and ambi-tious breed of conspirator. At the very least, the conspirators are said to have a Machiavellian streak a mile wide. They "have a prize worth cheating for and the will and ability to stop at nothing to get it," as Joe Uscinski and Joseph Parent put it. A common refrain among conspiracy theorists is *cui bono?*—who benefits? Anyone who stands to gain from some situation is automatically suspected of bringing it about. Adding to the intrigue, the villains often turn out to be the very individuals and institutions we normally expect to act in the public interest, such as our democratically elected leaders, health care providers, and the media. In many cases, vindication of conspiracy theories would justify the impeachment of whole governments, the disbandment and criminal prosecution of entire organizations and industries, and the rewriting of history.

Taken to extremes, conspiracy theories become "all-encompassing expressions of organized evil that leave the political corruption of Watergate looking like careless playground fibbing," as Jane and Fleming pithily put it. We are not dealing with garden-variety criminals. Their malevolent ambition goes far beyond everyday plots born out of self-interest, rivalry, corruption, cruelty, and criminality. These are villains who seem to have stepped out of the pages of a comic book. They are guilty of causing all the ills from which we suffer, committing abominable acts of unthinkable cruelty on a routine basis, and striving ultimately to subvert or destroy everything we hold dear. The world according to conspiracy theories is one of high stakes and moral absolutes. We are up against Evil Incarnate. "One could ironically say that [conspiracy theories] brought the Devil back," political scientist Paul Zawadzki wrote, "only this time it was a human Devil." If this sounds overblown, just listen to David Ray Griffin, the soft-spoken academic: "We have become entranced by demonic power, so focused on lust for wealth and control that almost anything becomes possible."

Anomaly Hunting

Richard Hofstadter noted the "heroic strivings" with which conspiracy theorists amass evidence in favor of their claims. "Conspiracy theorists do not see themselves as raconteurs of alluring stories," Jovan Byford notes, "but as investigators and researchers." There are entire cottage industries devoted to the Kennedy assassination, the 9/11 attacks, and endless other conspiracy theories. The most committed conspiracists possess an intricate knowledge of their subject, often far in excess of their debunkers. If you've ever debated a devoted 9/11 Truther, you may have been regaled with an endless list of facts and arguments ostensibly pointing toward conspiracy as the only possible explanation. The conspiracist style, however, does not treat all evidence equally.

At 4:54 Eastern Time on the afternoon of September 11, 2001, a BBC correspondent in New York City, with the distant, smoking ruins of the Twin Towers in shot behind her, reported that a third skyscraper had just collapsed—World Trade Center Building 7. The only problem with the report was that Building 7 hadn't collapsed. In fact, it could be seen in the background of the shot, over the reporter's shoulder, still very much standing. If that had been the end of the story, the mistaken report would have probably been long forgotten. But twenty-six minutes later, at 5:20—and just five minutes after the reporter's satellite feed to the BBC's London studio had mysteriously cut out—the building came down.

The premature report of Building 7's demise is a typical example of the sort of evidence conspiracy theories are built on. As far as the official story is concerned, the report is of no real significance one way or another. Things were confusing in Lower Manhattan, the building was known to be in bad condition, and the report of its collapse was simply a mistake. According to some conspiracy theories, however, the report is far from irrelevant to our understanding of the 9/11 attacks; it is *evidence*. Anomalies like this—seemingly odd details that the official story can't immediately account for—are the lifeblood of conspiracy theories. Each small oddity sets in motion a chain of reasoning that inexorably leads to the conclusion that the whole thing was a conspiracy. The mistaken report about Building 7, according to the conspiracy theories, suggests that the BBC *knew* what was about to happen, and the reporter got ahead of the script—one of those minor hiccups in an otherwise flawless conspiracy. And if the collapse of Building 7 was preordained, the Twin Towers must have been scripted to fall as well, which means the entire ordeal was meticulously planned from the get-go.

As philosopher Brian Keeley has pointed out, by weaving every niggling anomaly into a grand unifying theory, conspiracy theories can look stronger than the official stories by sheer virtue of completeness. Conspiracy theories "*always* explain more than competing theories, because by invoking a conspiracy, they can explain *both* the data of the received account *and* the errant data that the received theory fails to explain." But this apparent virtue, Keeley argues, is an illusion. You can find anomalies *everywhere* if you look hard enough. Our understanding of complex events will always contain errors, contradictions, and gaps. History is messy, people are fallible. "Given the imperfect nature of our human understanding of the world, we should *expect* that even the best possible theory would not explain *all* the available data," Keeley concludes.

Which is not to say that such anomalies are inherently worthless. Much scientific discovery and refinement proceeds from the discovery of errant data that current models can't account for. But the conspiracist style imbues each small anomaly with profound significance, using it to cast doubt upon the entire mainstream explanation. The true value of an anomaly can only be fairly assessed by putting it in the context of the facts it seems to call into question.

As a case in point, some JFK assassination buffs make much of the fact that some of the bystanders in Dallas's Dealey Plaza that day reported hearing more than three gunshots—which, if it were true, and given that Lee Harvey Oswald supposedly fired three shots, would call into question the Warren Commission's conclusions that Oswald worked alone. Accordingly, these eyewitness reports are given pride of place among the evidence for conspiracy. What the conspiracy theories neglect to mention (or attribute to the cover-up) is the fact that only 5 percent of witnesses reported hearing four or more shots. Eighty-one percent heard three.

Heads I Win, Tails You Lose

Earl Warren is best known for his titular role in the Warren Commission, the first official investigation of the Kennedy assassination. For his efforts, Warren became a key figure in many of the Kennedy conspiracy theories, starring as the figurehead of a vast cover-up. So it is not without irony that two decades earlier, Warren provided a stark—and particularly consequential—illustration of the final motif of the conspiracist style we will include in our definition. Conspiracy theories are constructed around an unassailable, irrefutable logic, according to which absolutely *nothing* can disprove the conspiracy—even evidence to the contrary.

On February 19, 1942, President Franklin Roosevelt signed into effect Executive Order 9066, authorizing the secretary of war to designate parts of the country "military areas" from which "any or all persons may be excluded." Despite the vague wording, the order was written with a specific group of persons in mind. More than one hundred thousand people with Japanese ancestry, more than half of whom were American citizens, were evicted from their homes and sent to internment camps. Such drastic action was deemed necessary because, as Order 9066 pointed out, "the successful prosecution of the war requires every possible protection against espionage and against sabotage" on the home front.

So what was the evidence that people with Japanese heritage were conspiring to sabotage the war effort? There had not been a single act of sabotage in the six weeks since the Japanese attack on Pearl Harbor, and the FBI had concluded there was no evidence of any security threat. When it comes to conspiracy theories, however, lack of evidence just means the conspiracy is working. Earl Warren, who was attorney general of California at the time, was one of the most vigorous campaigners for internment. "Unfortunately," Warren said in testimony to Congress, "many of our people and some of our authorities . . . are of the opinion that because we have had no sabotage and no fifth-column activities in this State since the beginning of the war, that none have been planned for us. But I take the view that this is the most ominous sign in our whole situation." The saboteurs, Warren told the committee, were merely biding their time, waiting for the right moment to strike. "I believe that we are just being lulled into a false sense of security."

9/11 Truthers have a similar suspicion of missing evidence, as illustrated by radio host Charles Goyette in a tense 2006 interview with Davin Coburn, a reporter for *Popular Mechanics* who worked on a book dispelling conspiracy theories about the attacks. The two disagreed over the significance of withheld evidence. "What the hell? It's five years later. When are the American people entitled to the evidence?" Goyette asked with exasperation. "I think there is plenty of evidence that exists out there to explain—" Coburn began to respond, but Goyette cut him off. "Well it's not the evidence that we've *seen* that we're concerned about, it's the evidence we *haven't* seen," he said. "It's the dog that didn't bark."

If absence of evidence is evidence of conspiracy, the existence of contradictory evidence can be even more damning. For many 9/11 Truthers, the official investigations were at best willfully biased and incomplete, at worst entirely fraudulent, while videos of Osama Bin Laden taking credit for the attacks were faked using a lookalike. According to conspiracist logic, an outright denial by the accused conspirators can even be construed as a tacit admission of guilt. A 1967 CIA memo on the topic of Kennedy conspiracy theories, sent to overseas intelligence agents, noted that any conspiracy worth its salt would have organized the assassination very differently. ("Oswald would not have been any sensible person's choice for a co-conspirator," for instance). For Lance deHaven-Smith, author of *Conspiracy Theory in America*, however, the fact that the assassination appeared sloppy is, paradoxically, evidence that it was the work of professionals. The assassination "actually had the hallmarks of true expertise," deHaven-Smith wrote, "which is the ability to apply expert knowledge and skills while appearing amateurish."

Thanks to this self-insulating logic, attempting to refute a conspiracy theory is like nailing jelly to a wall. Since conspiracy theories are inherently unproven, the theory is always a work in progress, able to dodge refutation by inventing new twists and turns. Each debunking can be construed as disinformation designed to throw truth seekers off the scent, while the conspiracy theorists' continued failure to blow the lid off the conspiracy merely testifies to the power of their enemy (and the gullibility of the masses). Conspiracy theories aren't just immune to refutation—they thrive on it. If it looks like a conspiracy, it was a conspiracy. If it doesn't look like a conspiracy, it was *definitely* a conspiracy. Evidence *against* the conspiracy theory becomes evidence *of* conspiracy. Heads I win, tails you lose.

A Working Definition

So we've laid out six crucial elements of the conspiracist style. Before we take stock and move on, however, a note of caution is required. Coming up with a checklist can give a false impression of objectivity, the feeling that we're in possession of an identikit picture of our quarry—what conspiracy scholar Peter Knight refers to as the "How-to-tell-if-your-neighbor-is-a-Communist" approach. But as Emma Jane and Chris Fleming point out, "conspiracies and conspiracy theories vary so dramatically in their believability, scale, and impact, they sometimes have the quality of Rorschach ink blots. Different analysts look into them and see very different things." Defining a concept as nebulous as conspiracy theories is a subjective business. Think of our six characteristics as useful rules of thumb, rather than immutable laws.

Moreover, while some conspiracy theories are elaborate, all-encompassing, extensively footnoted, book-length treatises, others are expressed in the form of a mere hunch—the "just asking questions" tactic (sometimes shortened to "JAQing off"). Rather than postulating a coherent narrative, the theorist merely poses questions that appear to raise problems for the "official story"—always with the implication that somebody isn't telling the truth—and leaves the task of figuring out the specifics up to the listener. This tactic, according to psychologist Mike Wood, seems to have gained in popularity with the rise of the Internet, where conspiracy theories can be debunked as quickly as they are postulated, and vagueness can serve as a useful shield from criticism. It's not a new strategy, however. Nor is it employed only as a cheap defense mechanism by people lacking in intellectual fortitude. British philosopher Bertrand Russell, winner of a Nobel Prize for literature, famously organized a Who Killed Kennedy Committee and published an article titled "16 Questions on the Assassination," which insinuated that Oswald was a patsy and the Warren Commission was a cover-up.

It's worth reiterating that none of the features we've talked about, in and of themselves, distinguish conspiracy fact from conspiracy fiction. Just because a claim meets our six criteria doesn't mean it can't be true. It's also worth noting that the conspiracy theorist faces some unique problems. For one thing, while conspiracy theories diverge from how the world normally seems to work, the only conspiracies we know about are the ones that weren't all that good—either they messed up, someone spilled the beans, or it achieved its goal and secrecy was no longer required. If a conspiracy really was as good as theorists say, we might never be able to prove it. For another thing, as Brian Keeley points out, unlike boring old scientists with their lab coats and test tubes, if conspiracy theorists are right about their theories, they are engaged in research that someone else is actively trying to hamper: "Imagine if neutrinos were not simply hard to detect, but actively sought to avoid detection!" (Exclamation marks are a rare sight in academic papers, but then it's not often that scholars have the opportunity to conjure up the mental image of a cabal of evasive neutrinos.) In this light, construing evidence against the conspiracy as evidence of conspiracy isn't necessarily all that irrational.

To unthinkingly dismiss every claim of conspiracy would be as misguided as uncritical acceptance. Sometimes appearances do deceive. Sometimes powerful forces do attempt to suppress evidence and sow misinformation. Sometimes even seemingly implausible and unimaginably malicious plots really do take place. The astoundingly ill-conceived (not to mention illegal and immoral) Operation Northwoods sounds like the stuff of the most fanciful conspiracy theories—except for the fact that it *really was* drawn up by high-ranking government officials. (Thankfully, higher-ranking officials refused to put the plans into action—but we'll see a troubling example of an immoral plot that really did go ahead later on, in Chapter 5.)

Calling something a conspiracy theory is often used to summarily dismiss a claim as ludicrous. I hope to have offered a less pejorative definition. That said, our definition isn't entirely neutral. It seems fair to suggest that there is probably an inverse relationship between the extent to which a theory demonstrates each of our six features and its plausibility. Broadly speaking, the more mundane the claim, the more likely it is to be true.

In any case, it is precisely *because* conspiracy theories exist along a spectrum of plausibility, *because* there is no neat line in the sand dividing conspiracy fact from conspiracy fiction, that conspiracy theories are so intriguing. In fact, all-encompassing theories of apocalyptic shenanigans entirely devoid of compelling evidence—the theories that best fit our portrait of a conspiracy theory, in other words—are in many ways the *least* interesting product of the conspiracist style. As we'll discover throughout the rest of the book, it's where the boundary between conventional and conspiratorial thought is blurriest—where the

plausible and the paranoid are hardest to tell apart—that we
stand to learn the most about how our minds work.

With all these caveats in mind, let's recap our portrait of a
conspiracy theory. The prototypical conspiracy theory is an
unanswered question; it assumes nothing is as it seems; it
portrays the conspirators as preternaturally competent; and as
unusually evil; it is founded on anomaly hunting; and it is
ultimately irrefutable. These characteristics do a good job of
teasing apart the two versions of 9/11 that we began the chapter
with. Even though saying that al-Qaeda hijackers conspired to
pull off the attacks poses a theory about a conspiracy, the claim
doesn't fit the bill of a conspiracy theory, whereas claiming it
was an inside job fits the description to a T.

More importantly, by seeing how conspiracy theories tick,
we've uncovered some clues about how conspiracy *theorists* tick.
Conspiracy theories are the way they are because they're a
product of someone's imagination, and they're popular because
they align with other peoples' imaginations. And our imagination—the kind of ideas we find attractive and plausible—is
constrained by our psychology. To buy into a claim that ticks
the boxes of our definition, it would help if, for instance, you
are open to any and all unproven allegations of conspiracy, if
you habitually shun conventional wisdom, if you suspect that
nothing happens by accident, if you're into grand stories about
good facing off against evil, if you have a penchant for connecting
the dots between anomalies, and if you can sustain your belief
whatever the evidence (or lack thereof).

What kind of people tend to think this way, and why? These
are questions that psychologists have been studying, in one guise
or another, for decades. The answer to the first question is all of
us, more or less. As for *why* we think this way—that requires a
little more explaining.

CHAPTER FOUR

Conspiracy Minded

"So... 'Conspiracy Theory Day'... an innocent get-together of like-minded folk, or something far darker?..." On the Internet message board of an obscure, now defunct, British satellite television channel—Controversial TV on channel 200—suspicion was mounting. "The more I think about this, the more unsettled I become," another user confided. "Is it possible," a commenter named Angryhead wondered, "that the forthcoming meeting in London is a silent step towards establishing the foundations for a future alienation and then victimisation of 'conspiracy theorists' through the State System?"

The meeting in question was to entail a series of talks on belief in conspiracy theories, given by a lineup of academics that included yours truly. In the run-up to the conference, however, the event's organizer noticed the scrutiny our agenda was receiving. In the spirit of openness and inclusiveness, he extended an invitation. Send us a speaker, he offered, to represent another point of view. They sent Ian R. Crane. Ian R. Crane, according to his website, is "an ex-oilfield executive who now lectures, writes and broadcasts on the geo-political webs that are being spun; with particular focus on US Hegemony and the NWO agenda for control of global resources."

A typical audience for these kinds of events is primarily composed of meek, scholarly types with an interest in the social sciences. Thanks to the message board controversy and Ian's headlining slot, however, our audience included a vocal contingent of Controversial TV fans who suspected that we were all government shills. The tension, at points, was palpable. I was the first speaker of the day—and I might add that at that point in time I was a fresh-faced grad student early into my Ph.D. This was my first foray into public speaking. Feeling somewhat thrown in at the deep end, I thought it would be a good idea to open with a joke. It was nice to see the other speakers, I said, because we hadn't all been in a room together since Bilderberg. It didn't go over too well.

The conference, I must say, was greatly improved by Ian's presence and the mix of viewpoints among delegates. There was some lively debate between the speakers and audience members throughout the conference, and Ian's talk, all about how 9/11 was an inside job, was an interesting counterpoint to the other lectures. Yet the moment that most stands out to me happened—like many of life's most interesting moments—in the pub afterward. I got chatting with an audience member who was pretty sure that 9/11 was an inside job. But he wasn't, it turned out, a huge fan of Ian R. Crane. I asked him, if the government really was behind 9/11, why is Ian allowed to go around telling everyone; why don't the conspirators just shut him up? He glanced over his shoulder and leaned toward me. It's quite possible, he said, that Ian R. Crane is *working for the government*, trying to discredit conspiracy theorists by making them look foolish.

This came as a surprise. I wasn't shocked that my academic pals and I were suspected of being government-sponsored disinformation agents. We were essentially saying that maybe there is no big cover-up, and, after all, that's presumably what somebody who is part of a big cover-up *would* say. But the idea that somebody claiming to *expose* the cover-up might be *part* of the cover-up is another level of deviousness altogether.

That was the first time I'd come across this kind of meta–conspiracy theory. It turns out, though, that it's a fairly common idea among committed conspiracists. In *Revelations: Alien Contact and Human Deception,* astrophysicist and UFOlogist Jacques Vallée argues that many claims of UFO sightings and alien abductions are part of an elaborate disinformation campaign designed to undermine the credibility of serious UFO scholars (like Vallée himself, naturally). Intimidating, paying off, murdering, or otherwise shutting up every conspiracy theorist who stumbles upon the incredible truth would presumably be fairly labor-intensive, the logic goes. It would be easier to discredit conspiracy movements from *within*, by actively spreading ever more convoluted, implausible, absurd theories, thereby manufacturing an atmosphere in which conspiracy theorists are invariably seen as unhinged wack-jobs who aren't worth paying attention to. As Vallée muses, you can't stop a speeding train just by standing in its way. A better tactic might be to hop on board and crank up the velocity until it loses control and jumps the tracks.

There's even a conspiracy theory for the popularity of the term *conspiracy theory*. According to Lance deHaven-Smith, the fact that the phrase came to be associated with faulty thinking "was planned and orchestrated by the government itself." Specifically, CIA agents started surreptitiously popularizing the term in the 1960s as a "whisper campaign against critics of the Warren commission"—shorthand for *the person making this claim is crazy*. According to Bob Blaskiewicz, who teaches a course on conspiracy theories at University of Wisconsin Eau Claire, this idea has been around since the late 1990s, and it has only gained momentum since then. DeHaven-Smith, in his 2013 book *Conspiracy Theory in America*, laments, "the CIA's campaign to popularize the term 'conspiracy theory' and make conspiracy belief a target of ridicule and hostility must be credited, unfortunately, with being one of the most successful propaganda initiatives of all time." (Though in the very next sentence deHaven-Smith acknowledges that more people doubt the lone gunman account than believe it, which seems, to me at least, to somewhat undermine the success of the alleged smear campaign.)

All this illustrates one of the central features of the conspiracy mindset. Conspiracism is a lens through which the world can be viewed, and it has the potential to distort everything in its field of view. Anything—even a humble academic conference—could be part of the plot, and anyone could be in on it, whether they are spreading conspiracy theories or debunking them. Of course, not everyone who believes conspiracy theories falls all the way to the bottom of this intellectual rabbit hole. Yet, as we'll see, the conspiracy mindset means that connoisseurs of conspiracy often tar everything with the same brush—even when it means thinking everything in the news is a conspiracy, believing made-up stories about energy drinks, or simultaneously entertaining theories that seem to flat-out contradict one another.

#FalseFlag

On December 14, 2012, Adam Lanza, a troubled young man who had been diagnosed with Asperger syndrome and obsessive compulsive disorder, went on a shooting spree. He killed his mother in their home in Newtown, Connecticut, and then drove to Sandy Hook Elementary School, where he shot and killed six adults and twenty children. When police arrived, Lanza shot himself.

It took investigators days to piece together the details and make the information public. In the hours following the tragedy, however, confusion reigned. The news media scrambled for exclusives, passing around unconfirmed rumors about the identity and motives of the person or people responsible, only to retract the claims minutes or hours later as the investigation unfolded. Over the course of the day, it was wrongly reported that a second gunman, a man spotted wearing military fatigues, had been involved; that the shooter was the father of a child at the school; and that the gunman's mother was a teacher at the school. Worse, for a few hours the actual gunman's brother, Ryan Lanza, was mistakenly named as the culprit, when in reality he was on a bus from his Manhattan office to his New Jersey home frantically protesting his innocence on Facebook.

Yet even in the panicked hours immediately following the shooting, some people felt that no further explanation was needed. They had already figured out who was behind the shooting: It was a false-flag operation staged by the United States government. Articles and comments quickly flooded conspiracy theory websites, proclaiming that the shooter (or more likely multiple gunmen) was a government patsy under the influence of mind control. Theorists asserted that the distraught parents of murdered children were "crisis actors" and said that President Obama faked tears during a press conference. Some saw the media's retraction of incorrect information as evidence of the cover-up. One theorist eventually sent a letter to Adam Lanza's father, reassuring him that his son had been drugged by the CIA and forced to commit his acts in order to generate support for gun-control legislation.

When events are caught on camera, the opportunity for amateur sleuths to suss out clues of conspiracy is even greater. On April 15, 2013, two homemade bombs exploded near the finish line of the Boston Marathon. Three people were killed, and more than two hundred others were injured. Within the hour, professional conspiracy theorist Alex Jones tweeted, "Our hearts go out to those that are hurt or killed . . . but this thing stinks to high heaven #falseflag." The same afternoon, in a nationally televised press conference, Jones's colleague Dan Bidondi asked Massachusetts governor Deval Patrick if the attack was "another false flag staged attack to take our civil liberties and promote homeland security while sticking their hands down our pants on the streets?" "No," Patrick responded flatly; "Next question."

Online, thousands of people trawled through closed-circuit TV images, news footage, amateur photos and videos, and eyewitness accounts from the scene of the explosions looking for anomalies. A widely circulated picture taken the moment one of the bombs exploded captured a guy apparently striding across the roof of a nearby building, leading to suggestions that the man had had something to do with the explosions. Another image captured two shady-looking men wearing hats and backpacks, presumed to be military contractors who had secretly orchestrated the attack. Another pointed out the resemblance between an injured man and a soldier who lost both his legs in Afghanistan two years earlier, which was passed around as evidence that the bombing had been staged, the victims merely acting. Writing for the *Wire*, Philip Bump reported that, as of 10:30 P.M. on the night of the bombing— just eight hours after the explosions—a Google search for "boston marathon false flag" returned more than eighty five thousand hits.

Events that take place elsewhere in the world receive similar scrutiny. At around two in the afternoon on May 22, 2013, two men attacked and killed British soldier Lee Rigby on a street in Woolwich, a suburb of London, attempting to behead him with a machete in front of horrified bystanders. Online, conspiracy-oriented commenters pored over photos and video from the scene, pointing out apparent anomalies, such as what they considered to be an insufficient amount of blood. Likewise, on the morning of January 7, 2015, two gunmen stormed the Paris office of the French satirical newspaper Charlie Hebdo, killing eleven people and wounding eleven more. As the gunmen fled the scene one paused to shoot a police officer in the head, at point blank range, as he lay on the ground pleading for his life. When a chilling video of the execution emerged, captured by a witness in a nearby building, some conspiracy theorists again complained that the apparent lack of gore proved that the event was faked. "Official narratives are inherently suspect because power always looks out for itself," one commenter wrote of the video; "This appears to be a good example—whether what it shows is relatively harmless or sinister—to remind us of that fact."

Even the weather might be part of the conspiracy. Hurricane Katrina, which struck the southeastern United States in August 2005, remains one of the worst natural disasters to occur on American soil. It's estimated that more than eighteen hundred people were killed, and the damage cost in the region of eighty-one billion dollars. The worst of it was in New Orleans, where levees burst, flooding the city. Conspiracy theories about Katrina flourished almost immediately and remain popular. Some merely allege that the levees were deliberately destroyed in an act of profiteering or ethnic cleansing; others claim that the hurricane was conjured up out of thin air by the Bush government using powerful secret military weather manipulation technology.

I'm not saying conspiracy thinking is a product of the digital age. Both the mainstream media and its critics struggle to satisfy the conflicting demand for truth and the desire for quick answers. The Internet has simply made it quicker and easier than ever before to share information as events are still unfolding. Within minutes of an event hitting the news wires anyone with an Internet connection can begin pontificating about how it is evidence of some kind of plot or cover-up. As psychologist Mike Wood noted, the Internet and twenty-four-hour rolling news provide the kind of raw material that conspiracy theories thrive on; "by sheer weight of numbers, there are bound to be some apparent inconsistencies that can be seized upon and used as evidence against the mainstream narrative of the event." On the other hand, the Internet allows conspiracy theories to be debunked as quickly as they are hatched.

The point is, the Sandy Hook shooting, the Boston bombing, the Woolwich and Charlie Hebdo attacks, and Hurricane Katrina are just a few relatively recent examples out of an endless parade of events that provide fodder for conspiracist imaginations. From shootings and bombings to aircraft disasters and disappearances to international conflicts to disease outbreaks, there's hardly an event in the news that doesn't provoke at least a short-lived flurry of conspiracy theories.

The fact that some people are so quick to come up with or buy into conspiracy theories, even in the chaotic minutes after an event when the explanation cannot possibly be known, hints that there is more to conspiracy thinking than impartial evaluation of the evidence. When it comes to events like the assassination of JFK, the moon landing, or even the 9/11 attacks, years have now passed, information has been gathered, and so people advocating conspiracy theories can reasonably claim to have surveyed the evidence. But in the confused aftermath of an event—as when the media wasn't sure how many gunmen had opened fire on defenseless children at Sandy Hook or who was behind the Boston bombing—there's often little evidence to go on, and the story can change rapidly as new information comes to light. In these situations, a claim of conspiracy made by someone with no access to special information can't be based on careful study of the evidence. It's as if the theories were prefabricated. As Emma Jane and Chris Fleming put it, "these are conclusions lying in wait for friendly 'facts.'"

One Conspiracy, Different Forms

The second hint that conspiracism is about more than mere evidence is that the various, seemingly unconnected events that give rise to conspiracy theories are rarely interpreted as the product of unrelated conspiracies planned by independent groups with their own idiosyncratic motives and goals. Instead, conspiracy theorists have a remarkable knack for weaving a multitude of seemingly unrelated events together, into a single rich tapestry.

In the case of the Sandy Hook shooting, many theories assert that the shooting was not an isolated event, but merely the latest in a string of false-flag operations that includes the shootings at Columbine High School, Virginia Tech, a cinema in Aurora, Colorado, a Sikh temple in Wisconsin, and a shopping mall in

Oregon, to name just a few. All these horrific events, they say, are part of the same singular plot: a ruse staged by government operatives intent on taking away the Second Amendment right to bear arms. (That way we the people won't be able to resist the implementation of the New World Order when the time comes.) The conspiratorial ties between events might even extend to using the same actors to stage different atrocities; Mike Wood points out that "several YouTube videos purport to point out people at the site of the Boston Marathon bombing who look vaguely similar to others who were involved in the Sandy Hook shooting, giving further support to the idea that both were the result of crisis-acted fakery."

And according to some of the people who think that Hurricane Katrina was part of a genocidal conspiracy, so too are the many other particularly destructive storms, tsunamis, and earthquakes. The source of just about any anomalous natural phenomenon, from devastating earthquakes to unusual amounts of precipitation, they claim, is HAARP—the High Frequency Active Auroral Research Program—a (recently decommissioned) U.S. military research facility that the government uses, so the story goes, to manipulate storms and conjure up earthquakes on a whim.

This urge to explain just about anything that happens in the world as one small piece in a much larger puzzle pervades all conspiracy thinking. When Jonathan Kay, a reporter with Canada's *National Post* newspaper, spent time interviewing 9/11 conspiracy theorists for his book *Among the Truthers*, he found that talk of 9/11 would inevitably lead to other conspiracy theories—often to do with who killed JFK. "Scratch the surface of a middle-aged 9/11 Truther," Kay wrote, "and you are almost guaranteed to find a JFK conspiracist." I found the same trend speaking at the Bilderberg Fringe Festival to a handful of people who collectively explained everything from global warming to the Black Plague as the machinations of some sinister conspiracy. (We'll hear more about the Bilderberg Fringe Festival in Chapter 6.) Perhaps the clearest example comes from David Icke. Icke is famous for giving marathon ten-hour-long, unscripted lectures to sell-out crowds, during which he explains the entirety of human experience as part of an interdimensional conspiracy. "People say I see conspiracies everywhere," Icke said during a 2014 lecture at Wembley Arena in London; "I don't. I see one conspiracy that takes different forms."

In short, people don't tend to buy into just one conspiracy theory. Rather, someone who believes a conspiracy was to blame for one event probably believes many other events are best explained as the result of similar plots, schemes, and cover-ups. By the same token, somebody who doubts any given conspiracy theory probably doubts many others.

This might not come as a surprise. We've all found ourselves debating someone who seems to believe everything that happens in the world is evidence of conspiracy. But it ought to be surprising. The question of whether a senseless shooting in France was scripted by government agents is unrelated in any obvious sense to the possibility that a British princess was assassinated by the monarchy, which in turn is unrelated to the issue of whether the American government possesses secret weather manipulation technology, which has nothing to do with the question of whether the footage of Neil Armstrong's giant leap for mankind was shot on the surface of the moon or in a terrestrial film studio. Presumably an impartial researcher might assign each claim a different degree of plausibility. Yet that doesn't tend to be the case. We've seen indications of this trend in the knee-jerk rush to label ongoing events as part of a conspiracy, and the tendency to see individual conspiracies as just one element of a larger plot. But it's important to make sure we're not being unfair, cherry picking a few unrepresentative examples. We need to back up the anecdotal observations with hard data.

Now, when it comes to measuring belief in conspiracy theories, psychologists don't simply ask people whether they reckon, say, 9/11 was an inside job, yes or no. This is an important point, because we're not just interested in the minds of the most devoted conspiracy theorists; we're interested in how *everyone* forms their beliefs. While there are certainly some people out there who are utterly convinced that 9/11 was an inside job— and people who are convinced it wasn't—most people's opinions lie somewhere in the gray area between complete rejection and complete acceptance. Perhaps you harbor a mild suspicion that it was a conspiracy; maybe you're pretty sure that it wasn't a conspiracy; or you might just be completely on the fence. Belief isn't a binary, all-or-nothing quantity, in other words; it's a spectrum. We want to capture this kind of variation, and so we don't just measure outright belief and disbelief. Neither do we measure belief in just one conspiracy theory. To find out if there's a pattern to the way people rate different theories we need to ask about a bunch of them.

In the abstract, this might sound complicated, but in practice it's pretty straightforward. Imagine (or better yet, jot down on a piece of paper) the numbers 1 through 7, written in a row, left to right. The number 1 means you're completely convinced 9/11 was *not* an inside job by the U.S. government, the number 7 means you're certain it *was*, and number 4 sitting in the middle means you're torn between the two, completely undecided. The numbers in between represent various degrees of doubt or certainty. What number would you circle? Now imagine a second identical row of numbers below the first. Let's say this one is for the assassination of JFK; the number 1 means you're positive Lee Harvey Oswald did it alone, 7 means you're certain he didn't, and so on. Now imagine another scale below that one for the moon landing, another for the idea that some small secret group secretly controls world events, and others for any conspiracy theory you like.

Is there a pattern to the numbers you would circle? There's no reason why your answers couldn't be all over the board. Indeed, some people's will be. But when we get large numbers of people to fill in scales like this, we find that people's answers, more often than not, tend to form a roughly straight line down the page. If you rate your belief in a 9/11 conspiracy theory as a 3, say, there's a good chance you'll rate all the others in the same ballpark. Someone who leans towards a 5 or 6 for the moon landing conspiracy theory is likely to rate 9/11, JFK, New World Order, and all the other theories in the same "mild belief" range. To put it more technically, belief in one conspiracy theory *correlates* with belief in others—even when there's no obvious logical connection between the theories.

With rare exception, almost every study that has looked at the relationships between beliefs in different conspiracy theories has found these kinds of correlations. Americans who believe that their government is hiding aliens at Area 51 are more likely to think vaccines are unsafe. Londoners who suspect a conspiracy was behind the July 7, 2005, bombings on the London Underground are more likely to suspect that the assassination of Martin Luther King Jr. was the result of conspiracy by the U.S. government. Austrians who believe there was a conspiracy behind a well-known crime, the kidnapping of Natascha Kampusch, are more likely to believe that AIDS was manufactured by the U.S. government. Germans who believe the Apollo moon landings were faked are more likely to believe that the New World Order is planning to take over. Visitors of climate science blogs who think climate change is a hoax are more likely to think that Princess Diana got whacked by the British royal family.

But perhaps the clearest demonstration of this predictive power is the fact that some people will even believe a conspiracy theory that psychologists have just made up out of whole cloth. For a study conducted in Austria, a team of researchers led by Viren Swami concocted a theory about the popular energy drink Red Bull. The theory alleged that Red Bull contains illegal substances (the aptly named extract "testiculus taurus") that make people want to drink more of the product, and, more alarmingly, caused lab rats to grow rudimentary wings (hence the slogan "Red Bull gives you wings"). The drink only made it to market, the theory suggested, because the inventor pays off the food inspectors. Red Bull wasn't an arbitrary choice—it was selected as the basis of the conspiracy theory because of its particular relevance to the Austrians taking part in the study. Red Bull was developed by an Austrian, and the brand's parent company is one of the most successful Austrian companies of the last few decades. As the researchers put it, allegations that the success of Red Bull rests on a conspiracy ought to provide a "good 'breeding ground' for a conspiracy theory." Sure enough, some people rated the claims as being plausible. And, as expected, the people who bought into these entirely fictitious conspiracy theories were the same people who thought JFK was killed by a conspiracy, 9/11 was an inside job, and the New World Order is trying to take over the world, and so on. On the other hand, people who doubted those established conspiracy theories were likely to doubt the new one, too.

In short, the details of the theories don't seem to matter much. If you know a person's attitude toward one conspiracy theory, you can predict his or her attitudes toward other conspiracy theories with a fair degree of certainty, even when there is no obvious connection between the theories.

Dead and Alive

Why is it that buying into one conspiracy theory means you're likely to accept all the others (or, on the other hand, doubting one means you're likely to reject the rest)? One possible answer, suggested by sociologist Ted Goertzel, is that the conspiracy mindset operates according to the slippery logic that if one conspiracy theory were true, it could be taken as evidence for the truth of all the others. If you reckon that government agents had a hand in JFK's assassination, they'd probably be up for something like 9/11, too. And if authorities would attack their own citizens in a sham terrorist attack, what's to stop them secretly poisoning us with chemicals in the water and toxins in vaccines? And if they have no qualms with lying to their citizens about their health and safety, then why not fake the moon landing and cover up the existence of aliens? And if a small renegade group of plotters can get away with all that, then maybe some secret group of elites plans everything that goes on in the world. And on and on it goes. Conspiracy theories, according to Goertzel, make for a self-perpetuating network of beliefs because they all support one another. If you aren't willing to take the first step in believing one theory, then the rest look equally implausible. But once you buy into one theory, it opens the door to all the others.

In theory, then, persuading someone that one conspiracy theory might be true ought to make them more receptive to other, ostensibly unrelated theories. Suppose, for instance, I tell you that there are reasons to be suspicious about the car crash that killed Princess Diana. It's an open secret that the British government didn't approve of her relationship with Dodi Fayed, an Egyptian Muslim, nor her increasing involvement in politics. Just three days before her death she was quoted describing the government as "hopeless." Politicians were baying for her blood, making scathing comments like, "What was this woman doing meddling in politics, why didn't she stick to old ladies and little children. She is a 'loose cannon.'" Knowing this, it's entirely reasonable to question whether her death was simply a tragic accident, or something more.

At least, that's what psychologists Daniel Jolley and Karen Douglas told half of the people who took part in a 2014 study. The other half read a similar set of claims, but flipped around to argue *against* the conspiracy theory: "It is no secret that Princess Diana's popularity made some members of the government uneasy. However, there is no evidence at all to suggest that the British government were involved in her death . . . her death was simply a tragic accident." People who read the pro-conspiracy version unsurprisingly reported believing more strongly that Princess Diana's car crash was an assassination. More interestingly, they were also more open to conspiracy theories in general, like the idea that the government routinely involves itself in secret international plots and schemes. As expected, presenting the Diana conspiracy theory as plausible seems to have opened the door to believing that other plots and cover-ups are rife.

The self-perpetuating, mutually supportive logic pointed out by Ted Goertzel may be one aspect of the conspiracist mindset, but it's not the entire story. Things get more interesting, as demonstrated by a curious paradox concerning Osama Bin Laden.

Shortly after the 9/11 attacks, President Bush evoked the imagery of the Wild West, vowing to take al-Qaeda mastermind Osama Bin Laden "dead or alive." A global manhunt was soon under way. Bin Laden evaded capture for almost a decade, until eventually the search led to a compound in Abbottabad, Pakistan. In the early hours of May 2, 2011, an elite team of Navy SEALs approached in stealth helicopters and stormed the compound, under the orders of President Obama. "After a firefight," the president later announced, "they killed Osama Bin Laden."

Or did they? What if Bin Laden had, in fact, died of natural causes a decade earlier? After all, it's widely known that he suffered a range of maladies, from an injured foot to diabetes. More importantly, some people think Bin Laden may have had

Marfan syndrome. People with Marfan syndrome are often tall and thin with unusually long, thin fingers and a curved spine— just like Bin Laden. It also causes heart valve problems that can kill sufferers without warning. This, according to some conspiracy theorists, is what really killed Bin Laden. And it happened back in late 2001 or early 2002, just months after the 9/11 attacks. The American intelligence community covered up his death, keeping his specter alive in the public consciousness for years as a terrorist boogeyman to justify their War on Terror. All the while, they secretly kept Bin Laden's corpse on ice, ready to be wheeled out at an opportune moment.

Or *did* they? What if Bin Laden is, in fact, still alive and well? After all, the U.S. government refused to provide any physical evidence that they really had killed him. They merely asserted that the body had been buried at sea in accordance with Muslim practices, and that releasing gruesome pictures of Bin Laden's corpse might incite terrorists into violent retaliation. Glenn Beck, an American radio show host who frequently dabbles in conspiracism, suggested that Bin Laden may have actually been captured alive, to be interrogated in some secret room about whatever plots al-Qaeda had in the works. According to others, the Americans might even be looking after Bin Laden. He was a U.S. asset all along, they said, recruited by the CIA back in the 1980s when U.S. intelligence aligned itself with mujahideen groups fighting against the Soviets in Afghanistan. Even Mahmoud Ahmadinejad, the president of Iran, got on board with this theory, speculating in an interview on America's ABC network (in 2010, a year before Bin Laden was reportedly killed) that Bin Laden was living safe and sound in Washington, D.C.

So we have three very different possibilities. There's the "official story"—Bin Laden was killed by the U.S. military on May 2, 2011. And there are two competing conspiracy theories—either he had already been dead for years when the raid took place, or he was still alive. Clearly both conspiracy theories can't be true. As the title of a paper by psychologists Mike Wood and Karen Douglas put it, Bin Laden can't be "dead *and* alive." And yet their paper reports something odd. When Wood and Douglas asked people how much they agreed with the two conflicting conspiracy theories, they found that the people who gave credence to one were likely to also suspect that its counter-point was true. In other words, people with a hunch that Bin Laden was already dead were more likely to suspect he was still alive; some people seemingly entertained the idea that Bin Laden might be some kind of Schrödinger's terrorist, alive and dead at the same time.

The possibility of entertaining contradictory conspiracy theories isn't exclusive to Bin Laden's uncertain demise. Wood and Douglas ran another study looking at belief in a handful of conspiracy theories about Princess Diana. Again, some of the theories contradicted one another. One alleged that Diana faked her own death to escape the spotlight, while another proposed that her death had been arranged by the British secret service. Like the people who seemingly thought Bin Laden was simulta-neously dead and alive, people who suspected that Diana faked her own death tended to also suspect that she had been assassi-nated by secret agents. Another team of researchers found that the more someone is inclined to think that the U.S. government had advanced knowledge of the 9/11 attacks and merely allowed al-Qaeda to carry them out, the more likely he or she is to also think that the government actively planned the whole thing. As Nicoli Nattrass notes, Thabo Mbeki, the South African presi-dent from 1999 to 2008, claimed that HIV had been manufactured by the CIA, while seeming also to entertain the notion that the virus is harmless, or that it doesn't even exist. Looking at conspiracism in the Middle East, Daniel Pipes points out that "when Washington and Baghdad get along, Tehran sees a conspiracy; when they go to war, it's another conspiracy."

Why is it that some people can seemingly believe that Osama Bin Laden is simultaneously dead *and* alive, Diana faked her own death *and* was murdered, the U.S. government both planned *and* didn't plan 9/11, AIDS is a bioweapon *and* a myth, and both war *and* peace are evidence of conspiracy? As the authors of the Bin Laden study point out, the positive relation-ship between these beliefs doesn't intuitively make a lot of sense. Surely the correlations between contradictory theories should be negative: The more you believe one particular conspiracy theory, the less likely anything that contradicts it ought to appear. Ted Goertzel's monological belief system, in which the assumed existence of one conspiracy serves as evidence in favor of other conspiracy theories, can't account for these correlations. There's no sense in which Bin Laden being dead makes it more likely that he's still alive.

The answer to the paradox was revealed by one more question that Wood and Douglas included in their study. How strongly do you agree, they asked, that the U. S. government is "hiding some important or damaging piece of information about the Bin Laden raid?" This more vague allegation—that the official version of events simply can't be trusted, for reasons unspecified—turned out to be the key to unlocking the contradictory beliefs. The more someone accepted that *something* was being covered up, the more likely he or she was to buy into the two contradictory theories. Once this was statistically accounted for, the relationship between the contradictory theories vanished. In other words, it's not that believing Bin Laden was dead all along makes you more likely to believe he was still alive, or vice versa. It's that believing that *something* fishy was going on makes you more likely to entertain *any* conspiracy theories—even two that contradict one another.

Conspiracy Minded

This brings us to the heart of the conspiracy mindset. How strongly you believe any particular conspiracy theory is shaped not just by the facts of the matter, nor, as Goertzel argued, simply by how each theory props up all the others. Rather, your feelings about each individual conspiracy theory are determined in large part by the extent to which you buy into an overarching set of all-purpose assumptions about how the world works, like the idea that somebody is always engaged in deception, there is always more to events than meets the eye, we are never told the whole story—in other words, we might say, by how *conspiracy minded* you are. Seen in this light, conspiracism is a lot like any other personality trait. Just as knowing a person's score on a measure of extroversion provides a clue about how he or she will behave in a range of social situations, knowing someone's score on a measure of conspiracism tells us how he or she is likely to react to a variety of conspiracy theories.

Describing conspiracy thinking this way—as a psychological disposition—tends to strike some people, particularly those who believe conspiracy theories, as being absurd. "It's not about psychology," they might protest; "the facts speak for themselves." And it's an entirely understandable objection. When we believe something, our belief doesn't seem like a product of some ineffable ideology; it just seems *correct*, independent of our personal foibles or preferences. But to say that there are psychological reasons for believing conspiracy theories is not to suggest they are unusual in that regard. On the contrary, our psychology shapes most, if not all, of our beliefs.

Nowhere is the judgment-clouding influence of ideology easier to spot than when it comes to politics. As an example, Joe Uscinski and Joseph Parent point to the restaurant chain Godfather's Pizza. Up until early 2011, Democrat and Republican voters liked the chain equally well, according to YouGov's BrandIndex score. Then, in May 2011, a former C.E.O. of the chain, Herman Cain, announced that he was seeking the Republican party nomination to run for U.S. president. Cain's stint as C.E.O. some fifteen years earlier became a talking point throughout his campaign. Suddenly a wedge was driven between Democrat and Republican pizza aficionados. Godfather's ratings rose among Republicans and tanked with Democrats.

It's tempting to think our political affiliation is a product of all our individual, impartial decisions and judgments about candidates and policies. But, in fact, it has become increasingly clear that ideology comes first, and colors our interpretation of the facts. Presumably Godfather's didn't start serving better pizza to Republicans and skimping on Democrats' pepperoni. The quality of the pizza didn't change. The only thing that changed was how the company jibed with people's underlying political ideology.

Likewise, when it comes to conspiracy theories it's tempting to think that our belief—or disbelief—is based on a fair assessment of the facts. But the reality is that our beliefs are shaped by our overarching worldview more often than we might like to admit. As I said, conspiracism is a lens through which we view the world—and we all have a different prescription. Few people credulously accept every theory, and few staunchly reject every suggestion of conspiracy. Most of us are somewhere in the middle, mildly skeptical of conspiracy theories across the board, but unwilling to write them off completely.

Understanding this fundamental feature of the conspiracy mindset is our first step toward understanding the psychology of conspiracy theories. We can begin to see why conspiracy theories spring up around events even before there is an official story, and why people who buy into one conspiracy often see it as just one point in a collection of connected dots. We can see why some people will even buy into a fake theory, or two claims that contradict one another. We can see why the spread of conspiracy theories might look like a conspiracy. And we can perhaps see why even a humble academic conference might look like a harbinger of the coming New World Order.

But this is just the beginning of our journey into the psychology of conspiracy theories. After all, it doesn't explain why some people are more conspiracy minded than others, or why we are conspiracy minded at all. These are the questions we must turn our attention to next, beginning with the idea that is bandied about most often: people who believe conspiracy theories are just paranoid.

CHAPTER FIVE

The Paranoid Fringe

Aldous Huxley's 1932 novel *Brave New World* has been giving conspiracy theorists nightmares for the best part of a century. In it, Huxley imagines a seemingly utopian future. There's no war, no poverty. Pretty much everyone is satisfied with life. But, of course, things aren't quite as rosy as they first appear. The apparent peace and happiness is all artifice, carefully manufactured by a tyrannical dictatorship that insidiously controls every aspect of its citizens' lives. The government ensures that its citizens never question the system by brainwashing them with subliminal messages encouraging unthinking conformity and addiction to the mind-numbing narcotic, Soma. People are treated as little more than cattle, bred simply to work, consume, and die.

Huxley's vision of the coming Brave New World, in short, contains all the ingredients of a jolly good conspiracy theory, and it's highly regarded among conspiracy-minded people as a prescient warning of things to come. It is fitting, therefore, that one of the most iconic symbols of conspiracism was the creation of Aldous Huxley's older brother, Julian.

In a 1927 short story by the lesser-known Huxley, an eccentric scientist stumbles upon the secret of telepathy. Eventually he discovers that he can use it as a powerful psychic weapon, capable of surreptitiously controlling people's minds across vast distances. The only hitch is that the person sending out the hypnotic commands is just as susceptible to them as his intended victims. Luckily, the scientist discovers a way to shield himself from the psychic energy. The trick is to insulate oneself with metal—specifically, by fashioning a makeshift head-covering out of metal foil. Thus was born the idea of the tinfoil hat as an effective—if not fashionable—line of defense against mind-control rays.

The tinfoil hat has since become inexorably associated with conspiracy theories and the people who believe them—a mocking symbol of irrational belief in invisible enemies and imagined plots. The trope has been played for comic effect in films like M. Night Shyamalan's alien-invasion movie *Signs* and television shows from *The X-Files* to *The Simpsons*. It was perhaps most entertainingly lampooned by the comic musician "Weird Al" Yankovic. His 2014 song *Foil* begins as an earnest tribute to the advantages of tinfoil for preserving leftover food. The second verse takes a sinister turn, however, when Yankovic dons the requisite headwear, confesses that he has uncovered a vast conspiracy, and urges listeners to fashion foil hats of our own in case aliens take an interest in the contents of our skull (among other bodily cavities).

As well as being sported by fictional conspiracy theorists, the tinfoil hat is often used to ridicule real people thought to be acting a little (or a lot) paranoid. Journalists regularly lean on the tinfoil trope when writing about conspiracy theories and the people who believe them. Even politicians occasionally get in on the game. In 2014, Missouri taxpayers became unwitting accomplices in a foil-based jibe. Some opponents of an initiative to introduce the Common Core school curriculum in Missouri schools accused it of being a plot to covertly collect data on children, or perhaps even to brainwash them. State Representative Mike Lair not-so-subtly mocked the Common Core critics by submitting a proposal to set aside eight dollars of taxpayer money in the state's education budget to buy "two rolls of high density aluminum to create headgear designed to deflect drone and/or black helicopter mind reading and control technology." (The Common Core opponents, unsurprisingly, were not amused by Lair's joke. They got payback when pranksters wrapped Lair's desk and everything on it in—you guessed it—tinfoil.)

The tinfoil hat is probably one of the first things that comes to mind when you conjure up a mental image of a conspiracy theorist. The cliché is part and parcel of the prevailing stereotype of conspiracy theorists: They are a handful of deluded kooks lurking on the fringes of respectable society, with a penchant for obscure Internet forums, talk radio, and tinfoil. For many armchair pundits, there is a simple answer to why these people believe conspiracy theories: They are hopelessly paranoid loons. But do conspiracy theorists deserve their reputation for paranoia?

The Paranoid Style

One man did more than anyone else to legitimize the view that conspiracy theories are the purview of the paranoid fringe. Richard Hofstadter was a professor of American history at New York City's prestigious Columbia University from the 1940s until his death in 1970. He had the classic look of a mid-twentieth-century intellectual, with short, neatly combed hair, clip-on bow ties, and scholarly horn-rimmed glasses. One of Hofstadter's students referred to him as "almost nondescript." But his unassuming appearance belied a passion for unusual ideas. Hofstadter won two Pulitzer prizes for his books on populism and anti-intellectualism in American culture, as well as tackling subjects like social Darwinism and status anxiety. As a fellow historian put it, Hofstadter devoted much of his career to understanding "the odd, the warped, the zanies, and the crazies of American life." It is understandable, then, that he would eventually turn his attention to conspiracy theories.

In 1964, Hofstadter published an essay in *Harper's Magazine* summarizing the role of conspiracy theories in American history and speculating about the possible causes of conspiracy thinking. In doing so, he became one of the first social scientists to contemplate conspiracy theories, transforming them into a topic fit for respectable academic discussion. Almost every analysis of conspiracism that has come since owes an intellectual debt to Hofstadter's pioneering essay. Beyond academia, his essay contributed to the stereotype of the paranoid, fringe-dwelling conspiracy theorist and it is still often quoted approvingly by pundits. Which is a pity, because as we'll see, Hofstadter's analysis was as flawed as it was insightful.

Hofstadter gave his essay the deliberately provocative title "The Paranoid Style in American Politics." In case that was too subtle, he happily explained that when he said "paranoid style," he meant it as an insult. According to Hofstadter, the paranoid style is a distorted way of viewing the world, characterized by delusional thinking, excessive suspicion, shoddy scholarship, exaggeration of the facts, and unjustified leaps of imagination. But the key feature, he wrote, is "conspiratorial fantasy." Hofstadter conceded that there are, of course, legitimate conspiracies in politics, and so merely speculating about the possible existence of conspiracies is not necessarily delusional. "The distinguishing thing about the paranoid style is not that its exponents see conspiracies or plots here and there in history," he argued, "but that they regard a 'vast' or 'gigantic' conspiracy as the motive force in historical events." In other words, people suffering from the paranoid style see conspiracies everywhere. "The paranoid spokesman . . . traffics in the birth and death of whole worlds, whole political orders, whole systems of human values," Hofstadter rhapsodized. "He is always manning the barricades of civilization. He constantly lives at a turning point: it is now or never in organizing resistance to conspiracy. Time is forever just running out."

The paranoid style, Hofstadter argues, has polluted the thinking of minority political movements throughout American history, and around the world. Even though these disparate groups have had very different agendas, the underlying features of the paranoid style always remain the same. "A mentality disposed to see the world in this way may be a persistent psychic phenomenon," Hofstadter speculates; "while it comes in waves of different intensity, it appears to be all but ineradicable." Thankfully, however, he concluded that it usually afflicts only a "modest minority of the population" in possession of "uncommonly angry minds." In other words, the paranoid style thrives on the fringes of respectable society.

Inspired by Hofstadter's vivid portrait of conspiracy theorists as a small brigade of fringe crackpots suffering from an apocalyptically paranoid way of thinking, much of the ensuing social scientific research set out to see whether people who are drawn to conspiracy theories really do have an unusually paranoid disposition. One of the first researchers to put Hofstadter's thesis to the test was Ted Goertzel, a professor of sociology at Rutgers University in New Jersey. In 1992, Goertzel and a team of researchers telephoned hundreds of Jerseyites at random, asking how they felt about a few conspiracy theories that were popular at the time. Then the researchers posed questions designed to measure one element of paranoid thinking: distrust. How much, they asked, do you trust your friends, family, neighbors, and authorities like the police? The results were clear; the less people trusted those around themselves, the more they tended to buy into conspiracy theories.

Other scientists have asked similar questions and found the same trend. Researchers have also found relationships with other indications of paranoia; people who believe conspiracy theories strongly tend to be a little more hostile, cynical, defiant of authority, anxious, and disagreeable than people who dismiss conspiracy theories. Between them, these studies have surveyed thousands of people, from rural African American churchgoers to young British undergraduate students. The findings aren't entirely clear cut; one study, for example, found that people who posted comments online debunking conspiracy theories were sometimes more hostile than people advocating conspiracy theories. On the whole, though, the pattern is pretty consistent. People who generally believe conspiracy theories tend to have a more paranoid disposition than people who generally doubt conspiracy theories.

So far so good for Hofstadter's thesis (and the tinfoil hat stereotype).

What about the other main element of Hofstadter's argument—his assertion that the paranoid style is primarily an affliction of people who dwell on the margins of society? In support of his thesis, Hofstadter had no trouble plucking instances of fringe political movements forwarding conspiracist claims from across three centuries of American history. Notable examples range from a rabble-rousing Massachusetts preacher warning, in 1798, of "impious conspirators" plotting to undermine the foundations of Christianity, to the Red Scare senator Joe McCarthy asking the U.S. Senate, in a 1951 speech, "How can we account for our present situation unless we believe that men high in this government are concerting to deliver us to disaster?"

How about other people exiled to the margins of society—people who don't necessarily have a political agenda? As well as asking his sample of New Jersey residents how distrusting they were, Goertzel asked how discontented they felt with society. He found that the more strongly people agreed with sentiments like "most public officials are not interested in the average man" and "it is hardly fair to bring a child into today's world," the more likely they were to buy into conspiracy theories. Other studies have found that the less satisfied with life people are in general, and the less control over their own circumstances they feel they have, the more likely they are to accept conspiracy theories.

Moreover, conspiracy theories appear to be especially popular among people with particularly good reason to feel powerless and discontented with society: members of racial or ethnic minorities (in the United States, at least, which is where all the research has been done). The main racial groups represented in Goertzel's sample of New Jerseyites were Hispanic, African American, and Caucasian. He found that Hispanics and African Americans tended, on the whole, to rate the theories as more plausible than did Caucasians. In 1999, a team of researchers at New Mexico State University found the same trend among their students. In 2006, another team of researchers randomly phoned more than one thousand Americans and asked what they thought about 9/11 conspiracy theories. Once again, minorities (in this case, African Americans, Hispanics, and Asian Americans) were generally more accepting of the theories than were Caucasians. And recent opinion polls show similar demographic differences for a host of theories.

So it looks like Hofstadter hit the nail on the head. Conspiracy theories seem to be popular among people suffering a surfeit of paranoia, as well as people who find themselves alienated from mainstream society and feeling like they are at the mercy of forces outside of themselves. And it's tempting to stop there, having neatly confirmed our stereotypes about the paranoid fringe. But if we did stop there, we would have seen only one small piece of a much bigger puzzle. For all Hofstadter's insight, he failed to grasp the true scope of conspiracism.

The Paranoid Masses

The glaring problem with Hofstadter's take on the paranoid style is simply that conspiracy theories are not exclusively a feature of the fringe. He wasn't wrong to point out that conspiracism thrives on the margins. His mistake was to stop there. As a consequence, he overlooked the fact that conspiracy theories thrive in the mainstream, too. Jesse Walker found so many examples woven so deeply into the fabric of America that he titled his book on the subject *United States of Paranoia*. In it, he pointedly subverted the title of Hofstadter's famous essay by titling a chapter "The Paranoid Style *Is* American Politics" [italics added]. The establishment, Walker points out, "has conspiracy theories of its own."

The foundling nation's first president, George Washington, could hardly be accused of being a fringe figure, for instance. Yet when an acquaintance accused Washington of *not* believing in an Illuminati conspiracy, he was quick to set the record straight, writing "on the contrary, no one is more truly satisfied of this fact than I am." A century later, presidents Theodore Roosevelt and Woodrow Wilson both felt there was a hidden hand behind government. "Behind the ostensible government sits enthroned an invisible government owing no allegiance and acknowledging no responsibility to the people," Roosevelt wrote in 1912; a year later Wilson warned ominously, "some of the biggest men in the United States, in the field of commerce and manufacture, are afraid of something. They know that there is a power somewhere so organized, so subtle, so watchful, so interlocked, so complete, so pervasive, that they had better not speak above their breath when they speak in condemnation of it." In the three decades after the Second World War, Lance deHaven-Smith notes, "U.S. officials asserted that communists were conspiring to take over the world, that the U.S. bureaucracy was riddled with Soviet spies, and that the civil rights and antiwar movement of the 1960s were creatures of Soviet influence." (Recall that one of Hofstadter's own examples of a "fringe" conspiracy theorist was Joe McCarthy, an elected United States senator. The implication was apparently lost on Hofstadter.) Even President Obama, in his 2012 reelection campaign, accused "secretive oil billionaires" of distorting his record and attempting to buy the election.

Of course, it's not just a few high-ranking members of government who occasionally fret about conspiracies. The conspiracy theories of the fringe often have Establishment counterparts. While slaves in antebellum America feared white doctors were plotting to kidnap and butcher them, plantation owners fretted about their slaves being manipulated into violent revolt by Northern abolitionists. And while turn-of-the-century populists worried that government was controlled by a cabal of international bankers, others denounced populism itself as a "cunningly devised and powerfully organized cabal." And every now and again whole swaths of the public get swept up in conspiracist frenzies. In the early twentieth century, the American public was gripped by fears of a vast, insidious conspiracy to kidnap innocent young white women and sell them into forced prostitution. Inspired by the lurid tales, President William Howard Taft quickly signed into law the White-Slave Traffic Act (now known as the Mann Act), which provided fifty thousand dollars to create the agency that would eventually be known as the Federal Bureau of Investigation. In the 1980s and '90s, a wave of "satanic panic" swept Britain and the United States, according to which a vast, insidious conspiracy of Satan-worshiping murderers was abusing and slaughtering innocent young children en masse.

It's worth noting that over time it seems Hofstadter came to suspect that conspiracism might be a bigger phenomenon than he had initially imagined. While an early version of his essay stated that the paranoid style affects only a "modest" minority of the population, he later upgraded his estimate to a "considerable" minority. But Hofstadter didn't have numbers to back up his claims, and even this more generous estimate still falls short of the true scope of conspiracism. The last few years have furnished us with dozens of opinion polls, and, far from being the purview only of a small handful of alienated paranoiacs, huge numbers of people believe conspiracy theories. When it comes to the 9/11 attacks, the death of Princess Diana, the moon landing, the impending New World Order, the fluoride in our water, the safety of vaccines, or the existence of aliens, for instance, somewhere between 10 and 30 percent of people believe conspiratorial accounts. And when it comes to who killed JFK, conspiracy theorists are the majority; according to some polls over the years, as few as one or two people out of ten have accepted that Lee Harvey Oswald acted alone.

But looking only at the numbers of people who say they believe a particular conspiracy theory can't tell us the true scope of conspiracy thinking. Theories fall in and out of fashion. Some grow in popularity over time, while others fade from view.

Some are a flash in the pan, forgotten almost as hastily as they were formed. As Joe Uscinski and Joseph Parent point out, there's no reason to suspect that measuring belief in "any one conspiracy theory is an accurate bellwether for conspiracy theorizing writ large—any more than the stock price of General Motors is a prime indicator of the stock market."

To get an indication of the prevalence of conspiracy thinking in general, we need to take a broader perspective. For one thing, we can look at the proportion of people who believe not just *a* particular conspiracy theory, but *any* conspiracy theory. Ted Goertzel, in his 1992 survey, found that almost everybody accepted at least one of the conspiracy theories he asked them about, and most believed several of the theories were definitely or probably true. More recently, a 2013 poll reported that 63 percent of the American public believed at least one political conspiracy theory. Likewise, a 2014 survey found that half of Americans believed at least one medical conspiracy theory.

These levels of belief stretch any definition of "fringe" well beyond breaking point. But even these substantial figures underestimate the true prevalence of conspiracy thinking. All they show is that the people who took part in the research believed at least one of the few conspiracy theories the polls specifically asked about. Goertzel asked about twelve different theories, the 2014 medical conspiracy survey contained six, and the 2013 political survey asked about just four theories. This is an unavoidable limitation. Asking people about every conspiracy theory under the sun would be more informative, but not many people would be willing to sit through the interrogation. If we *could* somehow carry out such an ambitious study, I suspect we would find that pretty much everyone believes one conspiracy theory or another. We're all conspiracy theorists, at least some of the time.

Everyday Paranoia

Why, then, is it still so easy to fall for the stereotype of the sweaty-palmed, fringe-dwelling, tinfoil-hatted conspiracy theorist?

Well, there *is* a kernel of truth to the stereotype. As we've seen, people who buy into conspiracy theories most enthusiastically really *are* likely to be more paranoid than people who dismiss conspiracy theories. The problem is the assumption that paranoia is all that unusual. Hearing the word, it's tempting to picture someone barely able to function, constantly tormented by the fear that everybody is out to get them. This kind of pathological paranoia certainly does exist, and it can be debilitating. Severe paranoia is a key symptom of mental illnesses such as schizophrenia and bipolar disorder. But this kind of debilitating paranoia is only ever experienced by a tiny fraction of the population. Pathological paranoia can't account for belief in conspiracy theories.

But that's not the kind of paranoia that the studies we talked about earlier measured. It's not what Hofstadter had in mind, either. In his essay, he explained that, although he was borrowing the term *paranoid* from a clinical syndrome, he didn't mean to label those he accused of demonstrating the paranoid style mentally ill. He was using the word *paranoid*, he said, in a more colloquial sense. Despite his qualified use of the term, though, Hofstadter's language was still stigmatizing. It doesn't make much sense to say that conspiracy theories are a product of "uncommonly angry minds," as Hofstadter put it, when they are so damn common.

Thing is, it doesn't take an uncommonly angry mind to be suspicious about those around you. Paranoid thoughts cover a broad spectrum of severity, and there is no gaping chasm separating the pathological from the prosaic. The kind of fully fledged persecutory delusions that haunt some people with schizophrenia are at one extreme, and they are mercifully rare. But the opposite extreme—never having a single fleeting paranoid thought cross your mind—is similarly rare. Have you ever found yourself on a crowded train and felt like a complete stranger was giving you the stink eye for no apparent reason? Maybe you've had the feeling that people at work are sending emails about you behind your back, or had a friend walk right past you without saying hello and wondered if they deliberately snubbed you? Or have you ever just been home alone at night and had a niggling sense that something was lurking in the dark somewhere, waiting to get you? If so, you've experienced paranoia.

But don't worry, you aren't alone. Just about everybody has paranoid thoughts, and more often than you might think.

Psychologist Daniel Freeman has devoted his career to studying paranoia. In 2005, Freeman and a team of colleagues asked more than a thousand perfectly ordinary college students how often they found themselves having mildly paranoid thoughts, such as wondering if someone is trying to take advantage of them, or if people are talking about them behind their back. Pretty much all of them admitted to having these kinds of suspicions once in a while. Perhaps more surprisingly, more than *three quarters* of the students admitted to having one or more paranoid thoughts on at least a weekly basis. Around a third of the students admitted to having paranoid thoughts even more frequently.

When Ted Goertzel and others measured paranoia, it was these kinds of everyday suspicions their questions were designed to assess. Doubts about people's motives, distrust and defiance of authority, and the hostility and cynicism that go along with suspecting that you live in a world where people can't always be trusted are all fairly common feelings among perfectly ordinary people. Of course, some people are relatively more prone to these feelings than others. And it's not hard to see how a relatively—but still only mildly—paranoid disposition could lead to a penchant for conspiracy theories. When you suspect people, especially authorities, of being untrustworthy, you're probably going to take "official" explanations with a grain of salt. If you think most people have sinister motives then conspiracy theories can make perfect sense. Paranoia goes hand in hand with conspiracy theories, but conspiracy theories aren't exclusive to the fringe, because *paranoia* isn't exclusive to the fringe.

Likewise, there's an element of truth to the idea that conspiracy theorists tend to feel relatively alienated and powerless. But this, too, is a more universal experience than the stereotypes about Internet-dwelling loners would have us imagine. Psychologists have long understood the importance of feeling in control, and it's not a desire exclusive to people on the fringes. We all want to believe that we understand our circumstances and are master of our own destiny. Yet the world has a nasty habit of reminding us that we're at the mercy of randomness. From losing your job in a recession to stepping on a rusty nail, there are countless random sources of misfortune that are impossible to anticipate or control, and can change the course of your life—or at least screw up your day—in an instant. We face constant challenges to our sense of control in less dramatic ways, too, in the form of shifting social alliances; discrimination; feeling left out, alienated, or unfairly disadvantaged; or just feeling that somebody has power over us.

And it is precisely when our sense of control is threatened that we are most likely to get a little paranoid. Realizing that the world is chaotic is, for most of us, deeply unsettling. The existential anxiety spurs us to find other ways to satisfy our need for order and control; when we can't be in control ourselves, we'll settle for thinking someone (or something) else is in the driver's seat. Psychologists call this *compensatory control*.

We have a few options when it comes to finding compensatory control. A popular one is to believe we have a powerful ally. Religions based around the idea of a benevolent, controlling God assure believers that everything happens for a reason. Or, keeping things more down-to-earth, we can put our faith in institutions like the government. Psychological studies show that when people's sense of personal control is eroded, they are more inclined to believe in an interventionist God (but not in a more hands-off deity) and to support increased governmental controls.

Another way to achieve compensatory control is to believe we have a powerful *enemy*. This might seem paradoxical—what could be more troubling than imagining people scheming against you? But having enemies has its perks. Remember, the thing we want to avoid above all else is seeing the world as haphazard. If things happen to us because of pure chance, we have little hope of comprehending, predicting, and controlling our fate. Believing that someone somewhere is in control—even if they don't have your best interests at heart—is preferable to thinking that the course of your life is dictated by nothing more than chance. Unlike faceless randomness, identifiable enemies can potentially be thwarted, managed, or at the very least understood.

This isn't a conscious decision. Our brains do most of the work for us, without us necessarily even realizing why we feel anxious to begin with. Roderick Kramer, another social scientist specializing in paranoia, describes how threats to our sense of control spur our brain into action. We become hypervigilant, scrutinizing people's behavior more carefully than usual and ruminating on the potential motives behind it, searching for clues to help restore order and understanding. Zealously gathering and dwelling on this ambiguous data makes us more likely to read sinister intent into innocuous events and to misinterpret innocent behavior as threatening. As a result, we can easily become fearful that somebody is untrustworthy or out to get us, which leads to even *more* heightened vigilance and rumination. Before we know it, our suspicions can run away from us, leading us to overestimate the degree to which other people or forces are in control and mean to do us harm.

A handful of recent experiments show how easy it is to set this process in motion. Psychologist Daniel Sullivan and colleagues, for instance, designed a series of experiments in which unsuspecting participants had their sense of control toyed with. In one study, the researchers asked people to rate how much control they have over things like "whether I am exposed to a disease," or "whether my family members suffer or not." A different group rated more innocuous statements, such as "I have control over how much TV I watch." The first group—the ones who had been subtly reminded of uncontrollable existential threats—were significantly more likely to buy into a made-up conspiracy theory about a rigged election.

Psychologists Jennifer Whitson and Adam Galinsky came up with another approach. In their study, test subjects simply had to recall either an experience over which they had no control, or one over which they had complete control. Afterward, everyone was asked to "imagine that you are one of the top administrators in your organization." Your job entails, among other things, monitoring the Internet and email use of all employees at the firm. You're soon up for a promotion, and the day before your big interview you notice an unusual spike in the number of emails flying between the co-worker who sits next to you and your boss. When you meet with your boss, you find out you're not getting the promotion, the scenario concluded. How likely is it, the psychologists asked, that the co-worker had something to do with the boss's decision? Compared to the people who were made to feel large and in charge, the people made to temporarily feel powerless were more likely to suspect that a conspiracy was afoot.

Outside the lab, Polish psychologist Monika Grzesiak-Feldman had students answer questions about a possible conspiracy fifteen minutes before an important exam was due to begin. Compared to students who were merely waiting for a lecture to begin, the nervous test-takers were more likely to endorse the conspiracy theories. Likewise, Roderick Kramer found that people who are new somewhere, are under intense scrutiny, or are in a relatively lowly position (such as first-year grad students and assistant professors) are more likely than their higher-status colleagues to suspect that people are scheming behind their back.

Prudent Paranoia

This leads us to a very different view of paranoia than the stereotypical notion that it is the product of "uncommonly angry minds." In all but the most severe cases, paranoia is not the product of malfunctioning synapses conjuring up sinister delusions. On the contrary, mild paranoia is common among entirely ordinary people, a product of our insatiable drive to understand the world and our place in it, and to feel like we're in the driver's seat.

And paranoia isn't always such a bad thing. After all, the world is often an uncertain and scary place. As Daniel Freeman points out, "walking down certain streets can feel threatening. Friends are not always good friends." Maybe people really *do* make fun of you behind your back. Maybe someone *is* out to get you. Being on your guard against the "potentially hostile intentions of others can be a highly intelligent and appropriate strategy to adopt." Roderick Kramer calls this "prudent paranoia." It is, he says, "the mind's early warning system," and it can serve as a "healthy defense against a genuine outside threat." But there is a fine line between healthy suspicion of potential threats and overzealous, unwarranted perceptions of sinister intent. It can be hard to know when we should trust someone and when we are being lied to—when someone is benevolent or indifferent toward us and when we are in danger of being taken advantage of. When in doubt, we tend to make what Kramer calls the "sinister attribution error." We err on the side of suspicion.

Imagine you're shopping for a new pair of sunglasses. You step into a nice little boutique, and try on a few pairs. Just as you slip on a particularly expensive pair, the salesperson says something like "that's a really good pair, they look amazing on you." How would you feel about this compliment? Of course, the salesperson might be sincere (and I'm sure they *do* look amazing on you). But then again, a salesperson has an ulterior motive to flatter you: There's commission to be made and sales goals to be met. Maybe he or she is buttering you up simply to try and part you with your cash. When psychologist Kelley Main and her colleagues put shoppers in this situation (without knowing it was part of the study, naturally), they were understandably suspicious of the salesperson's motives. Faced with an uncertain situation, and knowing that salespeople might have reason to be disingenuous, shoppers were prudently paranoid.

The real insight of the study comes from another scenario, in which shoppers received the same compliment from the salesperson *after* they had bought a pair of sunglasses. There was no longer such an obvious motive for the salesperson to lie about the shades; the shopper had already forked out for them. Yet shoppers still suspected that the compliment was disingenuous. A bit of residual suspicion is warranted, you might argue. The salesperson might be trying to drum up repeat business. But the compliment concerned the specific pair of sunglasses that the shopper was holding right then, right there. Before the sale, the compliment could directly influence the shopper's immediate decision—the motive to lie is strong. After the sale, it could only influence some hypothetical future behavior—the motive is much weaker. And yet the timing of the compliment made no difference whatsoever. Shoppers distrusted the flattery exactly as much whether it came before or after the transaction. This simple experiment shows how easy it is for justified suspicion to slip into unwarranted distrust. We're so good at spotting ulterior motives that we sometimes see them lurking behind innocent behavior.

In this light, we can begin to see why conspiracy theories are so widespread. The fact is, we have pretty good reason to be prudently paranoid when it comes to many of the perpetrators of the most popular conspiracy theories, among them governments, intelligence agencies, corporations, and secret societies.

We know that certain groups of people really are sometimes motivated to pull the wool over our eyes. Given a little prudent paranoia, our brains can go into overdrive, collecting and over-analyzing information until we see hidden motives and signs of deceit—whether or not they are really warranted. Like the shoppers who continued to distrust a salesperson even when the motive to lie wasn't there, our healthy suspicion of those in power can sometimes lead to perceptions of conspiracy.

Bad Blood

Consider again the research showing that, in the United States, racial minorities are generally more accepting of conspiracy theories as compared to Caucasians. It's not hard to see why members of racial or ethnic minorities might have cause for prudent paranoia, especially when it comes to predominantly white institutions and authorities. According to a study carried out in the Deep South state of Louisiana, black people who have been a victim of racial discrimination or police harassment are more likely to accept conspiracy theories than those who have not had these kinds of alienating experiences. An even stronger influence is the degree of control they believed that black people have in politics: Those who believe that black people can influence the political process are less likely to believe conspiracy theories, whereas those who feel excluded from the process are more accepting of conspiracy theories. Likewise, Ted Goertzel's study showed that, on the whole, African American and Hispanic people were less satisfied with society than were Caucasians. In his analysis, this surplus discontentment accounted for most of the difference in endorsement of the conspiracy theories.

Most of the research into conspiracism and race has focused specifically on African Americans. Conspiracy theories have been called "the life blood of the African-American community." There are theories alleging that prominent civil rights spokespeople like Malcolm X and Martin Luther King Jr. were assassinated by government agents; that certain brands of snacks, soft drinks, or cigarettes contain ingredients designed to sterilize black people; that the American government deliberately makes weapons and illegal drugs available in African American communities; and that birth control is part of an effort to keep the black population down. One of the most pervasive theories is the idea that the government and medical establishment don't tell people the whole story about AIDS, or even that AIDS is a biological weapon designed to selectively target black people. A 1992 *New York Times* article on the proliferation of conspiracy theories in the black community began, "bizarre as it may seem to most people, many black Americans believe that AIDS and the health measures used against it are part of a conspiracy to wipe out the black race."

The fact is, black Americans have more reason than most for prudent paranoia, particularly when it comes to their health and autonomy. In the antebellum South, white slave owners controlled their slaves' reproductive rights, and slaves and "free persons of color" were disproportionately used for medical experiments and dissecting-table demonstrations. After the Civil War, some whites seeking to maintain control over freed slaves stoked rumors of "night doctors," who supposedly stole, killed, and dissected blacks. Well into the twentieth century, lynchings were a form of public entertainment. Photographers sometimes set up in advance, and later sold postcards featuring the hanging corpse for fifty cents a pop. In the 1960s, civil rights organizations and leaders became a prime target of the FBI's counterintelligence program—referred to as COINTELPRO—which used illegal surveillance and infiltration in an attempt to "expose, disrupt, misdirect, discredit, or otherwise neutralize" their "subversive" activities. Even now, America is in the grip of renewed unrest over police treatment of black people. Following the killing, in August 2014, of an unarmed black teenager by a white police officer in Ferguson, Missouri, a Department of Justice investigation found evidence of deliberate racial discrimination in the town's policing practices.

Perhaps the most infamous and egregious mistreatment of blacks by whites in twentieth-century America was the Tuskegee Study of Untreated Syphilis in the Negro Male. The study started out with good intentions. In the late 1920s, the United States Public Health Service began developing syphilis testing and treatment programs for impoverished black people in the rural South. Before the treatment phase of the study could begin, however, the Great Depression of 1929 wiped out much of the study's funding, leaving the researchers lacking the resources to provide any treatment. In a last-ditch effort to salvage useful scientific data, the project was hastily reconceived as a study of the natural progression of the disease. As the experiment's originator blithely put it, "the Alabama community offered an unparalleled opportunity for the study of the effect of untreated syphilis."

Six hundred impoverished black sharecroppers signed up. Their poverty and the promise of free health care made them willing subjects. They were not told that they were being enrolled in a study of syphilis, or even whether they were infected (around four hundred of the men had syphilis; the rest served as uninfected controls). They were only told that they would be treated for "bad blood"—an all-purpose euphemism that referred to a wide variety of maladies. In reality, treating the men was never part of the plan. Initially slated to last just a few months, the study ultimately dragged on for forty years, thanks to the researchers' drive to satisfy their scientific curiosity, and their disregard for their patients' rights. Left untreated, syphilis can progress to neurosyphilis, infecting the central nervous system and causing confusion, blindness, numbness, paralysis, and dementia. When the study began, there was no reliable cure. The standard treatment was a year's course of arsenic and mercury injections. By 1943, however, a safe and effective treatment—penicillin—had been discovered. Instead of canceling the study and treating the infected men, the Public Health Service actively prevented them from getting treatment so the experiment could continue. The researchers were determined to follow their subjects to "end point"—meaning the autopsy table.

It wasn't until the 1960s that some people within the Public Health Service began to question the ethics of the study. With the civil rights movement winning increasing rights for black Americans, the Public Health Service realized that the Tuskegee study could be a potential PR problem. But the study didn't come to an end until 1972, when a whistleblower leaked the story to the press. The story sparked national outrage, leading to congressional hearings and, eventually, a formal apology issued by President Bill Clinton in 1997. Laws have since been passed to protect people who take part in medical research from harm.

Ethical committees must vet and approve study designs, and participants must consent to take part voluntarily, having been fully informed of the procedures and risks of the study. The Tuskegee study, we're assured, could never happen again.

Yet it has understandably left a lasting impression on the African American community. Black people who know about the Tuskegee study are more likely to believe AIDS conspiracy theories. More generally, surveys consistently find that African Americans are more likely than other demographics to feel that they could be used as guinea pigs without consent and to doubt that physicians fully explain research participation information. On their own, conspiracy theories may seem "bizarre," as the 1992 *New York Times* article put it. In the context of history, though, it's not hard to see why African Americans might be particularly wary of authorities not having their best interests at heart.

Just Because You're Paranoid

In *The Paranoid Style*, Richard Hofstadter described conspiracy logic as hinging on a "big leap from the undeniable to the unbelievable." Hofstader was right about conspiracy theories being based on a kernel of undeniable plausibility. Yet the fact is that, for many—perhaps most—of us, conspiracy theories clearly aren't unbelievable. The transition from prudent paranoia to preposterous allegations isn't so much a big leap as a gentle stroll. It can be hard to tell where one begins and the other ends.

Conspiracy scholar Peter Knight noted that the cliché of the tinfoil-hat-wearing paranoid kook is hollow: "Labeling a view paranoid has now become an empty circular description with a gloss of scientific rigor: the paranoid is someone who believes in conspiracy theories, and, conversely, the reason that people believe in conspiracy theories is that they are paranoid." We can now move beyond this flimsy caricature. We all get a little paranoid from time to time, especially when we have little control over our circumstances. Of course, some people experience it more than others—and sometimes with good reason.

Given what we know about the FBI illegally spying on anyone they considered subversive; military plans to assassinate foreign leaders and innocent civilians; and recent revelations about the National Security Agency's unprecedented snooping abilities, we can all perhaps be forgiven a little prudent paranoia. And yet, instead of being reassured when a plot comes to light, we are outraged, and horrified about what revelations will come next. Learning about one conspiracy, we can't help imagining other, as yet undiscovered, secrets. The more we learn, the more prudently paranoid we become. Conspiracies beget conspiracy theories. Paranoia never goes out of style.

In sum, you don't have to be a card-carrying member of the paranoid fringe to believe conspiracy theories, and you don't have to have a closet full of tinfoil headwear. Which is probably for the best, since it doesn't seem to work anyway. In 2005— almost eighty years after Julian Huxley coined the idea of donning metal to protect oneself from unseen psychic forces— scientists at the Massachusetts Institute of Technology finally put the idea to the test. The researchers rigorously analyzed tinfoil's ability to block potentially mind-altering electromagnetic fields, using the latest in high-tech equipment and a variety of hat designs, including the "Classical, the Fez, and the Centurion." Contrary to expectations, they report that, not only did foil fail to block radio waves, it actually *amplified* certain frequencies—notably frequency bands allocated to the U.S. government for GPS communications.

Just because you're paranoid, doesn't mean they're not after you. (But it doesn't necessarily mean they *are*, either.)

CHAPTER SIX

I Want to Believe

June 8, 2013. It's a warm early summer's day. I'm in a field in Watford, a short train ride north of London. Packed into the field with me are two thousand other people, double the number the organizers had planned on. At this particular moment, around half past six in the evening, a bombastic Texan is standing on a small stage at the head of the crowd, shouting into a microphone. He's leading all two thousand of us in a chant, directed at a hotel about half a mile away up a hill and half hidden behind some trees: "We know you are killers! We know you are killers! We know you are killers!"

Once a year, more than a hundred of the richest and most influential people on the planet are invited to attend a secret meeting, where they will discuss the fate of the world. No, really. It's called Bilderberg, named in honor of the first hotel to host the esteemed delegation in 1954, the luxurious Hotel De Bilderberg in Oosterbeek, in the Netherlands. (The group, it has been pointed out, always meets in a five-star hotel with golfing facilities.) From the beginning, the Bilderberg meetings were shrouded in secrecy. No reporters are allowed to attend. Who attends and what is said remains, for the most part, a tantalizing mystery.

According to the official Bilderberg website (okay, they're a little less secretive these days), the conference is merely "a forum for informal discussions about . . . major issues facing the world." Nothing sinister about it.

According to some critics, however, the Bilderbergers aren't just *discussing*. They're *deciding*. Deciding when the next recession will be, the next terrorist attack, the next war, making secret pacts and illicit plots, steering us toward a tyrannical globalist government—the dreaded New World Order. For years, a small group of dedicated conspiracists nipped at Bilderberg's heels. They tailed the Bilderbergers around the

world, figuring out when and where the next meeting would
be, attempting to infiltrate and document the meetings, trying
to raise awareness of the Bilderbergers' sinister machinations.

And awareness has been raised. In 2013, Bilderberg's
conspiracy-minded critics gathered en masse in this field in
Watford, adjacent to the very hotel—the Grove luxury hotel,
spa, and golf resort—hosting that year's meeting. They called it
the Bilderberg Fringe Festival: a party-slash-protest against the
secret rulers of the world. Some of the biggest names in conspiracism were in attendance, including David Icke, Luke
Rudkowski (founder of the 9/11 Truther group We Are Change),
and Alex Jones (the energetic Texan who struck up the "We
know you are killers" chant). At the organizer's tent there were
shirts for sale emblazoned with the slogan I WENT TO BILDER-
BERG 2013 AND ALL I GOT WAS THIS LOUSY NEW WORLD ORDER.

As I chatted with festival-goers between lectures, there was
one issue about which everyone was unsurprisingly in agree-
ment. The Bilderbergers, they said, are up to no good. When it
came to the specifics, however, I was regaled with a dizzying
array of allegations. Cumulatively, the plot was reckoned to
encompass everything from the assassinations of John F.
Kennedy, Robert Kennedy, and Abraham Lincoln, to global
warming, vaccines, pollution, food additives, chem-trails, child
abuse, the Black Death, and the British royal family. More
surprisingly, conspiracism was not the only ideology on offer.
While I waited in line for a pat-down from security, I got chatting with a practitioner of white magic. Inside the field there
were Hare Krishnas, hula-hoopers, reiki healers, pot smokers,
drum circles, people strumming acoustic guitars, a man dressed
as a Jedi, another carrying a ventriloquist's puppet, and another
sporting a pair of pointed ears ("I roll with a group of fairies,"
he explained). Next to the press tent, a middle-aged couple was
hawking bottles of colloidal silver and gold. Nearby, a group of
meditators sat lotus-legged in a wide circle, soaking up the positive vibes presumably emanating from an elaborate copper-pipe
pyramid at their center.

The intermingling of ideologies at the Bilderberg Fringe
Festival took me by surprise. I hadn't expected to find metaphysical New Age spirituality happily rubbing elbows with
the more down-to-earth allegations about human greed,

corruption, and deceit. But the melting pot of ideas at the Bilderberg Fringe Festival reveals a lot about the conspiracy mindset, it turns out. We've already seen that believing one conspiracy theory tends to mean believing others—but it doesn't stop there. Conspiracism is just one potential product of a much broader worldview.

Simple Minds

According to one way of thinking, the reason people believe conspiracy theories is simple—or rather, it is *simplicity*. Historian Kathryn Olmsted put it succinctly: "Conspiracy theories are easy ways of telling complicated stories." Binjamin Segel, a scholar of the *Protocols of Zion*, explained that, through conspiracy theories, "the most serious problems of a nation's existence could be definitively solved by means of this simple formula." As Michael Billig put it, "in essence . . . [conspiracy theories] are simple: events do not have multiple causes and the chance factor in history is discarded. All events are traced back to deliberate decisions taken by conspirators." Daniel Pipes likewise describes conspiracy theories as "streamlining" reality: "myriad troublemakers become a single hostile force." In other words, conspiracy theories render the inexplicable explicable, the complex comprehensible. They pave over messy, bewildering, ambiguous reality with a simple explanation: *They* did it.

Thus, the thinking goes, conspiracy theories presumably appeal primarily to people who lack the inclination or ability to entertain more nuanced explanations. This point of view goes back to the dawn of the modern conspiracy theory. In response to Augustin de Barruel's Illuminati conspiracy theory of the French Revolution, critic Jean-Joseph Mounier bluntly asserted, "to causes extremely complicated have been substituted simple causes, adapted to the capacity of the most indolent and superficial minds." Segel saw the success of Illuminati and antisemitic conspiracy theories in the same terms. "This ridiculously simplistic philosophy of history appealed to the thinking of simple people," he wrote, "because it made no claims on their critical faculties."

It's always tempting to dismiss people you disagree with as intellectually inferior, but is it true? It wasn't until 1999, two centuries after Mounier first insinuated that conspiracy theories are for dummies, that social scientists finally set out to test the hypothesis. A team of psychologists led by Marina Abalakina-Paap gave students a stack of questionnaires designed to assess their thinking style. They measured three traits: *need for cognition* (how much you enjoy puzzles, problem solving, and other intellectual challenges); *tolerance of ambiguity* (how comfortable you are with uncertainty); and *attributional complexity* (how willing you are to entertain complex, nuanced explanations for people's behavior). In line with prevailing stereotypes, the researchers predicted that the more the students bought into conspiracy theories, the lower they would score on each of these traits—which is to say, the more simplistic, rigid, and lazy their thinking would be. Contrary to expectations, however, the test uncovered no relationships at all.

More recently, psychologists Patrick Leman and Marco Cinnirella measured a similar trait, *need for cognitive closure* (the desire to quickly settle on explanation for something and thus stem the need for further intellectual effort). Again, there was no difference between advocates and opponents of conspiracy theories.

On reflection, it's not all that surprising that the stereotype doesn't hold up. In many ways, conspiracy theories are *more* complicated than the alternative. While conspiracy theories are simple in one sense, "at the same time, conspiracy theorists find solace in complexity," Daniel Pipes notes. "Tangled and baroque explanations hold no terror for them. In the conspiratorial universe, the rule of logic known as Occam's Razor"—which asserts that the simplest explanation is the most likely to be true—"is suspended." The best conspiracy theories are endlessly nuanced and complex. For the most dedicated conspiracists, the simplest explanation is never true. There is always another layer of unseen forces and hidden motives to peel back.

It seems like the people who explain conspiracy theories as hasty, simplistic explanations preferred by the intellectually lazy and incurious are falling for an oversimplified explanation themselves. The data simply doesn't provide much support for the idea that conspiracy theorists are intellectually inferior to conspiracy skeptics. Far from being the dullards of popular stereotypes, in fact, recent research suggests that if we pit conspiracy theorists against skeptics, the conspiracy theorists are in some ways *more* intellectually adventurous.

Open Minds

Openness is one of the so-called Big Five—the five fundamental traits that, according to personality psychologists, sum up everyone's personality. (The others are conscientiousness, extroversion, agreeableness, and neuroticism. If you want to remember them all, just remember their initials spell out OCEAN.) A few studies have found that the higher someone scores in openness, the more likely he or she is to believe conspiracy theories. The relationship was small, however, and a few other studies have failed to reproduce it. So whether conspiracy-thinking is related to openness in general is still up in the air, and if there is a relationship it's probably a small one. (I trust you'll have no trouble tolerating this disappointingly uncertain state of affairs.)

But there are a few different elements to openness. It involves being imaginative, adventurous, emotionally aware, intellectually curious, appreciative of the arts. You don't have to satisfy all the criteria to score highly on a general measure of openness. You might love traveling to new countries, but not be fussed on poetry. At any rate, none of those elements seems to have much to do with believing conspiracy theories. More likely is that conspiracy theories are linked to one last feature of openness: the tendency to scoff at conventional wisdom, to embrace the unorthodox. This insight comes from studies looking at what kinds of *other* things conspiracy theorists tend to believe. A consistent trend has emerged. The more someone buys into conspiracy theories, the more likely he or she is to accept a whole host of unconventional claims.

One of the most comprehensive studies to date was carried out by a team of psychologists led by Emilio Lobato. Lobato and colleagues barraged college students with claims representing three varieties of weirdness: conspiracy theories, pseudoscience, and the supernatural. The students rated how strongly they believed each claim, and then their answers were tallied up to give three separate scores. It turned out that all three were intertwined. The higher one score, the higher the other two tended to be. People who bought into the pseudoscientific notion that homeopathy can cure serious illnesses were more likely to believe that supernatural psychic powers are real and that the Kennedy assassination was a conspiracy. Likewise, someone who suspected that Elvis is still alive was more likely to believe that ghosts are real and that we only use 10 percent of our brains. If someone was skeptical of conspiracy theories, though, he or she tended to doubt pseudoscience and paranormal forces, too.

Other studies have uncovered even more of this patchwork quilt of quirky beliefs. For one thing, conspiracy theorists tend to be a relatively superstitious bunch. The more someone endorses conspiracy theories, the more likely he or she is to be wary of black cats, broken mirrors, and walking under ladders. For another thing, they're more likely to suspect that there's a grain of truth to urban legends, like the old chestnut about businessmen waking up in bathtubs full of ice with a kidney missing. Not only are conspiracy theorists more likely to accept pseudoscience such as astrology and alternative medicine, but they're more likely to reject mainstream science and its products, such as vaccines and genetically modified foods. And several studies provide data to back up my unexpected discovery at the Bilderberg Fringe Festival: Someone who believes conspiracy theories is more likely to be into New Age spiritualism—which includes all manner of metaphysical notions, such as karma, reincarnation, astral projection, energy healing, and the idea that the whole cosmos is some kind of unbroken living whole.

I'm not saying that everyone who tells you 9/11 was an inside job will invariably believe in ghosts, healing crystals, and little green men. To be clear, these are *statistical* relationships—degrees of probability. There are, of course, people who believe conspiracy theories but have no time for anything paranormal, and there are New Age gurus who have no interest in New World Orders. But as a broad trend, the more someone is open to one unconventional belief system, the better the odds that he or she is open to others.

The Truth Is Out There

In fairness, some of the correlations between eclectic beliefs aren't too surprising. After all, believing that the government is covering up the existence of little green men requires you to believe in the little green men. It makes sense to believe energy healing works if you think Big Pharma is interested in suppressing it. In these cases, the ideological overlaps are built in. But some of the correlations are a little harder to explain. There's no obvious reason why someone who believes the CIA killed Kennedy should be any more likely to entertain the possibility of ghosts and psychic powers than someone who thinks Lee Harvey Oswald did it. Neither is there any good reason why believing that knocking on wood brings you luck would have anything to do with your views on the science behind climate change.

The fact that unconventional and seemingly unrelated belief systems tend to crop up in the same circles is not a startling new revelation. Back in the 1970s, sociologist Colin Campbell wrote about an intellectual "underground of society," where all manner of weird and wonderful ideas flourish and mingle. He called it the *cultic milieu*. The term might bring to mind charismatic cult leaders enticing vulnerable people into handing over their life savings (or their lives). But these kinds of fully fledged cults, Campbell wrote, are just the tip of the iceberg—the most visible manifestation of a much broader, more nebulous, more pervasive way of thinking. The cultic milieu, according to Campbell, is an ever-present feature of every society. Wherever there is orthodox wisdom, there are people who are irresistibly drawn toward the unorthodox.

By way of example, Campbell cites a laundry list of cultic beliefs and collectives: "Unorthodox science, alien and heretical religion, deviant medicine . . . the worlds of the occult and the magical, of spiritualism and psychic phenomena, of mysticism and new thought, of alien intelligences and lost civilizations, of faith healing and nature cure." To that we might add claims about astrology, numerology, parapsychology, revisionist history, Creationism, apocalyptic predictions, near-death experiences, and miracle diets. Although on the surface this assortment of eccentric beliefs might seem endlessly diverse (and sometimes incongruous), they all share one key feature: They are rejected by the Establishment, opposed by the orthodoxy, off the intellectual beaten path.

The ethos of the cultic milieu is neatly summed up in *The X-Files'* mantra, "the truth is out there." There are answers to life's big questions, but you won't find them where the Establishment tells you to look; you've got to track them down for yourself. (The second meaning is equally applicable to the cultic milieu: the truth is *out there*—it's stranger than you can imagine.) Devotees of the cultic milieu, Campbell argues, are united in their personal quest for enlightenment. And for true aficionados, the journey is more important than the destination. There are many paths to the Truth, and there's no reason to stop looking just because you've found one fountain of arcane wisdom. Why put all your eggs in one basket? This is why unconventional but otherwise unrelated ideas so often go hand in hand, Campbell explains. In the cultic milieu, ideas feed off and nourish one another. "Visitors from outer space prove to be psychic," for instance, "and mediums confirm that there is life on other planets."

Campbell didn't mention conspiracy theories, but judging by the correlations we saw a moment ago, it would appear that they slot neatly into the cultic milieu. As Nicoli Nattrass notes, a brief foray into the world of conspiracy theories opens the door to "an organized network of activists who, through their linked websites, conferences, papers, books, documentaries, and public relations exercises, construct not only a rival ideology to science, but an entire alternative social world with its own heroes, values, beliefs, and practices." And the world of conspiracy often rubs up against other unorthodox ideologies, as when David Icke claims to receive psychic messages about the nature of reality, or when Alex Jones advertises alternative health products like "Super Advanced Vitamin B-12 with The Infowars Life Secret 12™ Proprietary Formula."

What's more, conspiracist logic, more than any other unorthodox ideology, essentially *requires* the believer to dive ever deeper into the cultic milieu. If mainstream sources of information are part of the conspiracy, then the very fact that an idea has been rejected by scientists, academia, or the media can be taken as evidence of its validity. In effect, conspiracy theories turn the cultic milieu into the only source of trustworthy knowledge.

Dare to Know!

From the comfort of the intellectual overground, it's easy to look down on Campbell's cultic underground as a strange intellectual twilight zone where, intellectually speaking, anything goes. In a book called *How Mumbo-Jumbo Conquered the World*, journalist Francis Wheen laments that "the values of the Enlightenment have been abandoned" by conspiracy theorists and their fellow "irrationalists." In *Among the Truthers*, Jonathan Kay declares 9/11 Truthers "enemies" of the Enlightenment, and worries that they might bring about the end of the Age of Reason. Wheen and Kay are representative of a fairly common view among skeptics of conspiracy theories and other unorthodox beliefs, casting people who strike out against mainstream wisdom as backward-thinking crackpots. As Emma Jane and Chris Fleming put it, this view of the cultic milieu "portrays conspiracists and their mumbo-jumbo-ing ilk as the intellectual equivalent of failed dieters: while the great thinkers of the Age of Reason whipped society's flawed and flabby thinking into shape, the masses have let themselves go." Before we get too carried away patting ourselves on the back, though, let's see just how much of a departure from Enlightenment ideals the cultic milieu really is.

French philosopher René Descartes kicked off the Enlightenment with his 1641 *Meditations on First Philosophy*, in which he resolves to reject all received wisdom, doubt everything he possibly can, and rebuild his understanding of the world from the ground up, trusting only his own critical faculties. Half a century later, British philosopher John Locke wrote, "we should make greater progress in the discovery of rational and contemplative knowledge if we . . . made use rather of our own thoughts than other men's to find it: for I think we may as rationally hope to see with other men's eyes as to know by other men's understanding." When German philosopher Immanuel Kant was invited to answer the question "What is Enlightenment?" a century later, he suggested as a motto, *Sapere aude!*—Dare to know!

None of the lofty intellectual aspirations of Enlightenment thinkers, you might notice, are a million miles from the defining traits of Campbell's cultic milieu, which he described as "attacking orthodoxy" and "defending individual liberty of belief and practice." Sometimes the resemblance is downright uncanny. After urging readers to "have the courage to use your own understanding," Kant proceeded to ridicule the intellectual laziness and cowardice of unthinking "cattle" who wallow in self-imposed ignorance by trusting what they read in books and allowing other people to do their thinking for them—centuries before the phrase "wake up, sheeple" came into vogue. "Far from representing a rupture from rationalism," Jane and Fleming write, "conspiracy thinking is actually embarrassingly consistent" with Enlightenment ideals.

The cultic milieu isn't some exotic antiscience wonderland where all logic is suspended. There aren't many people who reject the evidence-based approach to reality entirely, after all. Even someone like David Icke, who frequently reminds his audience that scientists are part of an evil, reptilian conspiracy, cites scientific studies when they happen to fit his thesis.

The cultic milieu is what happens when the desire for intellectual autonomy clashes with the reality of life in an increasingly complicated world. Jane and Fleming point out that the great Enlightenment thinkers lived at a time when orthodox wisdom came largely from the Church, and all the world's technical, scientific, and philosophical knowledge could reside comfortably within a relatively slim encyclopedia. In the seventeenth century, in other words, rejecting orthodoxy and electing yourself as the best judge of what is true was a viable goal.

Since then, our collective scientific understanding of the world has become exponentially more complex and specialized. It's increasingly difficult for nonexperts—and we're all not experts at most things—to know what is true and what is nonsense. The phrase "studies show" has become a meaningless cliché. Scientific papers are often deposited behind paywalls, and can be incomprehensible to someone without the relevant expertise in any case. It would take a graduate-level education in chemistry, engineering, biology, and nutrition just to truly understand the label on an average frozen meal at the grocery store. We're increasingly stripped of our intellectual autonomy, forced to defer to experts.

The cultic milieu allows us to hold on to our autonomy. It tells us that we can be experts too, we don't have to listen to what we're told, we can find the answers we're looking for only by journeying down the road less traveled. Wake up! The truth is out there! Dare to know!

Campbell called the cultic milieu a cultural underground, but conspiracy theories and other unorthodox ideas clearly aren't confined to some dingy intellectual netherworld. Few people immerse themselves in the cultic milieu to the point of signing up to a cult, but almost everyone dips their toes in. The popularity of *The Secret*, Dr. Oz, Deepak Chopra, and shows like *Ancient Aliens* testifies to the fact that huge numbers of people have at least a fleeting, superficial interest in the mysterious and unorthodox. And we can hardly be blamed. Possessing arcane knowledge holds a deep psychological appeal. There is fun to be had cracking codes, sifting through signs, and uncovering lost knowledge and secret plots, Susan Harding and Kathleen Stewart point out. As Richard Hofstadter wrote, the conspiracy theorist gets to be "a member of the avant-garde who is capable of perceiving the conspiracy before it is fully obvious to an as-yet unaroused public." Or as Damian Thompson put it, unconventional beliefs can be "a passport to a thrilling alternative universe in which Atlantis is buried underneath the Antarctic, the Ark of the Covenant is hidden in Ethiopia, aliens have manipulated our DNA, and there was once a civilization on Mars."

But we don't generally believe stuff just for the fun of it. For us to really *believe* something, it has to seem plausible. How can the bearers of cultic beliefs be so sure that their journey off the intellectual beaten path has led them to the truth, while the scientific mainstream is deluded or deceptive? It doesn't take some charismatic cult leader to lure us into the cultic milieu; sometimes all it takes is our own overly optimistic brain telling us we understand the world in far greater depth than we actually do.

"I Think I Know Less than I Thought"

Contemplate the humble bicycle. A bike is a fairly simple device: two wheels, a frame, handlebars, pedals, and a chain (for our purposes we can ignore all the complicated gears and stuff). There's a good chance you've owned one at some point in your life, or at least ridden one. And if you live in a city, you probably see them every day, adorning lampposts or hurtling toward you as you cross the street. You know a thing or two about bicycles, right?

So this should be a piece of cake. Below is a doodle of a bike, but it's missing a few key parts. I just want you to fill in the rest. Sketch in the missing bits of frame, the chain, and the pedals. It doesn't matter if your lines are a bit wobbly. This isn't a test of artistic ability. Do it in your head if you don't have a pen handy. I just want you to indicate roughly where the different bits ought to go to make the bike work.

How did you do? When psychologist Rebecca Lawson set people this challenge, around half of them got something wrong—despite the fact that virtually all of them knew how to ride a bike, and many had one sitting at home. And these weren't trivial mistakes. They were design flaws that would render the bike a useless hunk of junk. Some people drew the bicycle's frame connected to both the front and back wheels, which would make it difficult to turn the handlebars. Some drew the pedals attached to the center of one of the wheels, which would make it tough to reach them with your feet. The most common mistake was putting the chain in the wrong place; some people drew it looped between the front *and* back wheels, which would also make steering tricky. The right answer is the frame juts down from below the seat to a spot between the wheels, and connects from there to the back wheel and to the frame up by the handlebars, making two triangles. The pedals go in between the wheels, and the chain loops around pedals and the back wheel (see page 274). This setup allows the pedals to turn the chain and drive the back wheel, while leaving the front wheel free to turn. Did you make any mistakes? Was it harder than you thought it would be?

This deceptively simple task reveals that a lot of people lack a basic understanding of how bicycles work. By itself, that's not all that revealing. Clearly we can get by in life without under-standing the finer points of bicycle design. What's interesting is that we *don't realize* our lack of understanding—until we've been forced to demonstrate it by completing the doodle, and we find ourselves faltering. Before confronting people with the doodle, Lawson asked them how well they reckoned they understood the basic mechanics of a bicycle. On a scale from one (meaning "I know little or nothing about how bicycles work") to seven (meaning "I have a thorough knowledge of how bicycles work"), people rated themselves, on average, around a four or a five—rea-sonably knowledgeable. But for a lot of them, it turned out their understanding was an illusion. When their mistakes on the diagram were pointed out—when they were directly confronted with their own ignorance, in other words—the illusion suddenly faded. It was a surprising experience. One earnest test subject summed the sorry state of affairs: "I think I know less than I thought."

It's not just the mechanics of bicycles that we think we understand better than we really do. We're overly confident about how well we understand all sorts of things. In an extensive series of experiments, Yale grad student Leon Rozenblit and his adviser Frank Keil asked people how well they thought they understood devices ranging in complexity and familiarity from can openers to zippers to a helicopter. In each case, most people initially reckoned they had a reasonably detailed idea of how the thing works. When researchers asked them to write a step-by-step explanation of how exactly a can opener opens cans, or how a helicopter flies, however, many people came up short. Like Lawson's deflated cyclists, many of Rozenblit and Keil's test subjects expressed "genuine surprise and new humility at how much less they knew than they originally thought."

And it doesn't stop there. People overrate their understanding of simple physics problems, such as what trajectory a falling object will follow, and more complex natural phenomena, such as how earthquakes occur and why comets have tails or how rainbows are formed. People think they understand the law and political policies better than they really do. As Dan Simons and Chris Chabris note in *The Invisible Gorilla*, the tendency for projects like Boston's Big Dig to go staggeringly over budget and past deadline shows that even experts sometimes overestimate how much they know when they're planning a project.

We might think we understand something in depth, but when it comes time to put our money where our mouth is, it often turns out our understanding leaves a lot to be desired.

The Unknown Unknowns

Why do we so often misjudge the depth of our understanding? It doesn't seem to be that we're just telling ourselves a flattering lie, or trying to sound impressive. Offering people cold hard cash to assess their understanding or abilities honestly and accurately—even the princely sum of one hundred dollars—doesn't reduce their overconfidence. Neither does forcing them to justify their assessment of their own abilities to their peers, and thus face the prospect of appearing arrogant or foolish for an overconfident assessment.

The real reason for our overconfidence comes down to a metacognitive glitch. *Metacognition* is just a fancy way of saying "thinking about thinking." When you say something like "I'm good at math," or "I'm easily distracted," you have made a metacognitive insight. But, like licking your own elbow, it turns out thinking about our own thinking isn't as easy as, well, you'd think. There are limits to our ability to accurately assess what we know, and particularly to realize how much we *don't* know. Former U. S. secretary of defense Donald Rumsfeld famously summed up the problem:

As we know, there are known knowns; there are things we know we know. We also know there are known unknowns; that is to say we know there are some things we do not know. But

there are also unknown unknowns—the ones we don't know
we don't know . . . It is the latter category that tend to be the
difficult ones.

Rumsfeld's phraseology might get your brain in a twist (and he
took some flak from persnickety linguists for it), but the point
he's making is an important one. Let's go through each category
in turn. The *known knowns* are easy. What's the capital city of
England? I know the answer: It's London. When I read the
question, it's as if my brain types it into a mental search engine,
and up pops the answer. The *known unknowns* don't present
much of a problem either. What's the capital city of Namibia? I
don't know. But I *know* that I don't know. Clicking the search
button brings up a blank page with an error message, "Your
search did not match any documents." Leon Rozenblit found
that when it comes to simple pieces of trivia, such as capital
cities, we don't tend to overestimate our knowledge. We either
know the answer or we don't; we have no problem telling the
difference. We experience a known unknown as a neat little gap
in our knowledge waiting to be filled. (Thanks to a vastly
superior search engine, I have now filled my blank: The capital
city of Namibia is Windhoek.)

But then there are the *unknown unknowns*. The unknown
unknowns are sneakier. They're an intellectual blind spot, and
our brain loves to fill in blind spots. As Rebecca Lawson, Leon
Rozenblit, and others have discovered, we are especially prone
to blind spots when it comes to physical phenomena or devices
like earthquakes and bicycles, and complex systems like law or
politics. The problem, Rozenblit explained, is that most of us
are not bicycle mechanics or political scientists, but we all have
a passing familiarity with some of the surface features of bikes
and politics. This smattering of vague knowledge can get us into
trouble, because it takes a bit of expertise just to know how
much you *don't know* about something. Without it, it can be
hard to tell the difference between a deep pool of understanding
and a shallow puddle.

Psychologist David Dunning explains it more bluntly: "An
ignorant mind is precisely not a spotless, empty vessel." It's filled
with information—all the "life experiences, theories, facts, intuitions, strategies, algorithms, heuristics, metaphors, and hunches"

we've amassed over the years. When we're uninformed—and we're all ignorant about a lot of things—our brain indiscriminately uses whatever is at hand to plaster over the intellectual blind spot.

For Rebecca Lawson's test subjects who rated their understanding of bikes as pretty strong and then proceeded to mess up the diagram, how a bicycle works was an unknown unknown. When Lawson asked them to rate their understanding, they submitted a mental search, and it didn't turn up an empty page with an error message. Instead, they saw a page that appeared, at first glance, to be filled with a healthy amount of information—the names of the various parts, fuzzy memories of what their childhood bike looked like, experience of riding bikes, maybe even knowledge of how to fix a puncture. They mistook all this fairly shallow knowledge for a deep understanding of how the parts actually function together to make the wheels turn. It wasn't until they were forced to inspect the page more closely—when the pesky psychologist confronted them with their mistakes on a little doodle—that their illusory understanding faded like a mirage.

As Rozenblit and Keil put it, we sometimes mistake a skeletal, incomplete sketch for a "vivid, blueprint-like" sense of how things work. Or, to paraphrase Chris Chabris and Dan Simons, you think you understand how a bicycle works, when all you really understand is how to work a bicycle.

This might be hard to get your head around. After all, we have a blind spot when it comes to our intellectual blind spots. Maybe, though, you've experienced the uneasy feeling of having a blind spot of your own unexpectedly revealed. Perhaps while chatting with friends over a drink you've found yourself launching into a lecture on some topic you've recently become opinionated about. Mid-sermon, someone interjects with an innocent question, like *how* exactly *do* cap-and-trade policies influence global carbon emissions? Suddenly you find yourself at a loss. You thought you were on firm intellectual ground, but you discover that your understanding has departed terra firma and is stranded, like Wile E. Coyote, in midair. Sometimes we can't see where our understanding ends until long after we've merrily skipped over the cliff edge. If you've never had this experience, either you're a genius, or you only ever talk about things you have genuine expertise with, or you've got a particularly bad case of the unknown unknowns.

The University of Google

How do you feel about nanotechnology? Do you know enough to take an informed stance? "One might think that opinions about an esoteric technology would be hard to come by," David Dunning notes. "Surely, to know whether nanotech is a boon to humankind or a step toward doomsday would require some sort of knowledge about materials science, engineering, industry structure, regulatory issues, organic chemistry, surface science, semiconductor physics, microfabrication, and molecular biology." And yet opinions on the topic are far from limited to people with expertise in the relevant disciplines.

In one 2006 survey, the majority of people who took part admitted to knowing little or nothing about nanotech. When they were asked to weigh the risks and benefits of the technology, around half said they couldn't answer. For them, the potential pros and cons were a known unknown. But it only takes a little information to conjure up an illusion of understanding. In another study, psychologist Dan Kahan and colleagues were able to increase the number of people willing to offer an opinion on the pros and cons of nanotech to nine out of ten merely by providing a two-sentence-long, entirely nonjudgmental description of the technology.

To be fair, most people's stance was to sit on the fence; on the whole, people were unwilling to stray far from the midpoint of the scale, rating the benefits and risks as pretty much equally matched. A little more information, however, sealed the deal. Kahan had a different group of test subjects read two brief paragraphs about nanotech, one outlining some potential benefits, the other outlining some potential risks. In reality, the small amount of vague and ambivalent information was barely informative at all. But apparently it didn't seem that way to the people who read it. The number of people unwilling to offer an opinion was cut in half, from 11 percent down to just 5 percent. More importantly, it encouraged people to climb down from the fence. After reading the two vapid paragraphs, people tended to offer significantly stronger opinions one way or another. A little information—even when it is barely informative—can make us inordinately opinionated. And the same illusion of understanding that can make someone happily take a stance on a technology they know next to nothing about can lure some people toward the cultic milieu.

On September 18, 2007, Jenny McCarthy appeared on the *Oprah Winfrey Show* to promote her book *Louder than Words: A Mother's Journey in Healing Autism*. In it, McCarthy describes how her son, Evan, came to be diagnosed with autism, and argues that vaccines were to blame. Jenny McCarthy has a lot of strings to her bow—model, actress, author—but one thing she does not have is any formal medical training. So what qualified her to diagnose the cause of her son's autism? "The University of Google is where I got my degree from," she told Oprah. When Evan was diagnosed with autism, she said, "first thing I did—Google. I put in autism. And I started my research." When Oprah dutifully read a statement from the Centers for Disease Control and Prevention explaining that the best available science does not support an association between vaccines and autism, McCarthy had her counterargument already lined up. "My science is named Evan, and he's at home. That's my science."

Jenny McCarthy isn't alone in thinking she knows better than mainstream medicine. Christine Maggiore was a businesswoman from Chicago. In 1992, a routine blood test came back positive for HIV. Despite having no scientific training or college degree, Maggiore dived into the medical literature on AIDS. She arrived at the conclusion that AIDS, rather than being caused by the HIV virus, is caused by drug use, anal sex, or even the drugs prescribed to treat AIDS. She founded a group called Alive & Well AIDS Alternatives to spread her message. In 2000, the rock band Foo Fighters organized a sold-out benefit concert for Alive & Well in Hollywood. "I was told I had between five and seven years to live," Maggiore told the audience. "Eight years later, I'm living in perfect health without any AIDS medicines . . . The reason I have what I have today is because I did not follow doctor's orders. I questioned them. And I urge all of you to question what you have been told about HIV and AIDS." When Maggiore got pregnant, she took no medication to prevent the transmission of AIDS to her children. Her daughter, Eliza Jane, died of AIDS when she was three and a half years old. Maggiore herself died on December 27, 2008, at age fifty-two, of opportunistic infections common in people with untreated AIDS.

A Little Learning

The University of Google is well attended. After watching a few YouTube videos of controlled demolitions, it can be tempting to consider yourself sufficiently well versed in structural engineering to believe, contrary to the consensus of expert opinion, that the collapse of the Twin Towers was a controlled demolition. We've all seen movies where a guy getting shot is flung backward by the force of the bullet; it's tempting to conclude that we know all we need to know about forensic ballistics to deduce the location of an unseen assassin from the movement of John F. Kennedy's head back and to the left. We know that a dark, cloudless sky ought to have stars in it; it's tempting to think we can prove that the moon landing was faked simply by pointing out the conspicuous absence of stars in pictures of the lunar sky. Most of us aren't experts in structural engineering, or forensic ballistics, or astrophotography. But when we know a little, it's easy to mistake it for a lot. The illusion of understanding makes armchair experts of us all.

When we're forced to plumb the depths of our knowledge, we often hit bottom much sooner than anticipated. For the most part, though, we get by in life floating on the surface, never realizing all the things that we don't know we don't know. Our illusions often go unchallenged. We rarely encounter psychologists brandishing incomplete schematics of bicycles at us, our friends are often too polite to call us out, and we're good at surrounding ourselves in an intellectual echo chamber where the people around us reinforce our beliefs. By the time Christine Maggiore, Jenny McCarthy, and millions of other armchair experts have their ideas challenged, their illusion of understanding has blossomed into an unshakable conviction.

We began the chapter with two thousand people gathered in a field, shouting "We know you are killers!" at a distant hotel. Everyone I spoke to was fairly certain that the Bilderbergers were engaged in a murderous conspiracy, but when I pressed for specifics—what exactly are the Bilderbergers up to, how do they pull off their grand conspiracies, what can be done about it—people's answers were all over the map, and often disappointingly vague. In the words of one festival-goer, "Well it's basically exposing the truth. And obviously the truth can be different to different people, but I see it as being one singular thing, and any other versions of the truth are simply just mistruths. You know, it goes on a more deeper level than just these evil people over there, you know, it goes on to—" He trailed off. "I can't find the words to explain it."

The poet Alexander Pope wrote, in his 1709 poem *An Essay on Criticism*, "A little learning is a dangerous thing; drink deep, or taste not the Pierian Spring; there shallow draughts intoxicate the brain; and drinking largely sobers us again." Less poetically, but perhaps more pragmatically, Emma Jane and Chris Fleming make a compelling case for the value of accepting that you don't have all the answers. "To admit that we know less than we think we do, and that we may be more in the dark tomorrow than we were today," ought to be considered a virtue, they wrote. "Perhaps we should occasionally stop and say to ourselves, 'You know, maybe I have absolutely no idea what I'm talking about.'"

CHAPTER SEVEN

(Official) Stories

David Icke has always been a daydreamer. At school, he remembers, teachers would tell him to stop daydreaming, and he would think, "Well, I like daydreaming more than listening to *you*, so I'm going to go and daydream." Icke left school at age fifteen to pursue a career in soccer. When agonizing arthritis forced him to retire at age twenty-one, he turned to journalism. By the 1980s, Icke had become a household name as a sports presenter on the BBC. But despite his success, Icke confessed in his 1993 autobiography, he felt increasingly dissatisfied with life. He felt there must be more to it. That's when he began receiving psychic messages telling him the world is secretly ruled by an evil race of interdimensional reptiles.

Here's the story of reality as David Icke tells it.

There was once a golden age of humanity. It was a time of harmony and bliss. Our ancient ancestors lived in perfect interconnectedness with each other and with the universe. There were no wars, no famines, no pollution; everyone just got along. Then the peace was rudely shattered. A sinister power began casting a dark shadow over humanity. A conspiracy was afoot.

For millennia now, the conspirators have been secretly implementing an elaborate control system, designed to suppress our natural connection to the cosmos and keep us trapped in a state of constant fear and confusion. The modern world is a shrine to their hidden machinations. The mainstream media, the education system, science, politics, and Western medicine are all tools of the conspiracy, used to control our minds and keep us subservient. Everything that happens in the world—every war, recession, natural disaster, and terrorist attack—is engineered by secret cabals of dark-suited men in smoke-filled boardrooms. But that, Icke says, is just the outer rim of the rabbit hole. These earthly oppressors are merely the puppets of an even more sinister enemy.

The true perpetrator of this heinous plot, according to Icke, is a race of interdimensional reptilian aliens called Archons. And the conspiracy, he says, goes beyond our five senses. The Archons feed off human energy like vampires. They have a particular taste for fear and hatred, and they harvest our darkest emotions by keeping us trapped within a virtual reality prison. Our universe is nothing more than a hologram, Icke explains, and the Archons have hacked into the very fabric of the cosmos. By controlling our perception of reality they can manipulate our thoughts at the source, keeping us trapped under their spell, in a constant state of bewilderment and fear, unwitting slaves to unseen masters.

Things are looking bleak. We are within the Archons' evil clutches. Humanity is teetering on the edge of total enslavement. Game over: The reptiles win.

But that doesn't have to be our fate. There is a glimmer of hope. The Archons have one fatal weakness: They must work in the dark, in secret. When their plans are exposed to the light, Icke says, the spell is broken, and their control system will topple like a house of cards. And there's a change in the air. More and more people are opening their minds, waking up, beginning to shake off the shackles of the Archons and their humanoid minions. If we keep up the momentum, the Archons will be defeated, and the shadow will be lifted. There will be a new dawn. Humanity will come together again as one consciousness, and we will reclaim our rightful place in the cosmos.

Now, if you're not already a fan of David Icke, these might sound like pretty wild allegations, to say the least (and I didn't even mention the stuff about the rings of Saturn being a giant radio antenna and the Moon being hollow). As Loren Collins eloquently put it in his book *Bullspotting*, David Icke and his reptoids "have become the poster child for the fringiest of fringe thought"—the very epitome of crazy conspiracy theories that no one in their right mind could possibly believe. But Icke's appeal isn't limited to the fringe. He has a dedicated following. His Web forum is one of the busiest conspiracy sites on the Internet, he has published more than a dozen books detailing his ideas, and thousands of cheering fans show up to his day-long lectures at venues like Wembley Arena in London.

Why are so many people drawn to Icke's convoluted, all-encompassing theories? When all I knew about Icke was that he thinks the world is run by a cabal of politically ambitious reptiles, I dismissed his ideas as the fringiest end of the fringe, too. But once you get to know Icke's worldview—and the psychology of storytelling—another side becomes clear. I said this is Icke's story of reality—and the fact is, David Icke's theories are no weirder than some of the most enduring, successful stories that we all know and love.

Once Upon a Time . . .

The oldest story ever written down—or, rather, the oldest one anyone has found—is the *Epic of Gilgamesh*. Parts of the story are thought to have first been told as long as five thousand years ago. Eventually, sometime around the seventh century B.C.E, the epic poem was compiled, etched onto twelve clay tablets, and deposited in the library of the Assyrian king Ashurbanipal at Nineveh. Not long afterward, war broke out between the Assyrian Empire and the Babylonians. Assyria fell, Nineveh was razed to the ground, and the tablets lay beneath the desert sand for almost three thousand years. Then, in 1849, the English archaeologist Austen Henry Layard unearthed the ruins of the ancient city and the forgotten tablets. It took another two decades to decipher the wedge-shaped cuneiform alphabet. When the ancient poem was at last translated, the Victorian public was enchanted.

The hero of the story is the strong and wise king of Uruk named Gilgamesh. One of his adventures begins with a monstrous evil casting a shadow over his formerly peaceful kingdom. The source of the trouble is Humbaba, a ferocious giant with, according to various descriptions, the face of a lion, the horns of a bull, the talons of a vulture, and a body covered in thorny scales. He is "a terror to human beings," Gilgamesh's friend warns him; "Humbaba's roar is a flood, his mouth is death, and his breath is fire." Undaunted, Gilgamesh travels halfway across the world to confront Humbaba in his underground lair, and a climactic battle ensues. Humbaba is far more powerful than Gilgamesh. It seems there is no hope of victory. Then, just when the hero is almost overcome, he summons a superhuman feat and vanquishes the monster. Peace returns to the kingdom of Uruk.

The *Epic of Gilgamesh* is a good story—so good, in fact, that people have been unwittingly reinventing it for thousands of years. Consider the tale of *Beowulf*, spun by the minstrels of medieval England sometime between the eighth and tenth centuries. The hero of the story is a strong and wise warrior named Beowulf. The adventure begins with a monstrous evil casting a shadow over the formerly peaceful community of Heorot. The source of the trouble is Grendel, a ferocious giant with burning eyes, deadly claws, powerful jaws, and a body covered in impenetrable scales. Night after night, Grendel terrorizes the inhabitants of Heorot, snatching men from their beds and tearing them limb from limb. Beowulf travels across Europe to confront Grendel. It transpires, however, that Grendel was merely a prelude to a more terrible villain, his even more monstrous mother. The hero ventures to her underwater lair, and a climactic battle ensues. The monster is more powerful than Beowulf. It seems there is no hope of victory. Then, just when all hope seems lost, Beowulf summons superhuman strength, vanquishing the monster with a sword forged by giants. Peace returns to Heorot.

The tales of Beowulf and Gilgamesh were conceived entirely independently, thousands of years apart, in cultures alien to one another, and yet the similarities in the two stories are remarkable. Today's air-conditioned multiplexes and big-budget blockbusters seem a far cry from the drafty banquet halls and serenading minstrels of yore, but we're no less enchanted by stories about valiant heroes battling terrible villains. Think about Steven Spielberg's *Jaws*. A monstrous shark begins terrorizing a sleepy seaside town. The hero, police chief Brody, ventures out to sea to do battle with the shark. Victory seems uncertain, until Brody, in a feat of ingenuity, slays the shark. Think of *Star Wars*, in which the monstrous Darth Vader threatens the entire galaxy, until Luke Skywalker puts the kibosh on Vader's Death Star by using "the Force" to find its one weakness. Or think about every James Bond film ever. Evil villain threatens the safety of the Western world. Bond ventures to the villain's evil lair. Villain almost has Bond within evil clutches. Bond prevails.

It is tempting to assume the human imagination is limitless. From tales whispered around campfires to podcasts streamed from the Cloud, we've been telling each other stories for millennia, using any means available. Collectively, we've conjured up innumerable superhuman characters, fantastical creatures, and impossible events. In theory, there are as many stories as storytellers. And yet, as these brief synopses demonstrate, when stories are stripped down to their bare bones, some of them become virtually indistinguishable. It's not that storytellers have been lazily rehashing ideas or intentionally plagiarizing one another. Rather, the blueprints of certain stories seem to be etched into our minds. Carl Jung wrote about psychological archetypes, describing them as "the ancient river beds along which our psychic current naturally flows." Even children as young as three understand story structure. We're wired to find certain stories instinctively satisfying, and we've been spontaneously creating and enthusiastically consuming stories based on these archetypal plots since the dawn of humanity.

Scholars generally agree that the number of archetypal stories is surprisingly small, though precise estimates vary. According to author Ronald B. Tobias, there are twenty "master plots." Screenwriter Blake Snyder cut that number in half, arguing that every movie ever made fits into one of ten essential genres. Journalist Christopher Booker pruned that number even further. Booker spent thirty-four years of his life combing through countless stories from around the world and throughout history; his efforts resulted in a seven-hundred-page tome, *The Seven Basic Plots*. As the title suggests, Booker argues that all the world's stories boil down to variations on seven fundamental plots. Mythologist Joseph Campbell trumped everyone, arguing that there is but a single grand "monomyth," the hero's journey, which virtually every story draws on.

There is, of course, no definitive answer. Classifying and quantifying plots is a subjective business. As Tobias admits, "you can package plot any number of ways, and the way you package it decides what number you'll end up with." The point is that certain themes crop up again and again, independently of one another, in stories told around the world and throughout recorded history. These ideas don't just shape the stories we make up—as we'll see, they reflect the way we fundamentally understand and explain the world around us.

It is one of Christopher Booker's basic plots that's of most interest to us. He called it *overcoming the monster*. Every overcoming-the-monster story, Booker explains, unfolds essentially as follows. The story begins with a peaceful community learning of some menacing threat. A hero is called upon to battle the forces of evil. As the hero comes face to face with the evil, it seems that the evil is much more powerful than the hero. The hero may fall into the monster's clutches. But the monster has one fatal weakness. Just when it seems that all hope is lost, the hero is able to exploit that weakness and vanquish the monster. The shadow is lifted, and peace returns to the community.

We've already seen this pattern played out in Gilgamesh, Beowulf, *Jaws*, and Bond. And we saw it at the very beginning of the chapter, in David Icke's conspiracy theory of reality. Icke's grand conspiracy theory is a classic overcoming-the-monster story; it traces every twist and turn, from the peaceful golden age of humanity and the looming shadow of evil, to the climactic final confrontation and the promise of a return to peace. It's a dramatic, ongoing saga, and it casts us all in the starring role. And Icke is not unique. All conspiracy thinking plays on archetypes of good overcoming evil. We'll delve into the psychology of monsters shortly, but first let's see what makes for a good hero.

The Advantages of Disadvantage

Everybody loves a winner. There is a phenomenon known to psychologists as *basking in reflected glory*—BIRGing, for short. In a classic 1973 study, a team of researchers led by Robert Cialdini noticed that when a college's football team had won a game over the weekend, more students showed up to class on Monday in team apparel than when the team lost. More interestingly, when students talked about a game the team had lost, they tended to say things like "they lost," whereas when the team had won, fans were more likely to say "we won." BIRGing explains a lot of otherwise bizarre behavior, from our childhood desire to hang out with the "cool" kids, to wanton name-dropping and the popularity of expensive brand-name merchandise (and cheap knockoffs). We are known by the company we keep, and there aren't many people who like to hang around losers. We want to associate ourselves, however tenuously, with life's winners.

If there's one thing we love more than a born winner, though, it's an underdog—someone with the odds seemingly stacked against them. There's no better example than the Old Testament story of David and Goliath. Goliath is the ten-foot-tall, armor-clad, sword-wielding, seemingly invincible champion of the Philistines. David is a teenager with a sling and a handful of stones. David has no chance of victory and everyone knows it; even King Saul—the tallest man in Israel—tells him it's an unwinnable fight. But David isn't fazed. He strides confidently toward the battlefield and nails Goliath between the eyes with a pebble, killing him instantly.

David is the archetypal underdog. It's no coincidence that he is said to be the youngest of eight brothers. When J. K. Rowling came up with her underdog hero Harry Potter, she gave him glasses as a constant reminder of his vulnerability. J. R. R. Tolkein's Frodo Baggins is a three-and-a-half-foot-tall, peace-loving hobbit thrust into a dangerous world of orcs and dragons. From Rocky Balboa to the Little Engine that Could, some of the most enduring and beloved characters of all time are unmistakable underdogs, boldly overcoming disadvantage and facing down insurmountable odds through sheer passion and determination.

The appeal of the underdog isn't limited to fiction. Psychologist Joseph Vandello specializes in the psychology of underdogs. A month before the 2004 Summer Olympics, Vandello and colleagues made a list of the total number of medals a handful of countries had won over the history of the games, from Sweden with almost five hundred, to Belgium with one hundred forty, to Slovenia with just six. Then they asked American students which of two countries they would rather see win a hypothetical swimming contest. When it was Belgium versus Sweden, most people sided with the underdog Belgians. But the lure of the underdog can make us fickle. When it was Belgium versus Slovenia, the Belgians became top dog and most people wanted to see them lose to the underdog Slovenians. As Neeru Paharia and colleagues note, television coverage of the Olympics often highlights the underdog credentials of the competitors, "from swimmer Michael Phelps's single mother to gymnast Shawn Johnson's parents taking out a second mortgage on their home to pay for her gymnastics lessons." All told, Vandello and others have found that upward of three quarters of people will root for the underdog in a sporting match (assuming they have no skin in the game).

The same kind of story that has us rooting for an underdog athlete can influence how we spend our money. Marketers know that cultivating a company's image as a scrappy underdog can tempt consumers to pick their product over the corporate top dogs. Jill Avery, a lecturer at the Harvard Business School, notes that "brewery Samuel Adams reminds us how small it is compared with behemoth Anheuser-Busch—while avoiding mention of how big it is compared with most craft beer makers." Avery should know: She used to be a brand manager at Sam Adams. Likewise, Apple, Google, and Hewlett-Packard are all quick to point out their humble origins in a garage with nothing more than a big idea and the passion to make it happen.

Politicians know there are benefits to being seen as the underdog, too. In a 2009 paper, Vandello noted that political candidates often clamor to play down their credentials and advertise their apparent disadvantage. "When your name is Barack Obama, you're always an underdog in political races," Obama said in the run up to the 2008 election. He used the same tactic in the run-up to his 2012 reelection campaign; when an interviewer asked Obama if he was the underdog now, he didn't hesitate to embrace the label: "Absolutely . . . I'm used to being an underdog." Obama's Republican opponent Mitt Romney had the same idea. While lagging in polls, Romney said, "It's always a good thing to be seen as the underdog, to be fighting hard." Romney was right; Vandello found that we see a political candidate as more likable—and no less competent—when he or she is labeled as the underdog. (Though, in this case, it didn't help Romney beat the incumbent underdog.)

Framing one side or the other in a conflict as the underdog can even shape how we see a bloody international conflict. In a 2007 study, Vandello asked students how they felt about Israel and Palestine. In addition to a brief history of the conflict, the students were given a map of the region to aid their decision.

Half saw a map of the Israel–Palestine area alone; Israel took up almost the entire map, swamping the tiny Palestinian territories of Gaza and the West Bank. The other half saw a map of the greater Middle East, so that Israel appeared dwarfed by the surrounding countries. The difference in framing had a large effect. When Palestine looked like the underdog—purely in terms of geographic size—a little over half of the students sided with the Palestinians. When Israel was framed as the underdog, more than three quarters said they supported the Israelis.

We see underdogs as putting in more effort, having more persistence, guts, and heart. According to a study involving fictional job candidates, we even see an underdog applicant as more physically attractive than the top dog. Our love of underdogs clearly runs deep. In a 2008 study, psychologist Scott Allison and colleagues demonstrated just how deeply ingrained it is. The researchers created a simple, fifteen-second animation, showing two circles moving across a horizontal line with a bump in the middle creating a rudimentary hill. The light gray circle—let's call it the top dot—moves from left to right at a steady pace. The dark gray circle, however—let's call it the underdot—noticeably slows down when it encounters the hill, as if it's struggling to make it up the incline. That one small difference was enough to engage viewers' sympathetic underdog response; when asked how they felt about each circle, people said they liked the underdot substantially more than the top dot.

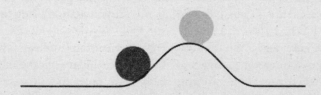

One more tweak to the video sealed the deal. In this version, the underdot didn't just struggle, it was actively impeded by the top dot; the light gray circle zoomed past the dark gray circle and halfway up the hill, then doubled back and shoved the innocent underdot back down the hill. This clip elicited the strongest reaction of all. Viewers were "visibly agitated when they witnessed the struggling underdog circle being harmed," Allison wrote. "After the study was completed, they reported to us that such an aggressive act directed toward an 'underdog' was completely out of line."

Allison's dots revealed the key to being an endearing underdog: You need to be at a disadvantage, and your disadvantage needs to be unfair—due either to lack of resources or to the malicious actions of an aggressive opponent. When we feel like somebody's disadvantage is self-imposed—when they have all the resources to succeed and still fail regardless—we dislike them even more than a simple loser. But unfair disadvantage arouses our sense of justice. We want to see top dogs taken down a peg; we want the downtrodden underdog to triumph. And when it comes to conspiracy theories, unfair disadvantage is par for the course.

"It Is a Dog Fight"

When we last saw Andrew Wakefield back in Chapter 2, his findings linking the MMR vaccine with autism had been discredited and his medical license withdrawn. But that wasn't the last the world heard of Wakefield. In the eyes of his supporters, Wakefield became a heroic underdog, courageously fighting a powerful, corrupt system that was out to destroy him. "If it is not clear to you this far, let me be frank about it," wrote the authors of an anti-vaccination book, *Vaccine Epidemic*: "The coverage of the vaccine/autism debate that you see in the media is not scientific debate or earnest investigation. It is a dog fight, and Pharma plays dirty."

In contrast to the monolithic pharmaceutical industry, with its government backing and billions of dollars, Wakefield is presented as a lone shining light, a valiant underdog nobly standing up for concerned parents. Describing Wakefield's research in the *Huffington Post*, Jenny McCarthy wrote, "Dr. Wakefield did something I wish all doctors would do: he listened to parents and reported what they said . . . Since when is repeating the words of parents and recommending further investigation a crime? As I've learned, the answer is whenever someone questions the safety of any vaccines." For his supporters, Wakefield's integrity is an unfair handicap; he is being vilified merely for having the courage to care. Wakefield himself has continued to defend his stance on autism and vaccines, earning not one, but two awards for "Courage in Science" from his admirers.

Wakefield isn't alone in being cast as a courageous underdog taking on a corrupt system. AIDS denialists have a renegade scientist in Peter Duesberg. Duesberg made important contributions to cancer research in his career as a molecular biologist, even getting elected to the prestigious National Academy of Sciences. In the late 1980s, however, Duesberg turned his attention to AIDS, claiming that the HIV virus by itself is harmless. AIDS, he argues, is caused by recreational drug use ("mainly the ones that are used by the gays"), or even by antiretroviral treatments. A biography on Duesberg's website paints Duesberg as a latter-day Galileo: "Prof. Duesberg's findings have been a thorn in the side of the medical establishment and drug companies since 1987. Instead of engaging in scientific debate, however, the only response has been to cut-off [sic] funding to further test Professor's [sic] Duesberg's hypothesis."

The 9/11 Truth movement has a renegade scientist in Steven E. Jones. In 2005, Jones, who was then a tenured professor at Brigham Young University, began arguing that the collapse of the Twin Towers was a controlled demolition. When the university distanced itself from Jones's remarks his supporters sensed foul play, suggesting that the "Bush administration had its dirty hand in forcing BYU to 'shut up' its professor."

Kennedy assassination buffs have an underdog attorney in the late Jim Garrison. In the late 1960s, Garrison became convinced that Kennedy had died at the hands of a CIA conspiracy. Despite the fact that Garrison's claims were dismissed by a jury, Oliver Stone, in his 1991 film *JFK*, presented Garrison as an underdog hero who sacrificed everything in pursuit of the truth. "Telling the truth can be a scary thing sometimes," *JFK*'s Garrison says, spoken like a true underdog.

The best conspiracy theories have all the trappings of a classic underdog story. The enemy is formidable. From the Elders of Zion to the New World Order, from the weapons-industrial complex to Big Pharma, the names given to the conspirators often play up their allegedly overwhelming power and influence. Like every villain, however, the conspiracy has one fatal weakness; if only their schemes can be exposed to the light, the enemy becomes powerless.

And the motive for the fight is noble. Christopher Booker notes that archetypal heroes act not to further their own interests, but on behalf of others. "David challenges Goliath because the giant is threatening his country, Israel; James Bond's villains are threatening England, the West, all mankind; Darth Vader, in *Star Wars*, is threatening to impose his tyranny over the entire universe." And according to conspiracy theories, the conspiracy is a threat to the freedom, liberty, and well-being of all mankind.

At first blush, it seems odd that someone would embrace a position of disadvantage. But as we've seen, there are upsides to being an underdog. Without conspiracy theories, people like Wakefield, Duesberg, Jones, and Garrison are just wrong. If there is an ongoing campaign to smear their reputations and discredit their findings, however, they become courageous heroes pushing the frontiers of science by selflessly battling a powerful, sinister foe on behalf of the unsuspecting public. Even more than making heroes out of a few renegades, though, conspiracy theories offer to make heroic underdogs of us all. A conspiracy theory is an invitation to join an enlightened but embattled minority—an elect few who bravely, selflessly speak truth to power.

As Joseph Vandello notes, our understanding of underdogs is "shaped by inspirational archetypal stories of odds overcome." In the real world, underdogs are, by definition, unlikely to prevail. In the stories we tell, however, the underdog always wins; good always triumphs over evil. Speaking of evil . . .

The Myth of Pure Evil

Villains come in all shapes and sizes. Some are literally monstrous, from the unusually bloodthirsty shark in *Jaws*, to the anatomically implausible Humbaba. Others are—or once were—human, from Voldemort's grotesque shell of a former person in the *Harry Potter* series, to the outwardly innocuous

Norman Bates in Alfred Hitchcock's *Psycho*. Despite their outward differences, however, all the best villains are cut from the same cloth. According to Christopher Booker, archetypal monsters represent everything in human nature that is somehow twisted and imperfect—the distilled essence of the very worst elements of the human psyche. They are driven purely by greed, self-interest, cruelty, cunning, ruthlessness, and egotism. And yet, for all their inhuman wickedness, the best baddies inspire not only feelings of repulsion, but fascination, curiosity, and even pleasure. Evil, it seems, has a paradoxical allure.

Social psychologist Roy Baumeister wrote the book on evil. Literally. He called it *Evil: Inside Human Violence and Cruelty*. He also wrote an essay on the psychology of some of the most evil characters ever imagined: the supervillains found within the pages of comic books. Comic book villains, Baumeister points out, gleefully perpetrate unconscionable acts of global or even cosmic significance on a weekly basis. And yet, supervillains rank among the most popular characters in all of fiction. In fact, a villain's popularity seems to be directly proportional to the depths of his or her depravity. An IGN.com list rating the one hundred best comic book villains of all time gave the top spots to the X-Men's archenemy Magneto and Batman's nemesis the Joker—ruthless villains boasting two of the highest body counts among all the various comic book universes.

Our love of fictitious supervillains is a little perplexing, Baumeister notes. In general, we're not fond of immoral people, and we don't take pleasure in hearing about morally objectionable acts. The supervillains' closest real-world analogs are such figures as Adolf Hitler and Pol Pot—individuals who are almost universally despised. So why do we delight in stories about psychopathic, indiscriminate killers? Why, Baumeister asks, do supervillains end up on posters on bedroom walls and children's lunch boxes? The answer, he argues, lies in our fondness for passing judgment on the character of others, and our reaction to moral deviants.

Imagine you and I find ourselves sitting in a psychologist's lab with ten crisp dollar bills on the table in front of us. The money is ours to take home, but here's the rub: I have been put in charge of deciding how to divvy it up. All you get to decide is whether you want to accept my offer. If you reject it, we both leave empty-handed. Psychologists call this the Ultimatum Game. In a perfectly fair world, I would offer you five dollars and keep five myself. You would presumably accept my amicable offer, and we would both leave five dollars richer. Encouragingly, this is the most common outcome; given the chance, most people offer an even split. Suppose, though, I offer you just one dollar. If you were being entirely rational, you should accept it—after all, you'll leave with a dollar more than you started with. But I'll bet the offer doesn't sound appealing. The thought of me skipping out with nine dollars, leaving you with a measly one, probably grinds your gears. Maybe you'd reject the offer, sacrificing your lonely dollar just to prevent me getting one over on you. If so, you would not be alone. Around half of players reject an offer that strays too far from an even split.

Foregoing the dollar to punish a greedy Ultimatum Game player might deviate from pure rationality, but it makes sense in a world where letting cheaters prosper could spell trouble for everyone. As a social species, our very survival depends on cooperating with others without being taken advantage of, and so natural selection made sure we are keenly attuned to other people's scruples. As the Ultimatum Game demonstrates, we're keen to condemn and punish people who mistreat us, even when we have to endure a small sacrifice to enforce justice. Being on the receiving end of an injustice doesn't just make us angry—it hurts. When people play the game inside brain imaging scanners, parts of their brain associated with pleasure and reward become active when they receive a fair offer, while regions associated with pain, distress, and disgust become active in response to unfair offers.

Even when we haven't just been slighted, we are constantly on the lookout for signs of other people's moral fortitude, using any information available to us. When we're around other people, we are constantly monitoring their behavior, even their fleeting facial expressions, for clues about their character. When someone isn't around, we gossip about him or her. According to psychologist Robin Dunbar, a primary function of gossip is to warn one another about potential miscreants, and something like two thirds of all conversation is devoted to gossiping about other people. The very moment we meet a stranger, we begin judging him or her, and the quality we value above all else is a person's trustworthiness.

A result of our ethical hardwiring is that we enjoy exercising our moral faculties—even on entirely make-believe villains. In fact, *especially* on entirely make-believe villains. The perennial popularity of overcoming the monster stories, Baumeister argues, is down to their moral clarity. In popular fiction, there is no mistaking the baddie. As if their heinous deeds aren't obvious enough, writers and filmmakers often give audiences a helping hand by providing unmistakable cues to a character's evil nature. The villains of silent-era melodramas had a penchant for twirling their mustaches in delight at their latest wicked scheme coming to fruition, while the villains in spaghetti Westerns donned black hats in contrast to the hero's white hat. Comic book villains take this trend to its logical extreme; a typical supervillain might wear a metal mask and go around calling himself "Dr. Doom," or flaunt a physical deformity to complement his moral depravity. Overcoming-the-monster stories give us an opportunity to engage in some easy mock moral judgment, jeering the obvious baddies and cheering the obvious heroes.

Literary critic Lionel Trilling pointed out that these kinds of stock characters, who had been a staple of high literature and theater well into the Victorian era, were largely retired from "respectable" fiction around the turn of the twentieth century. Serious authors sought realism, and such clear-cut villains have little basis in reality. "It became established doctrine," Trilling explains, "that people were a mixture of good and bad and that much of the bad could be accounted for by circumstances." Yet while writers who strive for realism tend to avoid cartoonish bad guys, the public at large still clearly adores a good baddie. Every one of the ten top-grossing films of 2014 had a villain of some form; five were comic book adaptations. In 2008, Heath Ledger's portrayal of the Joker in *The Dark Knight* was critically acclaimed and made for one of the highest-grossing films of all time.

Our seemingly insatiable appetite for stories with implausibly wicked baddies suggests that, even though they diverge from reality, archetypal villains correspond in some important way to how we see the world. Our thinking is subject to what Baumeister calls "the myth of pure evil." When *we* do bad things, we are good at rationalizing our behavior as a momentary lapse or a reasonable and justified response to circumstances. When *other* people do bad things, though, it's because they are just bad to the bone; we assume that evildoers are driven primarily by sadism and malice, inflicting harm for the sheer pleasure of doing so, while their victims are wholly innocent. The result is that, like Santa Claus, we have an irresistible compulsion to sort people into just two categories: good or bad, saint or sinner, naughty or nice.

Baumeister points out traces of the myth of pure evil not just in children's comic books, but in the stories we tell to make sense of everyday life, too. The nightly news tends to focus on stories about arbitrary attacks on unsuspecting innocents. In the wake of the Columbine High School shootings, *Time* magazine emblazoned its cover with smiling pictures of the two perpetrators, accompanied by the headline THE MONSTERS NEXT DOOR. President George W. Bush played into the myth when he said that the terrorists behind the 9/11 attacks were driven by pure hatred of "our freedoms"—adding "these terrorists kill not merely to end lives, but to disrupt and end a way of life."

Reality is complicated. Evildoers are rarely motivated by pure sadism and victims are not always entirely innocent. Violence is often the result of mutual provocation and escalating hostility. Heinous acts are often committed by people who are essentially ordinary, and who believe they are in the right. Through the myth of pure evil, however, we twist reality, with all its infinite shades of gray, into a black-and-white caricature of unassailable good versus irredeemable evil. "The myth of pure evil depicts malicious, alien forces intruding on the world of well-meaning, unsuspecting, virtuous people," Baumeister wrote. "The world often breaks down into us against them, and it almost invariably turns out that evil lies on the side of 'them.'"

As with any psychological foible, we're each drawn to the myth of pure evil to a greater or lesser extent. In 2011, psychologists Eric Oliver and Thomas Wood surveyed one thousand

Americans. Among questions about various conspiracy theories, they included one short statement about the fundamental nature of the political process: "Politics is ultimately a struggle between good and evil." More than a third of the people surveyed agreed with the sentiment. Revealingly, the more strongly someone agreed, the more likely he or she was to buy into conspiracy theories. A black-and-white worldview provides a perfect canvas for conspiracy thinking.

Joe Uscinski and Joseph Parent point out that conspiracy theories are far from an entirely alien way of viewing the world. Conspiracism, they argue, isn't all that different from everyday political discourse; it is merely intensified and stripped of nuance. "Where regular politicians highlight problems, advocate solutions, and call for concerted action soon, conspiracy theorists highlight an abysmal state of affairs, advocate titanic policies, and call for concerted action right now." There *are* genuine problems in the world; our liberty *is* sometimes threatened, bureaucrats *can* be self-interested. Through the filter of conspiracism, these issues take on the guise of a melodramatic struggle between good and evil, ripped straight from the pages of a comic book. From John Robison's claim that the Illuminati was intent on overthrowing all the governments of Europe, to currently fashionable theories about psychopathic bureaucrats with no qualms about murdering thousands of their fellow citizens, the best conspiracy theories are stories about manically evil villains, with the vaguest of motives, wantonly perpetrating outrageous evils on an innocent, unsuspecting public.

All the World's a Stage

In a 1987 essay on conspiracism, psychologist Serge Moscovici compared the world as portrayed in conspiracy theories to a theatrical performance. In the opening scene, we see society in a state of innocence and stability. Then a second group of characters enters, bringing with them conflict and intrigue. Like actors in a play, these evildoers are following a script laid out for them in advance, by some sinister producer who pulls the strings but always remains hidden behind the scenes. "Such a spectacle acted out in reality would be absurd," Moscovici concludes. "It is not absurd on stage, however. It is a performance stripped down to the essentials; it is the confrontation of elemental forces, which can only end in the definitive victory of one party over the other." In the world according to conspiracy theories, in short, "dualism is personified and acted out on the stage of society."

Listeners of Alex Jones's daily conspiracy-oriented radio show are greeted by the "Imperial March" from *Star Wars*—the unmistakably sinister theme tune that accompanies Darth Vader's appearance onscreen. Now and then, when coming back from commercials, a bombastic announcer reassures listeners, "*We're* on the march; *the Empire* is on the run." When I tuned in one Friday afternoon while researching this chapter, I caught Jones musing about the parallels between his understanding of the world and the plot of a recent superhero movie. "If you go see something like *Captain America*, it's almost like I co-wrote the thing," he said. "It's not that they're even copying me, it's that I understand how the system works."

At the trial of Timothy McVeigh, the Oklahoma City bomber, an accomplice explained how McVeigh had rationalized killing secretaries and receptionists and other government employees who had nothing to do with debacles like Waco. "He explained to me that he considered all those people to be as if they were the storm troopers in the movie *Star Wars*. They may be individually innocent; but because they are part of the Evil Empire, they were guilty by association."

"We are all tellers of tales," wrote psychologist Dan McAdams. Stories are how our minds work. They are the lens through which we make sense of the world and our place in it. They allow us to organize chaotic reality into something coherent and meaningful. There's no escaping stories. Even seemingly objective endeavors like science and history are ultimately exercises in storytelling. "No history is without an implicit sense of protagonists and antagonists," political psychologists Molly Patterson and Kristen Monroe point out; "no set of facts is without interpretations of what is important or relevant and what is not."

The stories we listen to can influence our beliefs and behavior. When you want to persuade someone, a story can be infinitely more effective than a mere list of bullet points. Psychologist Melanie Green and her colleagues have demonstrated that stories lure us in, bypassing our critical faculties. When we know someone is trying to persuade us, we are likely to scrutinize their arguments, but stories can shape our beliefs without us even realizing it. The better a story is, the more we are engrossed in it; the more engrossed we are, the more we are open to persuasion.

And when it comes to stories, "better" means conforming to the age-old archetypes that are etched into our minds like the grooves of a record. With that in mind, it's hardly surprising that stories have a habit of evolving in the retelling to more closely conform to our expectations. For example, the story, familiar to generations of American schoolchildren, of Christopher Columbus's discovery of the Americas has been embellished over time to play up Columbus's heroics (the journey was arduous, a mutinous crew almost threw Columbus overboard, he died penniless) while omitting some of the less savory details (such as his contribution to genocide and slavery). Sometimes a good story can eclipse reality.

Another way to improve a story is to ramp up the tension and conflict, bleaching out the nuance of reality until all that's left is a black-and-white story of good versus evil. David Icke's Archons are the perfect villain, driven only by greed and sadism. They are clever and well-organized, Icke says, but incapable of original thought. They can only feed off humans like parasites, sustaining themselves by harvesting our darkest emotions. In pursuit of their goals, they created a race of human-reptile hybrids that have literally had empathy deleted from their genome, Icke asserts, which is why they have no qualms about pulling off murderous stunts like 9/11 and engaging in blood-drinking, child-sacrificing rituals. By blowing the lid on the Archons' wicked schemes, Icke invites his listeners to join the fight, becoming underdog heroes, valiantly battling a monstrous conspiracy on behalf of the duped masses.

To be fair, the interdimensional reptile part of Icke's ideology seems to have relatively limited appeal. When Icke first went public with his psychic revelations in the early 1990s, he became a national joke. But over the last two and a half decades, he has crafted his theories into a grand narrative that explains everything from mundane political maneuverings to the very nature of reality. It's an epic saga, and one that perfectly traces the contours of an archetypal overcoming-the-monster story. With it, he has attracted a wide range of admirers. They might not believe *everything* he says, but Icke has legions of devoted followers who think he has something to offer.

Toward the end of one of his signature ten-hour lectures, Icke confided to the congregation, "they told me twenty-five years ago, 'You're finished. You can't go any further after all that ridicule.'" After surveying the crowd serenely, Icke offered a succinct response to his critics: "Watch me."

CHAPTER EIGHT

Connect the Dots

The "Zapruder film" is just twenty-seven seconds—four hundred eighty-six individual frames—of grainy 8mm footage recorded by a Dallas dressmaker, but it became one of the most iconic images of the twentieth century.

Abraham Zapruder almost didn't make the film at all. He left his high-end Zoomatic Director Series camera at home that morning, expecting rain. But the sky turned blue, and Zapruder's secretary insisted he make the short trip home to fetch it. When lunchtime came around he strolled outside and climbed on top of a raised concrete pedestal on the north side of Elm Street, where he would have a perfect view of the motorcade. Then he watched through his viewfinder as the president of the United States of America was shot in the head. According to his family, Zapruder never looked through the lens of a camera again.

Here's how the Zapruder film plays out. First, three police motorcycles round a corner onto Elm Street. There's an abrupt cut—Zapruder stopped the camera to conserve film—and suddenly President Kennedy's open-top Lincoln Continental is cruising along the street in front of delighted onlookers. Kennedy and his wife, Jackie, wave happily to the crowd. Then the car passes briefly out of sight behind a large street sign. When it emerges, something is wrong. Kennedy is clutching at his throat. He has already been shot once in the back. Moments later, a bullet rips through Kennedy's head. For one brief frame, a vivid orange-red cloud hangs in the air. The frame, labeled Z313, is so graphic that Zapruder agreed to sell the film to *Life* magazine only under the condition they never publish that frame; the public didn't see the complete film until Geraldo Rivera played it on late-night television in 1975. Kennedy slumps lifelessly toward his wife. Panic-stricken, she clambers from the seat onto the back of the car, moving toward

a Secret Service agent who mounts from the rear, as the motorcade speeds off. The short, silent film is horrifying and
haunting.

Rewind a few seconds and watch carefully, though, and you
might notice something odd. Just as Kennedy's car emerges
from behind the freeway sign, you can see a large black umbrella
protruding from the right side of the sign, half hidden in front
of it. There might be nothing odd about this, except for the fact
that it was a bright, breezy afternoon. Not one other person in
Dealey Plaza is holding an open umbrella, nor is anyone among
the hundreds of photos of crowds lining the motorcade's route.
The only open umbrella in Dallas happens to be right next to
Kennedy's car at the moment of his execution. What are the
chances?

It gets odder. Pictures taken by other people scattered around
Dealey Plaza show the umbrella's owner, an unremarkable
looking man in a dark suit, milling around before the motorcade arrived with the umbrella closed. As the president's car
approached, he opened the umbrella and held it conspicuously
aloft, thrusting it up and down and spinning it around. Just as
the car passed by this curious display, Kennedy was struck by
the assassin's bullets. Photos taken moments later appear to
show the man tranquilly walking away, the umbrella now at his
side, discreetly furled away.

Despite being one of the closest eyewitnesses to the president's murder, the Umbrella Man wasn't questioned by Dallas
police. Nor was he mentioned in the Warren Commission
Report. He simply vanished without a trace. It wasn't until
amateur assassination buffs noticed the anomalous umbrella that
questions began to be raised. For some skeptics, there was only
one possible explanation: the Umbrella Man was part of a
conspiracy. Some thought he must have been signaling to the
assassin(s) either that the moment was right to pull the trigger or
that their bullets had hit the mark. Others imagined he played a
more active role—perhaps the umbrella itself was a weapon,
hidden in plain sight. In 1978, Richard Sprague and Robert
Cutler published a detailed diagram outlining the deadly projec-
tile-firing mechanism they believed had been concealed within
the umbrella.

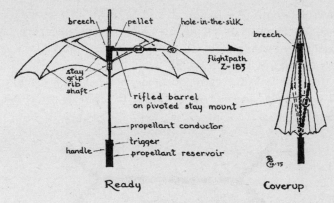

Ready   Coverup

THE PIECE

The mystery of the Umbrella Man was eventually solved; he and his umbrella were hauled in front of the U. S. government and asked to explain themselves. We'll find out what he was really up to later. For now, the curious tale illustrates a fundamental feature of any good conspiracy theory: the ability to weave seemingly unrelated and inexplicable anomalies into a coherent story about sinister conspirators and their hidden agenda. Conspiracy theories are an exercise in connecting dots. As we'll see, however, dot connecting is not the sole preserve of conspiracy theorists. The previous chapter was about the grand narratives that resonate with our deepest desires and darkest fears. This chapter, and the rest of the book, is about stories on a much smaller scale—about how we make sense of the world from one moment to the next. Reality is overflowing with dots. To make sense of it, our brain has to be good at quickly figuring out how they're connected. In its relentless quest to turn the chaos around us into meaning, however, our brain can conjure up seductive illusions. Sometimes our eyes deceive us, and sometimes our mind plays tricks.

Trick of the Eye

Let's begin with a familiar illusion. The two lines on the following page form one of the most famous illusions in the world: the Müller-Lyer illusion. You've probably seen it before. It consists

simply of two parallel lines, each bookended with a set of "fins."
The line with outward-facing fins appears to be incontrovertibly
longer than the one with in-turned fins, even though both are,
in fact, precisely the same length. Even when you *know* the lines
are the same length, even if you've measured them yourself, you
still can't help *seeing* them as different. Your brain is being
misled.

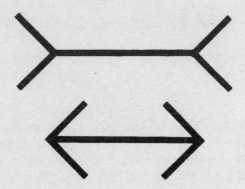

The Müller-Lyer illusion is a case of misinterpreting something that *is* there. Sometimes we see things that aren't there at
all. Another revealing illusion is the Kanizsa triangle. Named
after its creator, the Italian psychologist Gaetano Kanizsa, the
illusion appears to consist of two overlapping triangles resting
on top of three black circles (in a configuration that I, for one,
think would look at home adorning the stationery of some
sinister secret society).

The triangles and circles, however, only exist inside your
head. On the page, there is only an arrangement of discon-
nected, incomplete parts—three outward-facing arrowheads,
and three unfinished circles resembling a trio of hungry
Pac-Men. Your brain enthusiastically fills in the blanks,
conjuring up the illusion of complete shapes; the circles' missing
slices coupled with the spaces between the arrowheads give the
irresistible impression of a second triangle, upside down and
with no outline, lying on top of the first, covering bits of the
lower triangle's outline and slices of the circles. The most
striking thing about illusion is that even though neither triangle
really exists, and the paper is all the same color, you can vaguely

"see" the edges of the top triangle—it somehow looks as if it's whiter than white (though the edges vanish when you scrutinize closely the empty space where they should be).

From behind our eyes, it's tempting to think our retinas are a kind of cinema screen that our brain sits back and observes. But that's not how vision works. The brain doesn't just passively watch; it actively constructs. Simple visual illusions like these pull back the curtain, exposing our sense of sight for what it really is: a guess. An astoundingly good guess, for the most part—otherwise we would constantly be bumping into things and mistaking our reflection for an intruder—but a guess nonetheless. At any given moment, our eyes can see only a tiny area of the visual field with real clarity, roughly the size of our thumbnail at arm's length. The rest of the picture is largely blurry and lacks color. To compensate, our brain does a huge amount of work behind the scenes to create the impression that we're seeing a detailed, accurate picture of the world around us.

This sophisticated post-processing is so crucial to our sense of sight that around a third of our cortex is devoted to vision. Even so, generating a truly accurate and complete model of the outside world would be impossible, not to mention a massive waste of energy. The brain has an impressive repertoire of shortcuts and rules of thumb that it uses to make sense of the chaotic, ambiguous, and incomplete visual input it receives—sensible assumptions such as "light comes from above," "smaller means farther away," and "rapidly growing means coming toward." In other words, our sense of sight depends not just on the light hitting our retinas at any given moment, but on our brain's interpretation of that information.

This strategy frees up the rest of our brain to worry about what to have for lunch and other important things like that, and it usually works out fine. But occasionally it lets us down. We can fail to see something that's right in front of our eyes, like when you're looking for your keys and fail to see them sitting on the table right in front of you. We can misinterpret what's in front of us, like the deceptive Müller-Lyer lines. And occasionally, as the phantom Kanizsa triangle demonstrates, we can see something that isn't there at all.

When we look at illusions like the Müller-Lyer lines or the Kanizsa triangle, we know we're being tricked. In the real world, it can be harder to tell what's real and what's a figment of our imagination. Lacking an explanation for the strange things we see, we might be compelled to make one up.

Canals on Mars and Assassins in Bushes

For a few weeks in the late summer of 1877, Mars loomed unusually large and bright in the night sky. It was a Great Opposition, the point at which Mars's orbit brings it closest to Earth. A Great Opposition comes around just every seventeen years or so. Some of the world's leading astronomers had spent years preparing to take advantage of the uncommonly good viewing opportunity. One was an Italian named Giovanni Schiaparelli, director of the Brera Astronomical Observatory in Milan. In 1862, Schiaparelli had persuaded the Italian government to invest in a cutting-edge telescope. A new dome was constructed to house the ten-foot-long Merz refractor. Finally, when the sun set on August 23, 1877, Schiaparelli began the series of observations that would make him famous among astronomers and the public alike.

What Schiaparelli saw was incredible: There appeared to be an intricate network of long, dark, straight lines crisscrossing the Martian surface. Astronomers around the world rushed to confirm Schiaparelli's observations. Some saw the lines. Others didn't. A few high-profile astronomers, such as American astronomer Percival Lowell, championed the reality of the features, and suggested a sensational explanation. The lines, they said, were irrigation canals, and since canals don't build themselves, they could only have been made by intelligent (and presumably thirsty) beings. By the turn of the twentieth century, much of Europe and America was swept up in Mars mania.

Curiously, the canals proved immune to astrophotography. Curiouser, when different astronomers tried to map the features, their drawings often bore drastically different arrangements of canals. It was another Italian astronomer, Vincenzo Cerulli, who first suggested the lines might be an illusion. Martian cartographers had to stare for hours through their telescopes, waiting for rare moments of still air when the image was not distorted by Earth's atmosphere. Only then would they catch a fleeting glimpse of a tiny fragment of the planet's surface in focus and quickly sketch from memory what they had seen, gradually filling in the details across many viewings. This process provided ample opportunity for the astronomers' preconceptions to color their perception. Eventually improved observations proved Cerulli right; there are no canals on Mars. The long, straight lines Schiaparelli, Lowell, and others saw were nothing more than a figment of the brain's ability to find meaning in ambiguous images. As Carl Sagan noted, the canals were undoubtedly of intelligent origin—"the only unresolved question was which side of the telescope the intelligence was on."

The canals are not the only trace of life on Mars that can be chalked up to overactive imaginations. Since the 1970s, humanity has been putting cameras on and around the red planet. Among the many pictures of rocks and mountain ranges the rovers and orbiters have sent back, eagle-eyed anomaly hunters have spotted what seem to be a stone coffin, a tiny Bigfoot, a jelly donut, a surprising number of giant cartoon love hearts, a bust of President Obama, and a petrified iguana (petrified in the geological sense; it looks fairly calm, considering the circumstances). The most compelling sign of extraterrestrial intelligence, however, came from a picture taken by the Viking orbiter in 1976. The image shows an unmistakable, strangely ominous, human-looking face, seemingly sculpted into a hill on the surface of the planet. So mysterious was the face on Mars that when newer orbiters were sent to Mars decades later, one of their first tasks was to photograph the face. The higher-resolution images showed only a nondescript hill. As many people had suspected, the face on Mars was merely a trick of light and shadow.

As the assorted anomalies on Mars attest, some things are so important to us that we are particularly prone to seeing them in ambiguous images, including unnatural geometric patterns, people and other animals, and faces. The illusion can be so compelling that it leads to fanciful beliefs. Given the right circumstances, a portentous pattern can even nudge us toward conspiracy thinking. That's what happened to David Lifton, a journalist-turned-assassination-researcher, when he looked at a blurry Polaroid photo of the infamous grassy knoll in Dealey Plaza.

The Polaroid in question was taken by Mary Moorman. Moorman makes a cameo in the Zapruder film; you can see her standing directly across the street, next to her friend Jean Hill, who is wearing a distinctive bright red coat. Moorman has her camera held to her face. She knew the camera was slow to reload, and she would only have one chance to get a keepsake of the president's visit. The two friends were so intent on getting a good snapshot that they didn't even register the first two gunshots. As Kennedy's car passed by fifteen feet from the pair, Hill called out "Hey, we want to take your picture!" and Moorman pressed the shutter—just one sixth of a second after the third bullet struck Kennedy's head. In the foreground of the picture, Kennedy slumps toward his wife; in the background, the grassy knoll.

A year and a half later, David Lifton happened upon Moorman's photo in *Four Dark Days in History*, a collection of photos from November 22 and the three days that followed. What he saw in the blurry image stunned him. "There, visible on the printed page," Lifton wrote in his 1980 book *Best Evidence*, "was what appeared to be [a] puff of smoke . . . and, just behind it, a human form." He studied the page with a magnifying glass, and even hunted down the original negative. Not only did the improved quality confirm his suspicions about the puff of smoke, but he spotted *another* potential gunman elsewhere on the knoll, "visible from the waist up, and . . . holding something in his hands in a horizontal position." Other Kennedy assassination buffs found yet more assassins in the blurry picture. Gary Mack, curator of the Sixth Floor Museum in the Texas School Book Depository since 1994, identified what looks like a man in a police uniform standing behind a stockade fence, his badge glinting in the sunlight and his face obscured by the muzzle flash of a gun.

As far as forensic analysts can tell, the assassins are likely nothing more than film defects, highlights, shadows, or other anomalies, coupled with wishful thinking. One analysis of Gary Mack's Badge Man concluded that if he were an average-size person, he would have to be thirty feet behind the fence and four feet off the ground—an "untenable firing position," to say the least.

Lifton eventually realized what he was seeing might be an illusion. "It became evident that those who were already in disagreement with the Warren Commission conclusions found it far easier to 'see' people on the knoll than those who believed the Report," he admitted. Applying this reasoning to his own observations, he wondered "how certain could I be that my basic processes of perception were not hopelessly biased . . . Eventually I concluded that photographic enlargements had very limited use as evidence."

Trick of the Mind

It probably doesn't surprise you that we sometimes see things that aren't there, or misperceive things that are. Lying in bed at night, it's easy to momentarily mistake a coat hanging on the back of a door for a shadowy intruder. Looking for things that we know aren't really there can even be a pleasurable pastime. For millennia, humans have been whiling away afternoons pointing out familiar shapes in the clouds, and spending evenings imagining patterns in the stars to be people or animals. The twenty-first century is no different. Hours can be spent clicking through websites devoted to the many incongruous objects on Mars, or photos of everyday items that resemble faces. We know our eyes deceive us from time to time.

What we're less inclined to admit—or even realize—is that we are just as susceptible to illusions of *thought* as we are to illusions of *sight*. Much like we think of our eyes as faithful windows on the world, we spend our lives feeling confident that our brain is a dispassionate data processor. From inside our head, our thoughts and beliefs seem to be the product of an impartial, accurate understanding of reality. Once again, however, we have been tricked. Just as our ability to see the world depends on extensive behind-the-scenes processing and sophisticated guess-work, so too does our ability to understand the world. And much like the Kanizsa triangle or the canals on Mars, some of the most seductive cognitive illusions arise out of our brain's tireless hunt for patterns.

Read the following question out loud, and note the answer that comes to mind:

How many of each kind of animal did Moses take on the Ark?

According to a slew of experiments, around eight out of ten people confidently answer "two." Is that what you said? Given the fact that you're in the middle of reading about cognitive illusions, you may have suspected something was afoot and noticed the trick. The correct answer is "zero"; it was *Noah*, not Moses, who cajoled two of every animal onto his ark. As soon as the mistake is pointed out, it becomes glaringly obvious. So why do so many people fail to notice it right away, even though they *know* the story starred Noah, even when they can study the question for as long as they like—even, amazingly, when they've been warned that the question might contain a mistake?

Making sense of the world depends on drawing connections and finding patterns, and our brain conducts much of the search beneath the level of our conscious awareness. As you read a sentence, every word and idea automatically activates a host of associated ideas, like pebbles sending ripples across the surface of a pond. The illusion works because Moses and Noah happen to share several pertinent features: both are elderly biblical figures who figured in stories involving water. The pebbles land close enough together that the pattern of ripples is barely thrown off. You didn't realize anything was amiss, because your brain made sense of the nonsense behind the scenes. All you were aware of was the outcome. You read a question about Moses, but your brain interpreted it as a question about Noah.

Consider another variation of the question: How many of each kind of animal did Nixon take on the Ark? When the researchers tried this version, almost everyone noticed the mistake right away. The name Nixon activates a set of ideas (American presidents, hotel burglaries, not-a-crooks) very different from the rest of the sentence. The stray pebble throws the whole pattern off. Your brain can't easily make sense of the nonsense, and it flags up the problem. The misplaced Moses pebble fit the pattern well enough to slip by unnoticed, while the wayward Nixon pebble, true to form, made enough of a mess to get caught red-handed.

The insight offered by the Moses illusion extends far beyond misworded trivia questions. Our entire mental life is an exercise in pattern recognition. The brain tirelessly sifts through information looking for patterns, connections, and meaning. Usually the strategy works well. We can easily understand a simple sentence, even if we've never encountered that particular arrangement of words before. Sometimes it works a little *too* well. A mix-up between Noah and Moses can sneak by unnoticed. And sometimes we are so good at drawing connections that our brain finds meaningful patterns that aren't really meaningful at all.

From Coincidence to Cause

We're all suckers for a good coincidence. It's difficult not to be at least a little impressed when you have a dream about something and the next day it comes true, or when you get an unexpected phone call from someone moments after his or her name crossed your mind. The pattern-detection software in our brain is so sensitive that even the most trivial coincidence can seem incredible if it happens to *you*.

In an episode of the radio program *This American Life* devoted to coincidences, journalist Sarah Koenig tells a story from her early days as a reporter. Interviewing Esther Tuttle, a woman who had just celebrated her hundredth birthday, Koenig admits that she asked a rookie question: "What's the most amazing thing that happened in your life?" Esther thought on it a while, and then she said "the most interesting thing that happened to me was that on my first day at school, the principal said to me, what's your name? I said Esther Tuttle. And he said, I have a friend in Shelter Island by that name. I was twelve . . . and that to me was remarkable." Koenig confesses that she found herself disappointed by the answer. "This woman had seen the advent of cars, and movies, and computers, and space travel, and *this* was her answer?" After hearing so many coincidences from listeners while making the episode, however, Koenig says she had to reconsider. Coincidences stick with you, she admits, "even when the coincidence is barely a coincidence at all."

When it comes to pattern spotting, stories about spooky instances of synchronicity are just the tip of the iceberg. We tend to think of coincidences as these kinds of stories about prophetic dreams or shared surnames, but technically a "coincidence" merely denotes one thing apparently coinciding with another. In this sense, coincidences are all around us. You say something insensitive, for instance, and your spouse becomes upset. A farmer spreads cow manure on his field and enjoys a bumper harvest. Your granddad smoked two packs a day and lived to be a hundred. A company hires a new CEO and their quarterly earnings go up. A football team hires a new coach and has an abysmal season. Whenever one thing appears to coincide with another, whether it is an extraordinary dream coming to pass or a mundane quarrel over an ill-judged remark, our brain can't help taking note.

A coincidence by itself, however, is supremely unsatisfying, like an itch waiting to be scratched, or an unfinished tax return. Our brain wants to complete patterns, and spotting a coincidence is merely a prelude to learning something useful about the world. When we see some kind of connection between two events, we have potentially unearthed a clue about how things work. If one thing happens, the other is likely to happen; the relationship might be *causal*. Identifying causal relationships is an important business. Knowing what causes what allows us to predict and control the world around us. Coincidences like Esther Tuttle's stand out precisely because there is no obvious explanation. When we can't explain something that seems significant, the coincidence lingers in our mind. Our brain dangles it in front of us, taunting us with it until the pattern can be completed, until we have figured out the cause.

The trouble is that some coincidences are genuinely meaningful—others, not so much. Insensitive remarks often do rile spouses, and manure does nourish crops. It would be a mistake, though, to assume that cigarettes are good for your health just because you know one chain-smoking centenarian. Maybe the CEO is a genius and maybe the coach is lousy; maybe they are taking credit or blame for something that would have happened regardless. The pattern-detection software built into our brain is exquisitely sensitive, but there's no built-in quality-control program to keep it in check. To know whether one thing really causes another requires statistics and experiments, but the scientific method doesn't come naturally to us. Our brain evolved to interpret patterns quickly and decisively, which means treating every connection as meaningful by default.

Imagine one of our early ancestors strolling through the forest one day when she hears a rustle in the bushes and every bird in the area stops chirping. To discount it as mere chance, or to spend too long mulling over potential explanations, could be a costly mistake. There might be a dangerous predator in the area. The better an early hominid was at spotting patterns and quickly inferring plausible causes, the more likely she was to survive and pass on her pattern-prone genes. Our ancestors' legacy to us is a brain programmed to see coincidence and infer cause.

For the most part, our hypersensitivity to patterns and causes serves us well. With little pause or conscious deliberation, we are constantly learning how the world around us works, even when we don't know precisely *why* it works that way. Consider a simple cause-effect relationship: pushing a button and getting a response. As I walk to the New York Public Library to work on this book, I pass a crosswalk button. It's at the corner of Forty-first Street and Fifth Avenue, across from the big stone lions that lie placidly outside the library, posing for tourists' holiday photos. I give the button a push. A little while later, the traffic light over Fifth Avenue turns from green to red. The stream of traffic comes to a halt, and I continue on my way.

Even though the actual mechanism is hidden from me—some invisible magic happens in between the button and the lights—I have no trouble inferring the causal connection. I push the button, the light turns red. Cause, effect.

The trouble, as Michael Luo explained in a 2004 article for the *New York Times*, is that "the city deactivated most of the pedestrian buttons long ago." Getting traffic around a big city efficiently is a demanding, nuanced task. To keep everything moving, the lights need to operate according to a carefully choreographed schedule. Given power over when the walk signals light up, impatient pedestrians like me would really screw up the timing. The city would come to a standstill. So, in the 1980s, the Department of Transportation quietly switched to an entirely automatic system and deactivated almost all of the buttons. Many of the defunct buttons have been removed during reconstruction over the years. But going around and ripping out every single button, city officials decided, wouldn't be worth the expenditure. So many remain in place, enticing unaware passersby to give them a push, even though the walk signal comes up at set intervals, whether anybody is there to push the button or not.

The same is true, apparently, of the "door-close" button in elevators. "In most elevators, at least in any built or installed since the early nineties, the door-close button doesn't work," Nick Paumgarten wrote in a 2008 *New Yorker* article. "It is there mainly to make you think it works." One possible explanation is similar to the traffic problem: to keep wait times reasonable, the elevators in busy buildings need to work as a team, ferrying people up and down in a syncopated dance. People trying to shave a few seconds off their journey could throw the whole rhythm off kilter, and so the door-close button only works if you're a firefighter or a maintenance worker with a special key. At least, that's one explanation. Another possibility, according to an investigation by *The Straight Dope*, is that the button simply broke or was never wired up in the first place, and nobody has complained. At any rate, architects and elevator designers know that being hoisted hundreds of feet up and down a dark shaft in a metal box dangling from a cable can be disconcerting, particularly when we have virtually no control over the ordeal. And so they leave the dysfunctional door-close button in place as a benevolent deception—a placebo button that dispenses the illusion of control.

The ruse works. We push the button; eventually the doors close; ergo, our brain tells us, the button caused the doors to close. (And when the door doesn't close the very instant we push the button, mashing it a dozen times in quick succession usually feels like it does the trick.) Until some smart aleck tells us the button might not work, we have no reason to even consider the possibility. The button's sole stated purpose in life is to close the elevator doors sooner than they otherwise would, after all, and who would suspect elevator engineers of engaging in this massive public deception? Yet if our brain weren't so quick to spot patterns and jump to causal conclusions, the jig would be up the first time someone pressed a dysfunctional button.

This is how countless superstitions are born, from lucky charms to homeopathy. You wear your special socks to a job interview and get the position; you take some sugar pills and your cold clears up. In either case, the outcome may or may not have happened regardless of your actions, but your brain can't help connecting the dots and assuming that one thing caused the other. The illusion can be irresistible.

True, True, Unrelated

"As a young mother I, like most mothers, wanted to do the best job I could of caring for my new baby," Stephanie Messenger wrote. She breastfed him, she took him for regular check-ups. When she was told that it was time for him to get some vaccinations, she dutifully took him to the doctor that same day. Nobody at the health clinic mentioned possible side effects or adverse reactions, she says, and she didn't think to ask.

We met Messenger back in Chapter 2. She's the author of *Melanie's Marvelous Measles*. When her book caught the public's attention, in the wake of a measles outbreak at Disneyland at the end of 2014, Messenger became the target of ridicule and vitriol online. On Amazon.com, the book quickly received hundreds of mocking reviews. Commenters triumphantly declared their incredulity that anyone could think twice about vaccinating their children. But like many vaccine-anxious parents,

Messenger hadn't always opposed vaccines. Her concerns were shaped by tragedy.

In 1998, Messenger wrote an essay describing her first-born son as a happy baby who rarely even cried—until the day she had him vaccinated. "He screamed and cried for the rest of the day and had a very restless night that night," she wrote. He seemed to recover after that, she says, until four months later when he had more shots. "This time he screamed louder. I took him home, unable to console him at all. I would breastfeed him and he would vomit straight away (something he had never done), and still the screaming continued." Messenger says that he started arching his back, rolling his eyes, and his whole body would shake. After months of tests, doctors could not determine the cause but his prognosis was grim. Messenger took her son home "and watched him waste away to nearly nothing until he passed away six months later."

The connection seemed undeniable to her: "Jason's life was never the same from the day he was vaccinated." The coincidence lingered in Messenger's mind, crying out for an answer. Then, four years later, she was watching *The Phil Donahue Show*, a popular American talk show. That day's episode was about vaccination. One of the guests, a pediatrician, warned about the dangers of vaccination and said the risks weren't worth it, Messenger remembers. Another guest, a pediatric neurologist, said that most pediatric neurologists don't vaccinate their own children. "I was stunned," Messenger wrote. It was the explanation she had been waiting for. The pattern could finally be completed. The coincidence could be explained. She knew that vaccines had caused her son's illness.

Barbara Loe Fisher, another prominent anti-vaccine activist we met in Chapter 2, had a similar experience. "I trusted without questioning when I took my newborn to my pediatrician for baby shots in the late 1970s," she regretfully admitted in a 2004 essay for *Mothering* magazine. When her son Chris was two-and-a-half, Fisher took him for a routine DPT vaccination. Within hours of the shot, she wrote, her son "became a totally different child." Back home that evening, she realized the house was unusually quiet, so she went upstairs to check on Chris. "I walked into his bedroom to find him sitting in a rocking chair staring straight ahead, as if he couldn't see me standing in the doorway. His face was white and his lips were slightly blue. When I called out his name, his eyelids fluttered, his eyes rolled back in his head, and his head fell to his shoulder." Fisher says that the changes continued over the coming weeks. Chris had trouble paying attention to things, and couldn't remember his alphabet or numbers any more. "My little boy, once so happy-go-lucky, no longer smiled." Eventually, Fisher wrote, Chris "was diagnosed with minimal brain damage, including multiple learning disabilities and attention deficit disorder."

A year and a half later, Fisher watched *Vaccine Roulette*, the documentary that implied that the pertussis component of DPT was causing brain damage in hundreds of children. The lingering coincidence could be explained. "Chris is a vaccine reaction survivor," she later wrote. "He is among the walking wounded . . . whose futures are compromised in childhood when the risks of vaccination turn out to be 100 percent."

The medical community has an expression to remind themselves not to mistake coincidence for cause: "true, true, and unrelated." It is true that symptoms of developmental disorders like autism often become apparent between one and two years of age. It is also true that, if parents follow the recommended vaccine schedule, their children receive a large number of vaccines at the same time. The overwhelming weight of scientific evidence, however, shows that the two are unrelated. The connection is nothing more than a coincidence of timing. But our intuition is rarely impressed by statistics, especially when they tell us there is no sense to be made of a coincidence. Our intuition wants the dots to be connected.

According to a 2009 survey, more than half of American parents fear that vaccines have serious adverse effects. One quarter believe that some vaccines can cause autism in healthy children. Given our susceptibility to illusions of pattern and cause, it's not hard to see why. The Internet is an important source of information for many parents, and a few clicks of a mouse can produce seemingly endless stories, like Messenger's and Fisher's, of parents who are convinced that their previously healthy child transformed before their eyes after receiving a vaccine. A few more clicks lead to a movement of parents, pundits, self-proclaimed experts, and a handful of seemingly trustworthy scientists, all saying the dots are connected; vaccines are the cause.

An illusion of cause can be so compelling that it seems as though it should be as obvious to everyone else as it is to you. As a result, it can be tempting to think that anyone who denies a link between vaccines and autism might be lying—that there is a conspiracy to hide the indisputable danger of vaccines. In 2009, health anthropologist Anna Kata undertook a comprehensive survey of vaccine misinformation on the Internet. The results were remarkable. *Every* website she analyzed made some kind of conspiracist claim. The sites she selected weren't obscure; they were all among the first page of search results found by Googling neutral terms like "vaccine" and "immunization." Conspiracy theories act as a catalyst for vaccine paranoia. According to a 2014 study, one fifth of American adults—not just parents—believe that doctors and the government conspire to vaccinate children even though they know vaccines cause autism and other psychological disorders. A further 36 percent said they weren't sure. The debate rages on, fueled by conspiracy theories and sparked by an illusion of cause.

The anti-vaccine movement is not unique in creating conspiracy out of coincidence. Even coincidences that are orders of magnitude more tenuous than the illusory connection between vaccines and autism take on just as much sinister significance when viewed through the lens of conspiracy. Whether it is a terrorist attack that spawns a misguided war, a waving flag on an airless moon, or an open umbrella next to an assassinated president, coincidences are the lifeblood of conspiracy theories.

The best conspiracy theorists actively seek out seemingly inexplicable anomalies that can be construed as evidence of a conspiracy. In fact, "connecting the dots" is something of a mantra for conspiracy theorists. As a case in point, consider David Icke's 2007 book *The David Icke Guide to the Global Conspiracy (and How to End It)*. Emma Jane and Chris Fleming trawled through Icke's opus, counting up the number of times he mentions the word *connect* or its variants (*connected, connecting, connections*, and so on). They found a deluge; more than two hundred of the book's 625 pages made mention of connecting dots, and on many of those pages more than once. Within the first few paragraphs, for example, Icke tells his readers, "only when the dots are connected can the picture be seen." When Icke started a YouTube video series in 2014, in which he skims through the week's newspapers looking for hints of conspiracy, the choice of title must have been easy. He called it *David Icke: Dot Connector*.

"Bubbles in the Surface of Circumstance"

Which brings us back to where we started: an open umbrella and an assassinated president. Two tantalizing dots, beckoning us to spot the connection. Writer John Updike captured the irresistible lure of the Umbrella Man in a 1967 *New Yorker* column, describing him as equal parts "anomalous and ominous. He dangles around history's neck like a fetish."

Then, after fifteen years of speculation, the mystery was solved. In 1978, the U.S. House of Representatives was in the midst of a renewed investigation of the Kennedy assassination, called the House Select Committee on Assassinations. In an effort to track down the Umbrella Man, they released his picture to the press, asking anyone who recognized the man to contact the committee. Finally, after a tip-off from a friend, the identity of Umbrella Man was revealed. The enigmatic bearer of the anomalous umbrella, the man behind the mystery that had taunted assassination buffs for years, was, it turned out, an insurance salesman named Louie Steven Witt.

The committee didn't beat around the bush. "Did the umbrella in your possession on November 22, 1963, contain a gun or a weapon of any sort?" a panel member asked Witt. He closed his eyes, bowed his head a little, and solemnly shook it from side to side: "No." Incredibly, Witt still owned the umbrella in question. It lay on the table next to him, entered into evidence as Exhibit 405. A young woman on the committee staff was instructed to open the umbrella for examination. As she began to unfurl it in the direction of the seated committee members the chairman quipped, "Maybe you ought to turn *that* way with it." He gestured toward the press area. As the room burst into laughter, the umbrella skittishly splayed itself inside out, as if hit by a sudden gale. "I guess there is no gun in it," the chairman concluded, with a hint of disappointment.

So if Witt hadn't shot the president, what was his story? Under questioning, he confessed that he really had been there in Dealey Plaza. He really had carried an umbrella. He really had behaved strangely with it. It really had been a signal—but not to any coconspirator. His bizarre theatrics had been intended as a signal to Kennedy himself.

"In a coffee break conversation someone had mentioned that the umbrella was a sore spot with the Kennedy family," Witt told the committee. "Being a conservative-type fellow, I sort of placed him in the liberal camp and I was just going to kind of do a little heckling." John F. Kennedy's father, Joseph Kennedy, you see, had served as ambassador to England in the run-up to the Second World War, and had been harshly criticized for supporting British prime minister Neville Chamberlain's appeasement of Hitler. Chamberlain was noted for his habit of carrying around a black umbrella. By extension, the umbrella became a symbol of appeasement, and apparently something of a thorn in the Kennedy family's side. None of this was of particular concern to Witt; he claimed to have no strong feelings about appeasement, or even about Kennedy's own policies. He just happened to have a black umbrella to hand, and Kennedy happened to be passing through town. There was no conspiracy, just a mild heckle staged on a whim.

If there is a lesson to be learned from the story of the Umbrella Man, it is that sometimes the truth is stranger than anything we can imagine. Our desperate, deep-rooted desire to explain the inexplicable can lead us up garden paths, and down dark alleys. Updike wondered "whether any similar scrutiny of a minute section of time and space would yield similar strangeness—gaps, inconsistencies, warps, and bubbles in the surface of circumstance," the way normal laws of physics give way to quantum weirdness under a strong enough microscope. "The truth about those seconds in Dallas is especially elusive," he wrote. "The search for it seems to demonstrate how perilously empiricism verges on magic."

Our ability to see meaning in mayhem really is a kind of magic. From coming up with an apt analogy to inventing life-changing new technologies, creative thinking depends on spotting connections. It is the cornerstone of science, too. Learning about reality is an exercise in finding patterns in data, and sorting the real from the random. A brain biased toward seeing meaning rather than randomness is one of our greatest assets. The price we pay is occasionally connecting dots that don't really belong together.

For his part, Witt claimed to have no idea that his "little act of heckling" had earned him a starring role in so many conspiracy theories. He was clearly uncomfortable with the attention, and understandably remorseful about taunting Kennedy at the moment he happened to be publicly gunned down. "I think if the Guinness Book of World Records had a category for people who were at the wrong place at the wrong time, doing the wrong thing," he lamented, "I would be number one in that position, without even a close runner-up."

CHAPTER NINE

Intention Seekers

As Malaysia Airlines Flight 370 cruised out of Malaysian airspace in the small hours of March 8, 2014, its pilots calmly bade air traffic controllers in Kuala Lumpur good night—a standard radio sign-off. The flight had departed Kuala Lumpur International Airport forty minutes earlier, bound for Beijing, China. But MH370 never reached its destination. The plane, along with the 227 passengers and 12 crew on board, disappeared. A massive search operation was under way within hours. For days, twenty-four-hour news channels breathlessly covered the story around the clock. Yet, as I write this a year later, there is still no trace of the plane or its passengers.

But why let the lack of facts get in the way of a good story? Within hours, conspiracy theories about the plane's fate were rampant. Might it have been shot down by the military, or hijacked by government operatives? Had the plane been carrying some secret cargo worth killing for? Did it land in some secret location? Were the passengers being held hostage, or participating in a bizarre reality television promo? Had it been abducted by aliens? In lieu of substantive facts to report on, the proliferation of conspiracy theories became a story in its own right. More than half of a thousand Americans polled by CNN two months after the disappearance thought it likely that the plane had been hijacked by secret agents on the orders of a hostile foreign government. Almost one in ten thought it likely that the culprits were "space aliens, time travelers, or beings from another dimension." Even the former prime minister of Malaysia, Mahathir Mohamad, hinted that the CIA might know the whereabouts of the missing plane. "Airplanes don't just disappear," he wrote.

But MH370 is not the first plane to mysteriously disappear. On July 2, 1937, Amelia Earhart departed Lae, New Guinea, in her twin-engine Lockheed Electra. Earhart was an aviation pioneer, and one of the most admired women in America. Five years earlier she had become the first female pilot to fly solo across the Atlantic. Now Earhart and her navigator, Fred Noonan, were two thirds of the way into a grueling round-the-world flight. The next stop was Howland Island, a tiny atoll in the middle of the Pacific Ocean, just over a mile long, less than half a mile wide, and some 2,500 miles away. A United States Coast Guard boat was on location to guide Earhart's approach by radio, but communication was patchy. Eventually radio operators heard Earhart's voice: "We must be on you but cannot see you. But gas is running low. Been unable to reach you by radio. We are flying at one thousand feet." Earhart was lost, low on fuel, and there was no way to help her. After a couple more futile transmissions, there was nothing but static. A search effort of unprecedented scale was launched. For days, newspapers breathlessly reported every tantalizing lead and crushing disappointment. Almost eight decades later, no conclusive trace of Earhart, Noonan, or the plane has been found.

Over the years, however, a range of conspiracy theories have been put forward. Could the intrepid aviators have been secret government agents, shot down while spying on the Japanese in the South Pacific? Was the crash arranged in advance to allow the U.S. military to gather intel on Japan during the rescue mission? Did Earhart and Noonan fake their own deaths and secretly return to the United States? Were they abducted by aliens? In a 2012 survey, three out of ten Londoners rated an accidental crash at sea as the most likely explanation; however, support for conspiracy theories was considerable. The second most popular answer, endorsed by 14 percent of the people asked, was the theory that Earhart and Noonan had been executed by the Japanese military; third was the idea that they had faked their deaths and assumed new identities.

Conspiracy theories often cling to aviation disasters, even when there's wreckage to investigate. On April 10, 2010, a Polish Air Force jet crashed when attempting to land in dense fog at Smolensk North Airport in Russia. All ninety-six people on board were killed. Among the dead were President Lech Kaczyński; his wife, Maria; chiefs of staff of the army, air force, and navy; the president of the National Bank of Poland; and a host of other government officials and public figures. The delegation had been headed to Smolensk to attend ceremonies commemorating the 1940 Katyn Massacre, in which the Soviet secret police had executed twenty-two-thousand Polish prisoners of war. Official reports attributed the accident to the adverse weather and pilot error. Yet conspiracy theories of the crash abound in Poland, alleging that the crash was no accident—that it was a political assassination orchestrated by the Russians.

Closer to home, United Airlines Flight 553 crashed on December 8, 1972, when the pilot descended too quickly on approach to Chicago Midway International Airport. Theories that the plane had been deliberately shot down were stoked by the discovery that Dorothy Hunt, the wife of E. Howard Hunt, one of the Watergate burglars, was among the passengers killed on board. Trans World Airlines Flight 800 exploded over Long Island twelve minutes after taking off from Kennedy International Airport in New York on July 17, 1996. A four-year-long investigation by the National Transportation Safety Board chalked the explosion up to a mechanical malfunction, yet conspiracy theories alleging the plane had been shot down remain popular. In 2013, a group petitioned the NTSB to reconsider the possibility; but the NTSB rebutted the evidence and declined to reopen the investigation.

Until further evidence is discovered, it's impossible to say whether the disappearance of MH370 was down to mistake, malfunction, or mischief. As for the other disasters, all signs suggest they were tragic accidents. And yet whenever an airplane crashes, explodes, or disappears, conspiracy theories are sure to follow. When we're faced with disturbing, uncertain events, why is it so tempting to think that someone *wanted* it to happen? To find out, we need to explore one of our brain's most remarkable abilities.

Reading Minds

You have a superpower: You can read minds. Before you get too full of yourself, though, I should mention that I'm a mind reader too, and so is everyone else you know. I don't mean we literally tune in to other people's thoughts in a psychic, Mel-Gibson-in-*What Women Want* kind of way. That'd be creepy. We're more like Sherlock Holmes; we're ace detectives, with an innate, unstoppable compulsion to attempt to deduce what everyone else is thinking. Allow me to demonstrate:

Radharani/Shutterstock.com

See that little girl? You know what she's thinking, don't you? She's angry about something. You can even predict what she's going to do next: She's probably about to say some unkind words and stomp off in a huff. In *Thinking, Fast and Slow*, Daniel Kahneman offers this as an example of the effortless insight we have into other people's minds. Even though all you had to go on was a little black-and-white photo of a stranger's face, you instinctively knew roughly what's going on inside her head, and you had a premonition of her future behavior. What's more, it took no effort on your part at all. Your brain read her mental state from her expression and body language automatically. As Kahneman puts it, it felt more like something that happened to you than something you had to think about. You saw she's angry as effortlessly as you saw she has dark hair.

As good as our knack for reading minds is, though, we don't always get it right. Our intuition can mislead us. Sometimes we're less Sherlock Holmes, more a bumbling Inspector Clouseau. To see what reading minds has to do with believing conspiracy theories, we need to understand how our super-power works, and, more to the point, how it can go wrong.

Let's start with the basics. Our ability to read minds depends on a cognitive tool kit that psychologists (somewhat inelegantly) call *theory of mind*. It's your theory of mind that tells you that the guy sitting next to you on the bus isn't just some unthinking fleshy robot. His head is full of beliefs, desires, feelings, knowledge, abilities, and dispositions. In short, he has a mind, just like you do. Your theory of mind also tells you that the things he feels and believes and wants might be different from the things you feel and believe and want, and that it might be useful if you could figure out what's on his mind.

The tricky part is we can't *see* what's inside someone else's head. There's too much hair in the way, for one thing. We can only see their actions and hear what they say. So this is where our powers of deduction come in. To figure out what made someone say or do something we have to work backward, from the action we've observed (or learned about) to the thoughts and desires that the person in question might have been acting on.

This reverse reasoning is handled by a crucial tool in our theory-of-mind tool kit. Let's call it our intention detector. Our intention detector tells us if something was *intentional* (did somebody mean to do it?), and hazards a guess as to what exactly the intention was (why did they do it?). This is how we're able to reason our way inside other people's heads. Intentions are the crucial bridge between the actions we can see and the invisible thoughts that might have caused them. You watch little Suzy furrow her brow and purse her lips, for instance, and, as if by magic, your intention detector tells you she's in a foul mood.

This might not sound like much of a superpower so far. *Of course* other people have minds, and *of course* we can tell what someone is thinking by how he or she acts. It's a skill that comes so naturally to us that it's easy to take for granted. But imagine if I could flip a switch on the side of your head and turn your intention detector off. The world would suddenly become a very strange place.

Let's say I flip the switch when you happen to be watching a documentary about a day in the life of a doctor. First you see her sticking needles into the arms of crying babies. Then she brandishes a scalpel at some guy and slices off a weird-looking chunk of his flesh. Later she blasts someone else with radiation. To wrap the day up, she spends a few hours giving people advice and drugs. As psychologists Dare Baldwin and Jodie Baird point out, without an understanding of intentions it would be impossible to make sense of the doctor's routine. You would have no sense that there was any purpose behind the things she did. Each of her actions would seem as different from the last as brushing your teeth is from driving a car. If anything, it might sound like the diary of a sociopath with a short attention span. As soon as I switch your intention detector back on, however, everything makes sense again; you understand that the doctor's daily routine is the product of a single intention, to make sick people better.

Let's take another example, this time from literature (our intention detector helps us get into the minds of fictional characters as well as real people). Suppose I flip the switch and hand you a copy of *Romeo and Juliet*. One minute Romeo is whining about someone named Rosaline, the next he's whispering sweet nothings to Juliet at her bedroom window. A couple of days later, he stabs her cousin and skips town. Meanwhile, Juliet takes a powerful sedative (which she got off a guy with no formal training in medicine, I might add) and nods off, whereupon she gets stuffed in the family crypt. Romeo shows up and promptly chugs some poison, and Juliet comes around only to stab herself in the heart. It's one of the world's most famous and captivating stories, but without a functioning intention detector it just sounds utterly incomprehensible. To appreciate the romance and the tragedy, you need to understand that the characters' various actions were driven by intentions—noble intentions (like true love), dishonorable intentions (like the bloody feud between the families), and intentions that were thwarted or misunderstood (like the plan to fake Juliet's death that went tragically awry).

Intentions are the interpersonal Rosetta Stone that allows us to figure out why people do the things they do. Without our intention detector, we would have no way of understanding or predicting other people's behavior. Even the simplest of social interactions would be impossible. There would be no small talk or seduction, no irony or satire, no lectures or study groups or committee meetings, no business or politics, no sport or art or literature or reality shows. If we couldn't understand other people's intentions, there might be no society at all.

"The Circle Enters the Rectangle"

In short, intentions are kind of a big deal to us, so our intention detector is good at sniffing them out. I mean, *really* good. Actually, it turns out, a little too good.

Back in 1943, Fritz Heider and his student Marianne Simmel concocted what would become one of the most influential experiments in psychology. The two psychologists led test subjects one at a time into a darkened room, sat them in front of a screen, and showed them a short black-and-white silent film, just over a minute long. When the projector whirred to life, some people saw three rambunctious children cavorting around a playground, with two kids teasing an unlucky third or a bully picking on two smaller kids. One person saw a mother scolding her two children for coming home late. Another saw a fairy tale about a witch trying to trap two innocent young children in her evil lair. Some people saw a darker drama, in which an abusive father intimidated his wife and young child, or a cuckolded boyfriend reacted violently against his sweetheart and her new beau.

Here's the trick: Everyone had actually watched the exact same movie. In fact, all the film showed was three simple shapes—a big triangle, a little triangle, and a little circle—flitting around the screen, occasionally going in and out of a larger stationary rectangle with a section that opened and closed like a door. Like the phantom Kanizsa triangle we saw in the previous chapter, the bullies, mothers, witches, and lovers existed only in the viewers' minds.

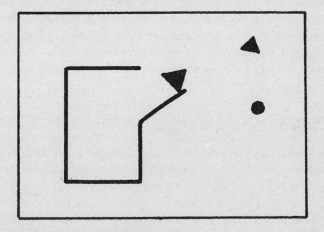

This classic experiment shows just how eager our intention detector is to translate actions into intentions. Only one person who took part in the experiment interpreted the film as just three polygons moving arbitrarily around a two-dimensional plane, nothing more. She described it in purely abstract terms: "A large solid triangle is shown entering a rectangle . . . Then another, smaller triangle and a circle appear on the scene. The circle enters the rectangle . . . The two move about in circular motion and then the circle goes out of the opening and joins the smaller triangle which has been moving around outside the rectangle," and so on. Everyone else saw not just three shapes but three *characters*, interacting with one another, expressing their own unique personality, motives, needs, and desires. You can find the Heider–Simmel video online. Watch it for yourself. Chances are you won't be able to *not* see a story.

I don't mean to say we're *wrong* to see the little shapes as acting out a story. After all, the shapes' movements aren't random; they were carefully choreographed. Heider and Simmel themselves describe the action as an anthropomorphic story, complete with chases, fight scenes, and a climactic ending. The point is, our intention detector is constantly on the lookout for signs of intent in the world around us. It only takes the slightest suggestion of deliberate movement to send it into overdrive. I said that our ability to read minds is a super-power—well, as the saying goes, with great power comes great responsibility. Yet as Heider and Simmel's film demonstrates, our intention detector doesn't have much self-restraint. It can get carried away, conjuring up personalities and motives, heroes and villains, even when we're just watching a crudely animated film of two triangles and a circle moving around a rectangle.

No Such Thing as an Accident

In fact, our intention detector seems to have a "shoot first, ask questions later" policy. It assumes *everything* that happens in the world happened because somebody intended it to.

Psychologists call this the *intentionality bias*. It's easy to spot in children. If you ask a four-year-old why somebody yawned or sneezed or tripped over the dog, she will probably tell you the person wanted to. Up until age four or five, children even sometimes make up intentions for their own involuntary actions, like the knee-jerk reflex, claiming they planned to move their leg after the doctor tapped their knee with the little mallet. The bias even extends beyond things that *people* do. Children see the natural world as having some underlying purpose, akin to the intentions that humans have. They tend to think the sun rises because it likes to make us warm, that the moon follows them around, and that pointy rocks are shaped that way so that animals can scratch themselves. Young kids, in short, have a habit of mistaking accidents and involuntary actions for deliberate acts.

You know better than to say these kinds of things are intentional, of course. You're well aware that people don't usually yawn or sneeze because they want to; yawns and sneezes are caused by involuntary reflexes. You know that people who fall over don't typically do so just for the fun of it; we're not always as graceful as we would like, and we're bound by the laws of gravity. And you certainly don't think the sun is terribly concerned about your comfort, or that rocks were put there for the convenience of itchy possums; you know it doesn't make sense to ask what rocks are for, or to say that inanimate objects have intentions.

Or do you? According to psychologist Evelyn Rosset, we never actually outgrow our childhood intentionality bias. When we decide that something wasn't intentional, it's not because our intention detector keeps quiet or tells us it was unintended. Even as adults, our trigger-happy intention detector deems everything to be intentional. We only come to see something as an accident by *overriding* our intention detector—by dismissing its default judgment and replacing it with a more reasoned decision.

Kids struggle with second-guessing their intention detector because they don't know that much about things like physics or the subtleties of human behavior. They just aren't aware of the biological nature of reflexes like sneezing, or of the forces that sculpt rocks and govern the orbits of celestial bodies. As we grow up, we collect knowledge and experience about these kinds of nonintentional causes. We have to *learn* this stuff. Our overzealous intention detector, on the other hand, comes preinstalled. Research with infants suggests that it's up and running within the first few months of life. When we're little, our intention detector tells us things are intended and, since we don't know any better, we believe it. As we get older, our intention detector remains as hyperactive as ever; we just become better at second-guessing what it tells us. When you see someone fall over, you *know* it was an accident, but part of your brain is still whispering "they meant to do that."

Rosset and her colleagues have discovered that it's not hard to scratch the surface of our grown-up facade and reveal the child-like intention-seeker within. In one study, she found that all it takes is a few drinks: Participants in the study chugged an ethanol cocktail equivalent of six shots of vodka, to be precise. Suppose you're at a crowded bar and somebody bumps into you, spilling Sauvignon Blanc all over your favorite shirt. According to Rosset's findings, your reaction could depend on how late in the night it is. If you're on your first drink, still sober as a judge, there's a good chance you'll write the incident off as a simple accident. The more you've had to drink, though, the more likely you are to suspect that the culprit was looking to pick a fight. In the good old days, you might have even issued the assailant an invitation to pistols at dawn. According to Eric Jager, author of *The Last Duel*, "hundreds of duels in the hard-drinking eigh-teenth century were provoked by bar-room quarrels at a time when inebriation was for many a permanent state." Gunslinger etiquette even made some concessions for the judgment-clouding properties of alcohol. According to one Wild West dueling manual, "intoxication is not a full excuse for insult, but it will greatly palliate."

Alcohol is not our only excuse for dubious inferences of intent. In another study, Rosset asked perfectly sober adults questions like whether "the sun radiates heat because warmth nurtures life," or if "finches diversified in order to survive." For the most part, people said no. Then she had a different group of people answer the same questions rapid-fire, with just three seconds to think each answer over. Under pressure, they became more likely to say that intentional explanations for natural phenomena were true. Another study found that even science professors at Ivy League universities—the last people you might expect to catch thinking about the world in terms of some kind of purposeful design—fell for these kinds of explanations when they were rushed.

The findings demonstrate, Rosset argues, that judging something to be intentional is automatic and effortless. Overriding that judgment, however, requires mental effort. When our faculties are impaired by alcohol, or when we just don't have time to think, we're more likely to settle for our intention detector's default assumption: Everything is intended. Even when we're not drunk or distracted, we don't always have the inclination or ability to second-guess our intuition. As a result, we can make all kinds of questionable attributions of intent. Consider the vast numbers of people who believe in ghosts, gods, angels, and aliens, or just have a vague inclination that the universe has a plan for everyone. As Jesse Bering, a psychologist who specializes in religion, points out, even people who don't believe in God can't help wondering what the meaning of life is—what was on our creator's mind. "It's an itchy rash that science can't seem to scratch."

And if you don't sign up for any of that, I guarantee that at some point in your life you've found yourself pleading with (and/or swearing at) an inanimate object, as if it's a misbehaving child and it'll behave if you just let it know how displeased you are. Just think about a time when your car wouldn't start, your computer shut down for no apparent reason, or your smartphone refused to respond to your prodding. You know it's just a machine, but you can't stop yourself from treating it as if it has a mind of its own—"*What are you doing that for?!*"—even if only in a momentary fit of rage.

When something happens that we can't immediately explain, there's a good chance we'll fall back on our hyperactive intention detector. We can't help thinking that someone (or some*thing*) meant for it to happen. Which brings us to conspiracy theories.

Someone Is Pulling the Strings

Well, it *almost* brings us to conspiracy theories. First I just want you to read a couple of sentences. Each describes something happening, but doesn't go into much detail. I want you to try to imagine the scene in as much detail as possible—what is happening, who is involved, what might have led up to it, and what is the outcome.

She kicked the dog.
The boy popped the balloon.

What came to mind when you read "She kicked the dog"? Did you picture something like a distracted woman tripping over Rover because she didn't see him lying at the bottom of the stairs? Or did you think maybe she was running late and deliberately kicked him out of the way? How about the popped balloon—maybe you thought of an excitable toddler inadvertently holding a balloon too close to a birthday candle with tearful results, or maybe you thought of an older boy brandishing a pin with a mischievous look in his eye. The details don't matter. The important thing is that there are two ways you could interpret each sentence: It could be describing something done on purpose, or something that happened by accident.

Which brings us to conspiracy theories. Those sentences themselves have nothing to do with conspiracies (unless you happened to think that the boy wasn't working alone when he popped the balloon—maybe there was a second boy on the grassy knoll). According to research I carried out with psychologist Chris French, however, the way you interpret innocuous sentences about unfortunate dogs and burst balloons predicts how likely you are to buy into conspiracy theories.

We had people read twelve ambiguous sentences, like the two you just read, and asked them to describe what came to mind. All we were really interested in, though, was whether they saw each one as intentional or accidental. Then we asked everyone about whether they reckoned the world is run by a shady cabal of conspirators. When we counted up the number of sentences each person interpreted as intentional and compared it against how they rated the conspiracy theories, it turned out that the two numbers were related. The more sentences a person interpreted as intentional, the more he or she tended to buy into conspiracy theories.

Another study revealed a similarly surprising relationship. Remember Heider and Simmel's little animated film of two triangles and a circle? A team of psychologists led by Karen Douglas dusted it off, uploaded it to the Internet, and had more than five hundred people watch the little shapes dance around their computer screens. Instead of having everyone narrate in detail what they thought the shapes were up to, Douglas and her colleagues just had them rate *how* conscious and purposeful they thought the shapes were on a simple scale. Then she asked viewers how strongly they believe conspiracy theories. Once again, the numbers were related; the more someone rated the shapes as thinking, feeling, mindful characters, the more likely he or she was to think Princess Diana had been bumped off and 9/11 had been an inside job.

These findings suggest that conspiracy theories owe some of their appeal to the way they resonate with our hyperactive intention detector. Remember, according to Evelyn Rosset's research, we all see *everything* as intentional by default. Some people are better than others at overriding this gut reaction, however. This predisposition—a bias toward either trusting or mistrusting your intention detector—colors your entire world-view. The intention detector, it seems, doesn't see much difference between a burst balloon, a dancing triangle, and claims about a cabal of secret puppet masters. People who habitually question their intuition tend to come up with more accidental interpretations of ambiguous sentences, to rate the Heider-Simmel shapes as less purposeful, and to see allegations of conspiracy as relatively implausible. People who listen to their intention detector, on the other hand, lean the other way. For them, the shapes are alive, the balloon was sabotaged, and the puppet masters are real.

To understand why conspiracy theories are so deeply appealing we need to weigh them against alternative explanations from the perspective of our intention detector. Picture an old-fashioned set of scales, balancing a conspiracy theory on one side and an official story on the other. Sometimes the weight of intent falls squarely on the side of the conspiracy theory. Princess Diana's fatal car crash was staged on the orders of the scorned monarchy; Elvis faked his own death to escape the pressures of fame; Amelia Earhart's plane was shot down because she was a spy. According to the official stories, on the other hand, these events were all essentially unintended. Weighing up the options, it's easy to see why our gut tells us the conspiracy theory is more plausible. The conspiracy theory fits what our intention detector has already told us, whereas believing the official story requires overturning the verdict.

Sometimes, however, the official story is one of intentions and motives, too. Take the 9/11 attacks. On one side of the scale is the official story: Al-Qaeda hijackers acted successfully on their intentions to crash airliners into several U.S. landmarks. On the other side of the scale is the conspiracy theory: Hidden conspirators within the U.S. government intentionally allowed or perpetrated the attacks. Here, both sides of the scale get some intent—but just because both explanations offer intent doesn't mean the scales are evenly balanced. We need to consider which story offers the *most* intent.

When the official story says that members of al-Qaeda intended the attacks, it implies that the seemingly monolithic, highly funded government agencies tasked with identifying and preventing terrorist threats were taken unawares; they expressly *did not intend for the attacks to occur*. The conspiracy theory, in contrast, offers a virtually limitless supply of intent. Not only were the buildings attacked on purpose, but the government was in on the entire plot, along with the seemingly endless parade of lackeys and disinformation agents who are part of the cover-up. Once we add this surplus intent to the conspiracy side of the scale, there's no contest. From the perspective of our intention detector, a conspiracy theory beats an official story every time.

Are You Thinking What I'm Thinking?

Our overactive intention detector might account for some of the appeal of conspiracy theories, but it doesn't tell the whole story. After all, merely supposing that something was intended doesn't mean you have to buy into a conspiracy theory. When a plane disappears or a beloved princess has her life cut tragically short, you could think it was intended in all sorts of ways. Maybe a ghost did it, or a vengeful god. Maybe it was the hand of a lone crackpot, or a posse of interdimensional aliens. The question remains, what is it that makes some people accept not only that something was deliberate, but that a conspiracy was behind it?

To find the answer, we need to look at another tool in our theory-of-mind tool kit: projection.

Now, when you hear a psychologist talking about projection you might picture Sigmund Freud, leaning sternly against a mantelpiece, twirling a cigar between his fingers, informing you that your subconscious mind is harboring such shameful urges that it won't even let *you* in on them; instead, it attributes them to someone else, as if *they're* the depraved one. Freud thought of projection as a defense mechanism, protecting you from realizing what a despicable person you truly are. Like much of Freudian psychoanalytic theory, however, it turns out this idea of projection was off the mark. Psychologists now understand that projection isn't about trying to deny some socially unacceptable urge. It's simply about trying to make sense of an uncertain world, and we all do it all the time.

We use projection because figuring out what other people are thinking based on their actions alone can be tricky. A lot of the time we don't have many clues to go on. Even when we know exactly what somebody did, it can remain frustratingly ambiguous. Imagine you see two men walking down the street, and one guy pushes the other. You instantly know the push was intended, but it might be impossible to guess whether it was a playful jostle or an aggressive shove. As enthusiastic as our intention detector is, it can't always get us inside someone else's head by itself. So our brain takes a more hands-on approach. Instead of agonizing over the possible interpretations of someone's actions, we mentally trade places with them and answer an easier question: What would *I* be thinking?

This isn't merely a lazy trick; projection is a cornerstone of theory of mind. Any time you see someone do something, your brain runs a quick simulation of sorts with you in the starring role. Seeing someone raise a glass of water to his or her mouth, for instance, activates the very same neurons in your brain that would fire if *you* were grasping a glass and bringing it to your own mouth. This sneaky simulation helps you figure out what your own intentions and desires might be when going through the motions, which you can use to guess what's on the mind of the person you are watching. In this case, you might guess the person is thirsty and planning to take a sip of water (as opposed to taking a bite of the glass, or smashing it over their head), because that's what *you* would most likely be planning.

Projection is an indispensable tool in our theory-of-mind tool kit, but it's not without flaws. Just as our overly enthusiastic intention detector can lead to some questionable judgments, projection can distort our view of the world. We are prone to neglecting the countless potential differences between ourselves and the people whose minds we attempt to read. As a result, our brain conjures up something psychologists call a *false consensus*—the illusion that most of the people around us are probably thinking what we're thinking.

Psychologists Daniel Katz and Floyd Allport provided one of the first demonstrations of the false consensus effect in 1931. They observed that students who admitted to cheating on exams tended to assume that college classrooms are teeming with cheating scoundrels, whereas students who didn't cheat guessed that most of their peers are similarly pious. Since then, studies have revealed that we imagine a false consensus for just about anything. If you think of yourself as outgoing you'll probably guess there are a lot more fellow extroverts in the world than someone who sees themselves as shy. Same goes if you support federal funding for space exploration, prefer brown bread to white bread, routinely donate blood, or make a lot of long-distance phone calls. When you're cold you think other people are bothered by the cold, and when you're thirsty you think other people are bothered by thirst. In one particularly creative study, researchers tried to persuade students to walk around campus wearing a large advertising sandwich board bearing the slogan EAT AT JOE'S (or, in another study, an admonition to REPENT). People who were willing to don the sign guessed that most other people would be similarly willing; those who declined predicted that most other people would refuse. Whatever the topic in question, we all tend to see our own preferences and peccadilloes as relatively commonplace.

Which brings us back to conspiracy theories.

It Takes One to Know One

Let's pretend it's the 1960s. You work for NASA. The Cold War is in full swing, the space race is reaching a crescendo, and you've been tasked with putting men on the moon before the Soviets. In a rousing 1962 speech, President Kennedy famously declared that the United States would land a man on the moon before the decade was out, not because it was easy, but because it was hard. But suppose it turns out getting people to the moon and back is *really* hard. It's going to take years. The Soviets already put the first satellite in space, and then the first human. Now they'll surely beat us to the moon. Just when all hope seems lost, new orders come in. We're going to fake the moon landing, they say. We've already booked the soundstage and paid for the fake moon rocks. Kubrick's agreed to direct. *Nobody will ever know.*

Would you take part in the conspiracy?

This is what psychologists Karen Douglas and Robbie Sutton asked unwitting college students: Had you found yourself in the position of the alleged conspirators, would you have faked the moon landing? For good measure, they also asked the students if they would have killed Princess Diana, staged the 9/11 attacks, covered up the existence of aliens, created the AIDS virus, and faked the data on climate change. Reassuringly, most said they wouldn't dream of it. On a scale from one to seven (one meaning "never under any circumstances," and seven meaning "probably yes"), the average response was a mere two. (Of course, some people might have just been *saying* they wouldn't so as not to come across as unconscionably evil, but the surveys were anonymous—people had no reason to lie.) There was something interesting, however, about the people who admitted to being open to the idea of conspiring. The more conspiratorial someone claimed to be, the more likely he or she was to believe the conspiracy theories were true.

According to Douglas and Sutton, their findings reveal projection at work. Finding conclusive proof for a theory, such as a confession by the alleged conspirators, is difficult. We're forced to look for other clues, and one thing we can easily do is project ourselves into the minds of the alleged perpetrators. Judging the probable guilt of an accused conspirator, we search within ourselves. Just like the cheaters who thought most people cheat, people who imagine themselves willing to conspire appear to see conspirators lurking in every shadow. And if you think the world is full of budding conspirators, then it is more likely that those accused did in fact go through with it.

It's worth pointing out, however, that we're dealing with self-confessed willingness to conspire. Douglas and Sutton's findings don't mean that, if it really came down to it, every conspiracy theorist is a conniving sociopath. Recall from Chapter 2 that the most committed conspiracists tend to *say* that violence against the government is an acceptable form of protest, but vanishingly few actually follow through on the sentiment. That said, there are some striking historical instances of conspiracy theorists taking on the trappings—and occasionally imitating the actions—of their imagined conspirators.

The Ku Klux Klan, for instance, was founded on a suspicion of secret plots among its enemies. By the 1920s, the Klan was as anti-Catholic as it was racist. The pope, they feared, was planning to declare war on Protestants, take over the federal government, and move the Vatican to Indiana. Catholics were said to be stockpiling guns in their churches, the steeples of which were built so high to provide a convenient vantage point for snipers. There was even a rumor that an arsenal of heavy artillery and explosives was hidden in the sewer system beneath Notre Dame University. Yet, as Richard Hofstadter pointed out, the Klan increasingly became a parody of its enemy, "to the point of donning priestly vestments, developing an elaborate ritual and an equally elaborate hierarchy." Daniel Pipes points out that, given the Klan's concerns about the secret machinations of Catholics, it is ironic that "not only did the Klan oppose a resolution condemning secret societies at the [1924] Democratic National Convention, but it used conspiratorial methods to defeat the resolution."

Philosopher Karl Popper noted that when conspiracy theorists find themselves in positions of power, their actions are often conspiratorial. As a case in point, Richard Nixon was famously paranoid. During his time in office, Joe Uscinski and Joseph Parent point out, Nixon was concerned with "Jews, the intellectual elite, the media, and the anti-war movement, whom he saw as conspiring against him and the country." His response? To conspire against *them*. In the midst of devising one plot, Nixon warned his aides, "we're up against an enemy, a conspiracy. They're using any means. *We are going to use any means.* Is that clear?" Nixon's exploits and lies led to his removal from office, but his plots were fairly tame compared to those of some other world leaders. Daniel Pipes notes that many Middle Eastern heads of state suffer chronic paranoia, and frequently resort to conspiring against their enemies. By way of example, Pipes points to the unlikely number of car crashes and other "accidents" that befell Saddam Hussein's political opponents.

And even that seems tame compared to Adolf Hitler, who incorporated visions of an apocalyptic Jewish conspiracy into his political platform and used it to justify his own conspiratorial machinations against Europe's Jews. For Hitler, the *Protocols of Zion* served as more than a glimpse into the enemy's tactics; it provided a model for his own quest for power. "I have read the *Protocols of the Elders of Zion*," Hitler is reported to have said—"it simply appalled me. The stealthiness of the enemy, and his ubiquity! I saw at once that we must copy it—in our own way of course . . . We must beat the Jew with his own weapon."

Pondering the curiously high incidence of conspiracy among conspiracy theorists, Daniel Pipes suggested that "what begins as a search for subversives ends in subversion; haters of the hidden hand take on the very characteristics they loathe." But with projection in mind, perhaps rather than us imitating the enemy, our imagined enemies are a reflection of ourselves. Conspiracists see a world crawling with conspirators, which in turn calls for counter-conspiracy. As Douglas and Sutton put it—channeling the wisdom of countless children in playground squabbles—*it takes one to know one.*

Manufacturing Motive

Having seen the ways our intention detector can misfire, and how projection can lead us to imagine a world full of conspirators, we can begin to see the appeal of conspiracy theories in the aftermath of a plane mysteriously disappearing. Consider one last study. When psychologists Preston Bost and Stephen Prunier presented participants in their 2013 study with a familiar conspiracy theory, people tended to evaluate it using whatever factual evidence they happened to be aware of. But when people encountered a theory that was completely new to them, they weren't able to marshal any facts on which to base their judgment. Instead, they relied on potential *motive*: Why might the accused conspirators have done it? What did they stand to gain? Would they be willing to go through with it? The absence of facts leaves our minds free to speculate. And sensing a plausible motive led people to believe a theory *just as confidently* as actual evidence. The disappearance of MH370 set off our intention detectors and provided a blank canvas onto which we could project our darkest impulses.

It shouldn't come as a surprise by now that we're so swayed by motives. In *The Happiness Hypothesis*, psychologist Jonathan Haidt explains that, in a practical sense, the world we live in is "not really one made of rocks, trees and physical objects; it is a world of insults, opportunities, status symbols, betrayals, saints and sinners." Figuring out other people's intentions is one of the greatest challenges we face. Whether people are enemies or allies depends on their abilities, desires, and motives. An event takes on an entirely different significance depending on whether it was accidental or intentional. As psychologist Adam Waytz put it, "a tree branch that another person drops on you is more noteworthy than one that the wind blows down on you." There is a huge difference between an airplane that malfunctioned and one that was sabotaged.

It makes sense that we evolved a brain that is highly attuned to the hidden realm of intentions, even if it occasionally mistakes mayhem for motive, or sees intent lurking behind accidents. In our evolutionary history, the cost of these errors was usually greatly outweighed by the cost of erring in the other direction. An early hominid who was predisposed to mistake a floating log for a crocodile was more likely to pass along her genes than was one who ventured too close to a hungry crocodile thinking it a harmless log. We could comfortably afford to err on the side of intent. Our inability to watch Heider and Simmel's dancing triangle without seeing it as a scorned lover or a boisterous child is another one of our ancestors' gifts to us.

In suggesting that conspiracy theories are seductive in part because they conform to our intuitions about intent, I'm not saying they are necessarily wrong. Sometimes a crocodile really is a crocodile. MH370 apparently changed course and continued flying for hours after its transponders were disabled, suggesting a deliberate act, though we are left to guess at the motive behind it. Maybe those who sense foul play will turn out to be right. Maybe there's a more innocent—if no less tragic—explanation. Or maybe, like the mysterious Umbrella Man, it will turn out that the truth is stranger than anything anyone has yet imagined.

CHAPTER TEN

Proportion Distortion

Over the years, eighty-two *specific* individuals—real people with names and lives and reputations and feelings—have been accused by conspiracy theorists of having shot President John F. Kennedy. All told, according to assassination researcher Vincent Bugliosi, forty-two groups or organizations, and 214 individuals, have been named as coconspirators.

The official story, of course, has it that one man, Lee Harvey Oswald, acted alone. Oswald was a disillusioned former United States Marine who briefly defected to the Soviet Union in 1959, only to get cold feet and return to America in 1962. A year and a half later, on November 22, 1963, he fired three bullets at the president from a sixth-floor window in Dealey Plaza in Dallas, Texas. The first bullet missed. The second struck Kennedy in the back (and then continued on to wound Texas Governor John Connally, who was seated in front of Kennedy). The third hit the president in the head, ensuring his death and Oswald's infamy.

There's plenty of evidence linking Oswald to the assassination. He worked at the Texas School Book Depository, where his improvised sniper's nest, rifle, and three spent cartridges were found. He was the only employee unaccounted for after the shooting, and was arrested a few hours later for shooting a police officer, J. D. Tippit, who had been looking for a man fitting Oswald's description. There's also the fact that seven months earlier Oswald had tried to assassinate another prominent figure in American politics, General Edwin Walker, a right-wing anti-Communist. An open-and-shut case.

But surveys over the years show that this version of events has never really held much sway with the general public. Suspicion flourished immediately. A poll conducted during the week after the assassination found that only one third of the American public thought Lee Harvey Oswald had acted alone; a little over half firmly believed a conspiracy was afoot, while the rest just weren't sure. Popular opinion wasn't budged much by the

Warren Commission Report, published in 1964, which found that Oswald had acted alone; in 1966 two thirds of the public still doubted the lone gunman story. By 1976 a cottage industry of Kennedy conspiracy theories was booming, and the conspiratorial version of events became the default view; from the mid-seventies to the turn of the century, polls found that around eight out of ten Americans suspected conspiracy. Now, more than fifty years after the assassination, people who believe that a conspiracy killed Kennedy are still a clear majority in the United States, and a sizable minority elsewhere.

Given these levels of suspicion, it's no surprise that a cavalcade of conspiracy theories has been put forward over the years to explain the assassination. Despite all the evidence placing Oswald at the scene of the crime, remarkably few theories have him actively colluding with other assassins or plotters. He is overwhelmingly relegated to the role of patsy—a mere scapegoat onto whom blame could easily be pinned. So who really killed Kennedy?

Unusual Suspects

Clandestine government agents, either foreign or domestic, play the villain in many theories. One story proposes a plot by the Soviets, who were stung over having to back down to Kennedy in the Cuban missile crisis. This theory hinges on Oswald having been recruited by the KGB, the Soviets' secret intelligence agency. But in 1964 a KGB agent who had dealt with Oswald's attempted defection to the Soviet Union defected to the United States himself. The agent, Yuri Nosenko, told the CIA what the KGB had thought of Oswald: not much. Realizing Oswald was a "mediocre, uninteresting, useless," and probably mentally unstable young man, the Soviets made no attempt to enlist him during his two-and-a-half-year stay. (For his trouble, Nosenko was illegally imprisoned by the CIA and kept in solitary confinement for three and a half years.) In fact, when Oswald first arrived in Moscow and declared his desire to renounce this American citizenship, the Soviet government tried to send him packing. It was only when he attempted suicide by slashing his wrists in a hotel room hours before he was due to be escorted out of the country that he was issued a visa. His handlers thought it easier to let him stay than risk the bad publicity of an American tourist dying on their watch.

At any rate, more theories point the finger closer to home. The CIA features in some of the most pervasive theories. Lending the idea of CIA involvement an element of plausibility, we now know that the agency had, in fact, drawn up plans to assassinate prominent foreign leaders in the early 1960s, foremost among them Fidel Castro. But would they employ the same shady tactics against their own commander in chief? Theorists assert that CIA leaders resented Kennedy for his handling of the Bay of Pigs fiasco, and that Kennedy himself was so embittered by the debacle that he planned to dramatically restructure the CIA, rendering it impotent. Not letting facts get in the way of a good story, the conspiracy theorists ignore the inconvenient truth that, once the Bay of Pigs dust had settled, Kennedy actually had an unusually close relationship with the CIA, increasing their budget and even shielding them from scrutiny in the face of allegations of misconduct.

The so-called military-industrial complex is another common culprit. Perhaps military chiefs and weapons manufacturers were nervous about the loss of revenue they would endure as a result of Kennedy's desire to withdraw all U.S. military involvement in Vietnam, and devised a plan to bump him off. If so, the scheme seemingly paid off; Kennedy's vice president and successor, Lyndon Baines Johnson, eventually escalated America's involvement in the Vietnam War dramatically. Never mind the fact that, at the time of the assassination, Kennedy had expressed no desire to withdraw, nor had Johnson stated a desire to engage. As recently as September 2, 1963, Kennedy had said in an interview, "in the final analysis, it is their [the South Vietnamese's] war. They are the ones who have to win or lose it. But I don't agree with those who say we should withdraw. That would be a great mistake." (Bugliosi points out that Oliver Stone included the first two sentences of this quote in his film *JFK*, but conveniently omitted the second two, which somewhat undercut the military-industrial complex conspiracy theory forwarded by the movie.)

Other theories blame the Mafia, which, understandably enough, didn't care for the Kennedy administration's clampdown on organized crime. As Oswald was being transferred from police headquarters to the county jail on November 24, a gunman lurched out of the crowd of onlookers and shot him in the chest. The man was Jack Ruby, a local strip club owner noted for his volatile temper and desperate quest for attention and respect. Theorists assert that he was also a wannabe gangster whose big break came when he was tasked by mob bosses with silencing the patsy they had enlisted to kill Kennedy. No less a figure than G. Robert Blakey, chief counsel to the House Select Committee on Assassinations, left the investigation certain that Mafia dons had orchestrated a hit on Kennedy, and that Jack Ruby's execution of Oswald provided (figuratively as well as literally) the smoking gun.

These theories at least have a veneer of plausibility. Others scrape the barrel of believability. Shortly after the assassination, three homeless men were found inside a railway car a few blocks from Dealey Plaza. They were photographed and taken into police custody, but then seemingly disappeared into the ether. Obviously, some conspiracy theorists said, the authorities had whitewashed the men's identities to hide their role in the shooting. And the theorists were only too happy to fill in the details, retrospectively identifying one of the men as a contract killer and the other two as Watergate burglars Frank Sturgis and E. Howard Hunt. But it later turned out that the Dallas Police Department had, in fact, jotted down the men's names when they were picked up. They were Harold Doyle, Gus Abrams, and John Gedney, and when they were tracked down by the FBI in the early 1990s, it was clear they had been nothing more than three drifters riding the rails.

According to the wackiest theories, you need look no farther than Kennedy's own motorcade to find his killer. Perhaps the conspiratorial mastermind was riding two cars behind Kennedy, waving genially to the crowd: none other than Vice President Johnson, who, according to the theorists, hatched a murderous plot to foist himself into the Oval Office. Another story insists that the fatal, gruesome head shot was accidentally fired by Secret Service agent George Hickey, who was riding in the car immediately behind Kennedy's. Of course, the Warren Commission conspired to cover up Hickey's mortal error.

Some even place the assassin inside JFK's own car. The man driving the presidential limousine, Secret Service agent William

Greer, can be seen in the Zapruder film briefly turning to look at the president as the first two shots rang out. Then, if you squint very hard, and with a bit of imagination, it almost looks like he brandishes a pistol and fires, point blank, into Kennedy's head. Or maybe, according to one theory, the killer was the last person anyone would suspect, the person sitting right beside Kennedy: his wife of ten years, Jacqueline Bouvier Kennedy. This yarn suggests that Jackie was, unbeknownst to her husband, a highly trained assassin, blackmailed into executing the president using a specially made gun hidden in her navy blue handbag.

The Usual Suspect

That's enough of that. My goal here isn't to prove or disprove these—or any of the myriad other—theories. The reason I mention them, and the opinion polls that show that a majority of people believe some conspiratorial version of the assassination, is to show just how popular, plentiful, and elaborate Kennedy conspiracy theories are. Conspiracist speculation has been ceaseless and voracious. As conspiracy scholar Timothy Melley exhaustively details, the assassination has been the subject of "two federal investigations of breathtaking scope; numerous smaller investigations by state, private, and federal agencies; several thousand essays, articles, and books; scores of novels, films, and plays; countless news stories; endless re-enactments, debates, and television news specials."

As a point of comparison, consider another presidential shooting. On March 30, 1981, John Hinckley Jr. fired six bullets at President Ronald Reagan from just ten feet away. All of the bullets missed Reagan, but one ricocheted off the bulletproof limousine and hit him in the chest, piercing a lung and missing his heart by an inch. Reagan came close to death, but doctors were able to remove the bullet and stem the internal bleeding, narrowly saving the president's life. The official story has it that Hinckley was mentally ill, and the shooting was a desperate attempt to impress the young actress Jodie Foster. He had pursued her for years, stalking her and sending her letters. Eventually, influenced by the film *Taxi Driver*, which starred Foster and featured the character Travis Bickle (played by Robert De Niro) planning to assassinate a U.S. senator, Hinckley decided the best way to impress Foster would be to kill the president. He wrote her a note on the morning of the shooting, pleading, "Jodie, I would abandon this idea of getting Reagan in a second if I could only win your heart and live out the rest of my life with you." An open-and-shut case.

Conspiracy theorists, on the other hand, would have us believe . . . Well, actually there are hardly any conspiracy theories about Reagan's attempted assassination. There has been a smattering of tenuous conspiracist allegations over the years; you can find obscure websites proposing that Hinckley was a mind-controlled Manchurian Candidate, manipulated into shooting Reagan by a sinister cabal. But the overwhelming majority of people were satisfied that Hinckley was a lone nut, and never thought twice about a conspiracy. Set against the Kennedy assassination, there's no comparison. Conspiracy theories about Kennedy are mainstream; conspiracy theories about Reagan never got off the ground.

Why is there such an imbalance between the popularity of Kennedy theories and Reagan theories? There are plenty of differences between the two events. Kennedy was a Democrat, Reagan was Republican. Kennedy was a sprightly forty-six years old, Reagan was a stately seventy. Oswald was infatuated with Marxism, Hinckley was infatuated with a movie star. But the foremost difference has to be the simple fact that one of the assassins succeeded and the other failed. As a result, the Kennedy assassination was an infinitely more momentous event. A charismatic, popular president was killed, and the course of history was forever changed. The Reagan assassination attempt was, relatively speaking, a nonevent. A charismatic, popular president lived to preside another day. The popularity of the respective conspiracy theories would no doubt be very different if Hinckley had been a better shot; ditto if Oswald's final shot had missed and Kennedy had merely been wounded.

That might sound obvious, but the reason for it lies in a fundamental quirk of how our brain works. We are guided by a mental shortcut called the proportionality bias. We want the magnitude of an event to match the magnitude of whatever caused it. When the outcome of an event is significant, momentous, or profound in some way, we are inclined to think it must have been caused by something correspondingly significant, momentous, or profound. When the consequences are less far-reaching, more modest causes appear more plausible. Put simply, we reckon big things have big causes.

Now, this isn't always a bad rule of thumb. A lot of the time, big events really do have big causes. If you pick up a rock and give it a gentle toss, you won't be surprised to find that it doesn't get very far. But reel back, wind up, put everything you've got into it and it'll go much farther. If you really try, you could even break something or hurt someone. We know the bigger effort will produce a bigger effect. Likewise, in the realm of complex global events, significant things often take a lot of effort. The development of the atomic bomb, for instance—a pretty big deal, both in terms of the physical result of a detonation, and in terms of its geopolitical ramifications—was the result of the Manhattan Project, a huge effort involving over 130,000 people over the course of seven years, at a cost equivalent to twenty-six billion dollars in today's money.

But it's not always true that the size of the cause matches the size of its consequence. Sometimes one small twist of circumstance can change the course of our lives. Sometimes one seemingly insignificant person can have a huge effect on the course of history. By leading us to overlook or dismiss instances of small causes having big effects, the proportionality bias can steer us toward belief in vast, insidious conspiracies despite overwhelming evidence to the contrary. But this kind of irrational reasoning doesn't apply only to conspiracy theories. The proportionality bias subtly influences the way we think about all kinds of things all the time.

Magnitude Matching

Imagine rolling a die. First, I want you to roll a low number—let's say a one or two. Really imagine going through the motions. Maybe you'd give the die a little shake, and blow on it for luck. Now let it go. All right, now imagine throwing your die again, but this time try to get a really high score, like a five or six. Was there any difference in your throwing technique? Keep this in mind—we'll come back to it in just a moment.

For now, let's assume that dice tend to obey the laws of physics and probability rather than responding to the thrower's hopes and wishes. The outcome of any particular roll is a matter of chance rather than skill. Yet sometimes we can't help acting as if we're in control—feeling like the way we throw the dice might influence what numbers come up.

In 1967, sociologist James Henslin demonstrated this in the most obvious, sensible, and straightforward way possible: by posing as a cab driver and infiltrating a group of St. Louis cabbies as they met in the early hours of the morning between shifts, in parking lots or grotty apartments, to engage in some illegal gambling. (Sociologists have all the fun.) Their game of choice was craps, in which players roll a pair of dice and place bets on the outcome. Henslin was interested in the superstitious rituals that gamblers used in an attempt to control their fortune in games of chance, and he found an elaborate set of rituals. A prime example was the belief that a player can influence the outcome of a roll by adjusting how hard he throws the dice. The cabbies would roll gently when they needed a low number, and throw more forcefully when they wanted a high number. Occasionally players would berate themselves for not adhering to the rule; Henslin quotes a player named Little Joe lamenting, "shot too hard that time."

Did you do something like this when you imagined rolling the die a moment ago? I certainly did when I played Snakes and Ladders (known as Chutes and Ladders in the U.S.) as a child. If I wanted to roll a low number to tiptoe one or two squares and land on a ladder, I would shake the die delicately and tip it gently onto the table. If I wanted to throw a high number and dash across a string of treacherous snakes I would launch the die across the table. I didn't have to be taught this strategy; the idea came naturally to me, as it does to St. Louis cabbies, and to gamblers and board gamers the world over. The more vigorous action is somehow expected to produce a higher number. A big number must have a big cause. The idea that the velocity of the die somehow influences the number that comes up shows the proportionality bias in action, guiding our beliefs and behavior about an outcome that, in reality, is totally random.

This is just one example to get us started. The proportionality bias goes much deeper than merely influencing how we roll a die. It shapes the way we think about life, the universe, and just about everything. When big things happen to us, we look for big causes. Maybe you can catch yourself thinking like this about events in your own life. If something important happens, like winning fifty thousand dollars on a scratch card or meeting the love of your life in a chance encounter, you can't help thinking there must have been some big reason for it. Perhaps the winnings were a karmic reward for some earlier good deed. Maybe fate brought your lover to you. Likewise, when we're faced with a personal tragedy it can be tempting to think that it is part of some divine plan, or maybe the work of the Devil.

Even if we don't really believe in fate or karma, God or Satan, most of us can't help thoughts like these crossing our mind from time to time. This is especially true, psychologists Michael Lupfer and Elizabeth Layman found, when events are beyond our control and have life-altering repercussions. It is supremely unsatisfying to think that our good or bad fortune is nothing more than blind chance, or that we met our soul mate not because of some cosmic plan, but merely because we drank too much wine and happened to vomit on an attractive stranger's shoes.

Even scholars, who ought to be bastions of rationality and objectivity, are susceptible to the proportionality bias. Many historians argue that grand historical events, such as the First World War, were essentially inevitable. Europe was poised for conflict, they say, and even if events hadn't transpired in precisely the way they did, *something* would have initiated the global conflict. But is this a justifiable notion?

The crucial event precipitating the outbreak of the First World War was the assassination of the Austrian Archduke Franz Ferdinand while he was on a state visit to Sarajevo. A radical organization called Black Hand conspired to bump the duke off. Six assassins were stationed by the roadside, equipped with bombs to lob at Ferdinand's motorcade as it passed. The first two got cold feet and failed to act. The third hurled a grenade at Ferdinand's vehicle, only to watch it bounce off and explode underneath a different car. The would-be assassin swallowed the cyanide pill he had been provided and hurled himself into a nearby river. Unfortunately for him, the dose of cyanide was sufficient only to cause violent fits of vomiting, and the river was only half a foot deep. He was promptly roughed up by the crowd of bystanders and taken into custody, while the remaining assassins quietly skulked off in defeat. Barely fazed, Ferdinand decided to continue his visit. Later in the day his motorcade took a wrong turn, and momentarily stopped to back the parade up. As chance would have it, Ferdinand's car stopped right outside the café where one of the foiled assassins, Gavrilo Princip, had retreated to lament his failure. Stepping outside and finding himself a few feet from the archduke, Princip seized the opportunity. He drew his handgun and fired two bullets into the car, killing Ferdinand and his wife.

It's easy to imagine how a slight alteration to the sequence of events could have allowed Franz Ferdinand to cheat death. If only Ferdinand had cut short the visit, if only his driver hadn't turned down the wrong street, if only Princip hadn't chosen that restaurant, or hadn't walked outside at just the right moment, the assassination would never have been completed. It's harder to imagine what the wider ramifications of this small tweak to history might have been. Could the entire war have been averted? According to studies by political scientist Richard Lebow, scholars of history or political science often reject out of hand the notion that something as seemingly trivial as a careless driver taking a wrong turn could have radically changed how world events unfolded. But maybe their reasoning is clouded by the proportionality bias. Seeking to match the size of cause and consequence, they find it irrationally hard to acknowledge that such a minuscule rewrite could completely change the course of history. Europe may well have been a tinder box poised for conflict, but without the spark of the assassination to ignite the conflict, hostilities may have subsided, and war might have been averted.

It's not surprising that academics can be influenced by the proportionality bias. We all are, all the time. Its subtle influence may have even shaped how we communicate. Linguists point out that saying words like *little*, *petite*, *diminutive*, and *itsy-bitsy*, *teenie-weenie* (*yellow polka-dot bikini* notwithstanding) involves narrowing the throat and lips, while words like *large*, *huge*, *vast*, *rotund*, *enormous*, and *humongous* involve expanding our vocal apparatus. (This holds true in other languages, too. For example, compare the Spanish *gordo* versus *chico*, or French *petit* versus *grand*.) If we want to convey the idea of bigness, we make a big sound. To indicate smallness, we make a small sound. On a very basic level, it seems, the wiring of our brains forces us to seek consistency between how we think about magnitude and how we express it.

Crisis (Averted)

We've seen how the proportionality bias can shape our behavior, as well as the explanations we prefer for events in our own lives or things that have already happened in the world. But does it influence the way we interpret events going on in the world around us? Since ethics committees generally don't approve of psychologists surreptitiously engineering major world events just to see how people react, academics looking at the proportionality bias have settled for merely making up stories. Sticking to fiction allows the researchers to systematically tinker with the details, keeping everything the same except the size of the outcome. In most studies, two separate groups of people read the same story, but each group gets a different ending. For one, the story ends with a bang; the consequences are momentous. For the other, the story ends with a whimper; things fizzle out, and there are no major consequences.

A 2010 study led by psychologist Anna Ebel-Lam, for instance, involved stories about an explosion in an airplane's cargo hold. In one version of the story, the pilot struggled to maintain control and make an emergency landing, but the plane ulti-mately crashed, killing everyone on board. In the other version, the only difference was that this time the pilot was able to successfully land the aircraft. When everyone was given a list of possible causes to choose from, people who read the version ending in death and destruction tended to assume that the explosion must have been the result of a terrorist plot or endemic malpractice among the airline's technicians. People who read the version with less severe consequences, on the other hand, were more likely to blame the explosion on a more mundane cause, such as an electrical malfunction. It's important to note that the outcome of the story—whether the plane crashed or landed—was down to the pilot's actions rather than the explo-sion itself. There's no reason the outcome should have affected judgments about what caused the explosion. And yet, the bigger outcome was given the bigger cause.

In another study, Ebel–Lam and colleagues created stories in which a disease outbreak swept through an accounting office. According to both stories, dozens of employees were infected and had to be taken to the hospital. For one set of readers, the story ended with everyone making a full recovery and returning to work—no harm done. But for the other group, the story ended on a much bleaker note, with the disease killing many of the people it infected. Again, readers rated the likelihood of potential causes. Some were big: perhaps the outbreak was an act of biological warfare, or the result of an unusually infectious superpathogen. Others were more ordinary: maybe the outbreak was caused by a mundane bacterial infection, or was the result of a single employee who picked up a bug while traveling overseas. As expected, people who had been told that the outbreak had large consequences deemed the big causes more plausible, while those who were told that the consequences were smaller rated the relatively mundane causes as more plausible.

The magnitude-matching principle even extends to a preference for *physically* larger causes for extreme events. In my personal favorite proportionality study, Robyn LeBoeuf and Michael Norton concocted a story about an outbreak of an unusual disease among the animals at a zoo. In one version, the infection marauded through the zoo, killing most of the animals before it could be contained. In another version, zoo workers brought the disease under control quickly, so that only a few unlucky animals died. The source of the plague was narrowed down to two suspects: a newly obtained bunny rabbit, or a newly obtained fully grown bear. When readers had been told that most of the animals had died, the *literally* larger cause—the ginormous bear—was more likely to be deemed guilty of unleashing the outbreak. When few animals had died, on the other hand, more people deemed the bunny to be the culprit.

Other studies show that people prefer extreme causes for extreme crimes, such as a brutal murder, for particularly destructive natural disasters, like tornadoes, and for devastating accidents, like a plane crash involving a large number of fatalities. More mundane attributions are favored for lesser crimes, less extreme disasters, or accidents in which nobody is killed. It's interesting to note that the kinds of stories the researchers used concern precisely the kinds of events—disasters, diseases, and crimes—that generate some of the most popular conspiracy theories. Conspiracy theorists claim that HIV/AIDS is a biological weapon, that weather-manipulation technology was behind Hurricane Katrina, that mass shootings like the Sandy Hook school shooting were staged by the government, and that flight TWA800 was brought down not by a simple fuel-line malfunction but by the U.S. military. The studies we've seen so far didn't directly ask people if they thought a conspiracy was to blame—but other studies have.

Hits and Misses

Suppose the next time you check your phone, you see the headline of a breaking news alert: MAN SHOOTS AT THE PRESIDENT AND KILLS HIM. With just this headline and nothing more to go on, what are the chances you might suspect the gunman was not working alone? Now suppose you had seen a slightly different headline: MAN SHOOTS AT THE PRESIDENT AND MISSES. Are you more or less likely to sense a conspiracy? If you're like the test subjects in a 1979 study by psychologists Clark McCauley and Susan Jacques—one of the first psychological studies to look at belief in conspiracy theories—there's a far greater chance you'll suspect that the successful assassination was down to a conspiracy, and the unsuccessful attempt was the work of a lone gunman.

Nearly three decades later, in 2007, University of London psychologists Patrick Leman and Marco Cinnirella repeated the experiment, and found the same pattern. But they acknowledged an alternative explanation for the results. Perhaps people were simply reasoning that an assassin who tries to kill the president and fails is more likely to be a lone, unskilled kook—surely evil conspiracies have more stringent hiring practices. If this were true, the pattern of results might be less down to an unconscious proportionality bias than a logical, reasoned inference. In fact, McCauley and Jacques had found some evidence that this might be the case. When they simply asked their study participants how effective they expected an assassin working for a conspiracy to be, they reckoned he would be pretty damn effective. On the other hand, they guessed that a lone gunman would be less competent. This difference alone could account for the fact that the successful assassination was more likely to be attributed to a conspiracy.

With that in mind, Leman and Cinnirella added two new scenarios. In one, the president was reported to have been hit by an assassin's bullet, but miraculously survived—by pure chance, a mocked-up news article reported, the bullet narrowly missed the president's heart, leaving him with only a minor flesh wound. In another article, the assassin's bullet missed, yet shortly after the assassination attempt the president died of a heart attack. In these new scenarios, the president's ultimate fate is unrelated to the assassin's competence. Yet despite breaking the causal relationship between assassin and outcome, people's beliefs about the assassin *still* seemed to be influenced by the proportionality bias. When the president died, the would-be assassin was judged likely to have been part of a conspiracy, even though his bullet had missed (and the news report specifically mentioned that the heart attack was brought on by the president's busy schedule, not by the assassination attempt). When the president survived, the assassin was more likely to be viewed as a lone gunman, even though he had scored a direct hit, and it was only by pure chance that he failed in his task.

In another study, Robyn LeBoeuf and Michael Norton (the same researchers behind the study in which a disease swept through a zoo) crafted assassination scenarios in which the causal chain between assassin and outcome was even further removed. They made up more fake news reports, this time claiming that a British newspaper had criticized the recently assassinated president of an unspecified foreign country, thereby inciting terrorist attacks against Britain. One version of the story had dire consequences, reporting that Britain had declared war against the country as a result of the attacks. In a second version, the consequences were minor: the British prime minister responded peacefully, thereby subduing the attacks. Thus, the consequences of the assassination were arbitrarily determined by the prime minister's reaction. Despite the absence of a direct link between the initial assassination and the size of its ultimate consequences, people reckoned the assassination was more likely to have been a conspiracy when the magnitude of the consequences was large.

When the consequences were relatively insignificant, people were more likely to write the assassin off as a lone gunman.

One more experiment by LeBoeuf and Norton ditched the pretense of fictional assassinated presidents, and instead explicitly mentioned JFK. Readers were told either that Kennedy's death had prolonged the Vietnam War, resulting in the deaths of an additional forty thousand American soldiers, or that the assassination had had no effect at all on the war or the number of casualties. Even without the claim about additional casualties, 64 percent of the test subjects endorsed a conspiracy theory of the assassination. But when the consequences were ratcheted up, the number of conspiracy theorists rose to 75 percent. As LeBoeuf and Norton point out, their findings show that it's not just whether an assassination succeeds or fails that determines the magnitude of the event, but the wider ramifications for society.

The most extensive investigation of conspiracism and the proportionality bias to date was carried out by Dutch researchers Jan-Willem van Prooijen and Eric van Dijk. They made up newspaper reports detailing an unfortunate series of events that supposedly had befallen a man named Yayi Godo. Godo, the newspaper reports explained, was a powerful political opposition leader in the African country of Benin, and was likely to win the elections due to take place the next month. (Benin is a real country, but, as the researchers explained to participants after they had completed the study, Godo and the events that transpired were entirely made up.) In one study, the fake report claimed Godo had been involved in a car crash. For one group of test subjects, the report claimed that Godo had died, and that the upcoming elections would be postponed until further notice. For the other group, Godo miraculously survived with only minor injuries, and the elections would proceed as planned. In a second study, the report claimed that a motorcyclist had pulled alongside Godo's car as it sat at a traffic light, and opened fire. As usual there were two parallel endings: either Godo was hit in the head and died, or he was hit in the arm and survived. As you might expect by now, when Godo died, either in the crash or the drive-by shooting, readers were generally more likely to endorse a conspiratorial explanation.

But van Prooijen and van Dijk added another variable into the mix. A key factor in whether the proportionality bias influences our reasoning, they found, is the degree to which we empathize with the people affected by the event in question. When test subjects were instructed to make an objective judgment of the likelihood of conspiracy, the size of the consequences (whether Godo lived or died) had no effect on whether they bought into a conspiracy theory. When they were asked to imagine themselves in the shoes of a citizen of Benin, however, they became much more likely to explain the bigger event as the result of conspiracy. In another study, rather than directly manipulating whether or not subjects took the perspective of the people affected by an event, the researchers measured each participant's natural ability to emphasize with others. Before reading the bogus newspaper article, participants took a test of perspective-taking ability, in which they had to guess the emotion a person was feeling by looking at a picture of the person's eyes, with the rest of the face obscured. The higher participants scored on this test, the more their judgments tended to fall in line with the proportionality bias.

Earlier we saw how the proportionality bias can affect the way we explain events in our own lives. We write little things off as happenstance, but when something life-changing befalls us we chalk it up to fate. What van Prooijen and van Dijk's findings suggest is that when we are drawn to conspiracy theories about big events—even ones that happened halfway across the world and have little direct impact on our own life—it might be because we can't help imagining ourselves in the place of the real victims. When we're asked to be objective, we can write off somebody else's misfortune as mere chance. When we see it as a personal attack, the proportionality bias clouds our judgment.

President Dead

All told, these findings help explain why the most popular conspiracy theories surround some of the most momentous events in history. When big things happen in the world—the untimely death of a public figure, an unprecedented revolution, a tragic aviation disaster, a shocking terrorist atrocity, an epidemic of a deadly new disease—the "official stories" often leave us cold. To be told that the death of Princess Diana was just a senseless car accident, the AIDS epidemic is down to a tiny pathogen, the horror of 9/11 was the result of nineteen minimally competent hijackers, or that the French Revolution resulted from the haphazard coming-together of many independently inconsequential resentments and aspirations—these causes don't live up to the magnitude of their consequences. Conspiracy theories allow us to scratch the unconscious itch.

In a 1975 article in the *Washington Monthly*, journalist Tom Bethell captured the incongruity of President Kennedy's death. The "official" version of events, Bethell wrote, requires us to believe that the assassination and all its consequences—including, perhaps, the disastrous Vietnam War—was the doing of one man "who had, as it were, gotten out of bed on the wrong side that morning, and found a gun lying there. The cause doesn't fit the effect." Assassination buff Kenneth Rahn put it similarly. "It's preposterous on the face of it," he wrote, "to believe that a mousy little guy with a $12.95 rifle could bring down the leader of the free world." The uncomfortable reality is that small things can have big consequences. Sometimes kings are struck down by peasants. When that happens, we can't help longing for some alternative explanation more befitting the effect. "In the case of the Kennedy assassination," Bethell concluded, "this means looking for a conspiracy—preferably a large one."

CHAPTER ELEVEN

I *Knew* It

Steve Regan sets the scene: Dense fog rolled across the desolate English moors. It was the mid-1990s, and Steve was a flight sergeant with the Royal Air Force Regiment. He was stationed at Barnham Camp, a training area on a barren heath at the edge of a forest a few miles from the small town of Thetford. That night it was Steve's turn on guard duty—a twelve-hour shift spent sitting in a small guard room with nothing for company but a small TV and a kettle.

Barnham Camp had a spooky reputation, Steve tells me. Mustard-gas bombs had been made there during the Second World War, and then it was repurposed to store nuclear bombs during the Cold War. The bomb dumps had long since been decommissioned; the dilapidated old buildings were fenced off and falling apart. It looked like the set of a scary movie, he says. And then there was the fact that the camp was right in the middle of the so-called Thetford Triangle—East Anglia's answer to the Bermuda Triangle. The Triangle was a hotbed of UFO sightings at the time. Witnesses often pointed to Barnham Camp as the source of strange activity.

Steve gazed out the guard room window at the featureless wall of fog, barely able to see the camp's security gate a few yards away. He tells me that despite the long hours and austere conditions, the overnight guard shift was coveted among the officers at Barnham, because it was so uneventful. It was a quiet little camp in the middle of nowhere. Nothing ever happened. But that night, something happened. Steve was about to become the villain in someone else's conspiracy theory.

It began with a flurry of flashing blue lights appearing out of the fog. The intercom crackled to life, and the guard manning the gate announced "there's a load of police just turned up." Two police officers—a man and a woman—came into the guard room while the rest waited in their cars. Steve can't remember their names now, so let's call them Mulder and Scully, in honor of the conspiracy-chasing FBI agent and his more skeptical partner from *The X-Files.*

"We've had an incident," Mulder explained. "We got a number of reports from different sources tonight that a UFO took off from Barnham Camp, flew over Thetford, and relanded on Barnham Camp. We need to investigate it." Steve's response was prototypically English: "Do you want a cup of tea?"

It would take a while to get authorization to let anyone— even the police—onto the training area, so the three of them sipped tea, waited, and chatted. Steve got the impression that Scully didn't put much stock in the UFO story, but being a junior member of the outfit she had to go along with it. He remembers that when he asked what the officers thought the UFO might have been, she looked embarrassed. Rolling her eyes, she said, "You know, aliens." Mulder, on the other hand, seemed to think a conspiracy was afoot from the start. (See why I picked the names?) "All I'm saying," he mused, "is there are too many occurrences around here to be just a coincidence. We want to know if you're testing anything secret." Steve joked, "If we *were*, I wouldn't tell you; that is the definition of secret." He soon realized his mistake: Mulder was growing more and more convinced that Steve was covering up Barnham's sinister secrets.

Eventually they were granted permission to head out onto the training area. The trio climbed into Steve's Land Rover, and he drove across the rugged terrain at a slow crawl while Mulder and Scully squinted hopelessly into the fog. Steve knew it was futile: "Even if we were hiding an airship here at the moment, you're not going to find it, are you?" But the officers insisted on carrying on. Mulder was fixated on the spooky old bomb dumps, but there was no way Steve could take him there. The fog made navigating the rudimentary tracks dangerous, the buildings were off-limits because of residual contamination, and they wouldn't be able to see anything in the fog anyway. Steve had the sinking feeling that every time he said he *wasn't* hiding something, Mulder grew more convinced he *was* hiding something. Steve offered to get special clearance for the officers to come back the next day when the fog had cleared—they could search the entire place with dogs if they wanted, he said. But Mulder sensed subterfuge. He seemed to think Steve was deliberately delaying the search, that the evidence could be shipped

out by the next day, that perhaps the fog itself might have
somehow been conjured up to hide the truth.

Eventually they came across the group of recruits who were
out training on the heath. Steve asked the instructor what they'd
been doing. The fog had put a hold on things, he said, though
they had tried a pyrotechnics demo earlier, firing off a few flares
and things like that. On a hunch, Steve asked if they could fire
another one, just like they had earlier. The instructor fetched a
parachute flare and fired it into the air. It disappeared into the
fog. A moment later there was a distant pop, and a great ball of
orange light appeared, hanging in the sky, rippling eerily
through the layers of fog. Then the light started to move. It must
have hit an air current high above the ground, Steve says. First,
it drifted far away from the camp toward the town of Thetford.
Then another air current turned it around and brought it back
toward the camp. It slowly descended and landed back within
the bounds of the camp. The flare had done exactly what the
reports said the UFO had done. For a while, Steve says, everyone
just looked at each other in silence.

According to Steve, Scully was satisfied that the source of the
UFO sightings had been identified, but Mulder was far from
convinced. He seemed to think the flare demonstration was *too
convenient*. Maybe it wasn't what the UFO witnesses had seen.
Maybe it had been *set up*. Maybe Steve was still hiding something. Maybe the answers were just out of reach, hidden away in
that spooky old bomb dump that happened to be off-limits and
shrouded in fog.

Steve Regan's close encounter with two members of the
Thetford police department illustrates a familiar, but remarkable,
fact of life. Two people can look at precisely the same set of facts
and come to radically different conclusions. Once we have a
hunch about something—whether it's a conspiracy theory about
mysterious UFOs or a feeling about which brand of litter our
kitty prefers—we have a deeply rooted tendency to prove
ourselves right. We like to think our beliefs are founded on a
fair survey of the best available evidence; first you find out the
facts, then you come to a rational conclusion. But the reality is
that our brains often work in reverse. The conclusion comes

first, then our brain seeks out and shapes the evidence to fit what it already believes. And it does all this behind the scenes, leaving us with the illusion that we've diligently reviewed the evidence and arrived at the only reasonable conclusion. This tendency is called *confirmation bias*, and it colors our thinking in three distinct ways.

Seek and Ye Shall Find

Confirmation bias kicks in as soon as we get an idea in our head. When we go looking for evidence to test out a hunch, our brain doesn't treat all potential evidence equally. Rather, we use what psychologists call a *positive test strategy*: We seek what we expect to find.

In the 1960s, psychologist Peter Wason invented a game that shows this lopsided search strategy in action. Imagine you're a test subject in his study. Wason tells you, "I've made up a simple rule for constructing sequences of three numbers. I'll give you a clue: '2-4-6' fits the rule. Your job is to figure out what the rule is by coming up with other strings of three numbers. For every sequence you come up with, I'll tell you whether it fits my rule or not. When you're sure you have the solution you can stop testing and tell me what you think the rule is."

What sequence would you try first? If you're like most of Wason's subjects, your first hunch might be that the rule is something like *even numbers increasing by two*, so you might guess "6-8-10."

"Yes," Wason tells you, "that sequence meets the rule."

"Aha," you think. Next you try "14-16-18."

"Yes," Wason says.

"AHA!" You churn out a few more for good measure: "10-12-14; 46-48-50; 184-186-188."

"Yes, yes, and yes."

By this point you're pretty sure that you've nailed the rule. Channeling Sherlock Holmes, you announce, "It's elementary, my dear Wason. The rule is *even numbers increasing by two*."

Bzzt. "No," Wason says, "that's not the rule."

"How can that be?" you mutter. "I had so much evidence!"

In fact, the rule is simply *any three increasing numbers*. Few people guess the rule right away, but that's not what's interesting about the game. The interesting thing is what it reveals about our intuitive hunch-testing strategy. We set about gathering evidence by trying out sequences of numbers that *fit* our imagined rule. Since the real rule in this case is more general (it could be *any* ascending numbers), our guesses are all met with positive feedback, just as we expected—that's why it's called a positive test strategy. With each "yes," our confidence grows; we feel like we're getting ever closer to the truth. But our confidence is misplaced. The idea of trying to *disprove* the rule by testing a sequence that we *don't* expect to fit (something like "2-3-5," or "8-13-21") doesn't come so naturally to us. That kind of negative test strategy is potentially more informative—a "no" would be good evidence that we're onto something, a "yes" would send us back to the drawing board. Left to our own devices, however, most of us will collect "yes" after "yes" instead of looking for a single "no." As a result, a speculative hunch can become a confidently held belief, regardless of whether the hunch was justified.

This is how confirmation bias sets in. Merely finding evidence that appears to fit our preconceptions doesn't always mean we're right, but if we don't check for evidence that we're wrong, we have no reason to question our beliefs.

We don't just rely on the positive test strategy in psychological guessing games. It rules our lives. It's no coincidence that cat fanciers read *Cat Fancy* magazine and dog lovers read *Modern Dog*. (For the more exacting cynophile there are periodicals catering to the narrowest of canine interests, from *The Retriever Journal* to *Just Labs*.) The news sources we read, the links we click online, and the views of people we surround ourselves with online and in the flesh all align, more often than not, with what we already believe. We build a fortress of positive information around our beliefs, and we rarely step outside—or even peek out the window.

In one illustrative study, political scientists Charles Taber and Milton Lodge gave people a choice of essays to read arguing for or against tougher gun laws. There were essays by the National Rifle Association (NRA) and the Republican party, and essays from the Democratic party and Citizens Against Handguns (which was described to test subjects as a Maryland-based group devoted to the elimination of handgun sales in the United

States. Actually, the researchers had made up the organization, modeling it on various real gun-control groups). Test subjects were free to read whichever articles they wanted, but the researchers practically begged them to look at both sides of the argument, with pleas to "set your feelings aside," "consider the arguments fairly," and "be as objective as possible." But it was to little avail. People who already favored guns overwhelmingly chose to read the pro-gun essays. People already opposed to guns chose to read anti-gun arguments.

When it comes to conspiracy theories, the situation is no different. The world is a busy place. The amount of information out there is endless. But, as we've seen, our brains carefully curate the information we seek out, favoring a positive test strategy. And if you go looking for evidence of even the most far-fetched conspiracy theory, it's not hard to find.

This was playfully illustrated by historian Rob MacDougall. MacDougall came up with a game he called "The Paranoid Style" (named in honor of Richard Hofstadter's famous essay, which we talked about a few chapters ago). You can play at home. First, get a few friends together, and have everyone pick one well-known historical figure—it can be anyone they like. The object of the game is to find evidence that the figure was secretly part of a "conspiracy of vampires that has pulled the strings behind the world for hundreds of years." There is, as far as I know, no such conspiracy; MacDougall just made it up. But that doesn't stop people from finding evidence anyway. The first time he played with some historian colleagues, he says they quickly spun a yarn in which Henry Ford instigated the Industrial Revolution in the hope that factory smoke would blot out the sun, and Thomas Edison invented the light bulb to get humans used to living in the dark. (MacDougall notes that people got hung up on the "rules" of vampirism, like avoiding sunlight. These days he plays the game with extraterrestrial conspirators instead of vampires, since "we have fewer preconceptions about what aliens are like and what the alien conspiracy wants to achieve.")

MacDougall calls finding evidence of a nonexistent conspiracy in the real historical record "historical apophenia"; "People are creative, and good at finding patterns, and history is full of information that can be made to seem significant." The illusion of conspiracy can be eerily convincing. "That 'click' when disparate facts seem to fit together is a powerful and even uncanny feeling," he says. "The evidence starts to line up all too well with the fantasy you have just concocted, and you skate right up to the edge of believing."

The best conspiracy theorists are playing "The Paranoid Style" without realizing it. Remember David Icke, who we met a few chapters ago? The conspirators leave subtle symbols of their plot lying around, Icke says, and "when you know what you're looking for, it starts jumping out at you." Of course, for Icke this isn't evidence of an involuntary cognitive bias, it's evidence that the conspiracy is real. Here are just a few of the things Icke looks for as evidence of the conspiracy: people covering one eye (he has a collection of photos of popular musicians covering one eye), the number thirteen, pyramids (especially pyramids with thirteen levels, like the one on every American one-dollar bill), triangles (he has more photos of celebrities gesticulating in a triangular manner), circles, crescents, squares, cubes, hexagons, the number six, six-pointed stars, crosses, pillars, columns, crowns, horns, fire, sticking one's tongue out (cue more celebrity snapshots), the letters E and L, the planet Saturn, spiders, goats, and bearded men (including, but not limited to, Santa Claus). For David Icke, it's practically impossible to walk down the street *without* seeing evidence of a conspiracy.

It's not just professional conspiracy theorists who tend to see what they're looking for. As Wason's number game shows—not to mention our magazine subscriptions, browser histories, and Twitter followers—most people can't help unwittingly seeking out information that fits our hunches. When we get an idea, a proverbial light bulb lights up above our head, and we go looking for evidence only where the light is brightest, like the drunkard looking for his keys beneath a lamppost: "Is this where you lost your keys?" "No, but the light is so much better here!"

But that's just step one. After all, when it comes to issues of any substance, the evidence is usually a mixed bag. Our brains can do their best to insulate our beliefs in a protective bubble of positive evidence, but the world has a habit of brandishing other points of view at us. You might think this could burst our bubble. Coming across information that challenges our beliefs might force us to change our mind, or at the very least dent our confidence. But another component of confirmation bias comes to the rescue.

Depends How You Look at It

How do you feel about nuclear weapons? More specifically, are you in favor of nuclear deterrence—the government keeping a stockpile of nukes to use against our enemies if they try to nuke us? Supporters say it makes the world safer for everyone; nobody will fire the first shot, because doing so would guarantee their own destruction. Critics say we ought to rid the world of nuclear weapons, and nuclear deterrence just perpetuates the problem. Where do you stand?

Now consider this. At three A.M. on November 9, 1979, it looked like the Cold War was about to heat up. U. S. National Security Adviser Zbigniew Brzezinski was awoken by a dreaded phone call. The Soviet Union, he was told, had launched a full-scale nuclear attack against the United States. Early warning systems showed two and a half thousand nukes headed toward mainland U.S.A. Nuclear command centers across the country sprang into action. Retaliation would be swift. Planes loaded with nuclear bombs took to the skies. Missile officers in underground silos readied their launch keys. Then, just as Brzezinski was about to alert the president to the imminent nuclear apocalypse, he got another call: It was a false alarm. A test program that simulated a Soviet nuclear attack had somehow transmitted fake attack data to the regular warning displays as if it were real. The panic had been caused by a computer bug. Crisis averted.

How do you feel about nuclear deterrence now? More worried about our safety, or less? On one hand, the system malfunctioned and brought us to the brink of an apocalyptic disaster; maybe nukes are more of a liability than an asset. On the other hand, safeguards were in place and caught the error before any harm was done; maybe the risks of a malfunction are small compared to leaving ourselves defenseless. What we can conclude based on an event like this is not a simple, objective issue. Despite the different possible interpretations, however, it's not hard to predict how any given person will react. As psychologist Scott Plous demonstrated, all you need to know is how the person felt about nuclear weapons to begin with.

Plous designed a clever set of studies to see how people update their beliefs after learning about nuclear near-disasters. He found that people who started out on opposite sides of the ideological fence saw the same event very differently. People who opposed nukes tended to see malfunctions as "evidence of system vulnerability," whereas people in favor of nukes "tended to view the breakdowns as successful tests of system safeguards." As a result, nuclear advocates feel safer after learning about a near-disaster, while nuclear critics feel more vulnerable. And the stronger a person's prior belief, the more skewed their interpretation. When Plous tested college students with only a weak preference one way or the other, they were more ambivalent about the breakdowns. When he compared a group of Air Force cadets (who were strongly in favor of nuclear deterrence) and a group of peace campaigners (who were strongly against nukes), the bias was much stronger.

The trend isn't unique to laypeople sitting in a psychologist's lab. Plous's study was inspired by a real 1981 government inquiry into nuclear warning system malfunctions (there were quite a few of them during the Cold War). One committee member, Congressman Frank Horton of New York, saw cause for grave concern: "The recent false missile alerts . . . it seems to me, are a serious threat to our national security." General James V. Hartinger, on the other hand, claimed to be reassured: "I really have more confidence in the system now because it was demonstrated that we could cope with such a fault." Horton, it is worth noting, had opposed nuclear weapons throughout his political career. Hartinger was commander in chief of the North American Aerospace Defense Command (NORAD), the agency in charge of monitoring the skies for incoming attacks.

This is what psychologists call *biased assimilation*: We interpret ambiguous events in light of what we already believe. Think about the inevitable media response to a mass shooting. For pundits who already favored stricter gun-control laws, mass shootings are clear evidence that guns should be harder for people to get. For pundits who already supported the right to bear arms, mass shootings demonstrate that *more* people should carry guns. (As Wayne LaPierre, a leader of the NRA, put it, "the only thing that stops a bad guy with a gun is a good guy with a gun.") Even relatively mundane events can prompt biased assimilation. Two people on opposite sides of the political aisle can watch the same debate and both leave convinced their side came out on top. For football fans, whether the referee is a keen-eyed professional or an incompetent jerk depends on which team a penalty call favors. Fans of the Chicago Bears and the Green Bay Packers could be watching the same game, but when a dodgy call is made they might as well be in different universes.

Biased assimilation also kicks in when we're confronted with complex, conflicting evidence about some topic we have an opinion on. In 1979 a team of Stanford University psychologists looked at students' opinions about whether the death penalty deters would-be murderers from murdering. The students read two scientific studies, one showing that there *is* a deterrent effect, and the other finding that there *isn't*. In fact, the studies were both fake; the researchers had simply made up the details so that they could carefully control the quality of the evidence people saw for either side. The students tended to carefully scrutinize and dismiss the study that contradicted their preconceptions, while uncritically accepting the study that matched their preconceptions—even though both studies were equally open to criticism.

More recent studies have focused on peoples' prejudices about homosexuality, views about affirmative action, tax policies, abortion, gun control laws, and secondhand smoke, and even belief in psychic powers. In each case, the findings show what you've no doubt noticed in everyday life: When it comes to all these kinds of hot-button issues, people tend to see evidence or arguments that fit their preconceptions as much more rigorous and persuasive than evidence that challenges their beliefs. As a result, both sides of the ideological divide think their beliefs are based on the best available evidence, and it's rare that anyone feels the need to change their mind.

In 1995, psychologist John McHoskey put together another study of biased assimilation, but he wasn't interested in nuclear weapons or the death penalty. McHoskey wanted to know what people thought about the assassination of JFK. First, he asked two hundred fifty college students who they thought killed Kennedy: Was it Lee Harvey Oswald alone, or was it a conspiracy? Next, he showed the students a handful of arguments supporting each side. There was the fact, for example, that many eyewitnesses thought they had heard gunshots from the grassy knoll; some experts said Oswald didn't have time to fire all the shots, and that the "single-bullet theory" couldn't account for all the wounds inflicted on Kennedy and Governor Connally; Kennedy's head moved back and to the left when it was hit, suggesting a shot from the front; and the 1979 House Select Committee concluded that there was evidence of a conspiracy. A seemingly compelling case for conspiracy. But the arguments for Oswald acting alone were compelling, too: Oswald was strongly motivated to kill JFK; witnesses saw him at the book depository at the time of the shooting; he owned the rifle used to kill JFK; his fingerprints were on the gun and the sniper's nest in the book depository; recent reenactments demonstrate that the "single-bullet theory" *could* explain all the wounds, and that Oswald *could* have fired all the shots in the allotted time.

What to believe? The selection of evidence was deliberately designed to be a mixed bag, not amenable to any firm conclusions. Yet that didn't shake people's confidence in their initial beliefs. It will come as no surprise by now that both sides felt like they had been right all along. People who suspected a conspiracy found the pro-conspiracy evidence to be more convincing than lone gunman evidence, and vice-versa. In the end, many of the students left McHoskey's lab feeling *more* confident that they knew who killed Kennedy than they had when they'd walked in the door.

When we're faced with a murky pool of evidence, biased assimilation filters out anything that doesn't fit what we already believe, leaving behind the illusion that the truth is crystal-clear (and just so happens to fit what we knew all along). But questions like whether gun ownership restrictions, nuclear deterrence, and the death penalty are right or wrong have no clear answer; they are moral issues that come down to differing values. Then there are questions, like who killed JFK, that *do* have an answer, but for which the evidence remains (at least to some extent) open to debate.

What happens when there *is* a clear answer? What if we know for a fact that someone is simply misinformed, and we can offer incontrovertible evidence that ought to set him or her straight? Surely people will change their minds then?

Controverting the Incontrovertible

Barack Obama, the fourty-fourth president of the United States of America, has been on the receiving end of his fair share of misguided rumors. Some of the earliest and most enduring rumors question his very identity: Was he born in Hawaii, as he claims, or was he actually born in Kenya? For the Birthers, as the people who question Obama's origins have become known, this is no minor quibble. They claim that if Obama isn't a "natural-born" American citizen, he might be ineligible to be president, an impostor-in-chief.

Now, we could be charitable to the Birthers and assume their concerns are based on an innocent misconception. It ought, then, to be an easy mistake to correct. During his 2008 election campaign, the Obama team launched a website called *Fight the Smears* and uploaded a picture of his short-form birth certificate, confirming his U.S. citizenship. Yet the rumors persisted. In July 2009 the director of Hawaii's Department of Health put out a press release verifying that Obama's birth records really are on file there. Still the rumors refused to go away. Finally in April 2011, Obama made his long-form birth certificate available on the White House website—definitive, undeniable proof that the rumors were false. What more could the Birthers ask for?

As the years went by, Adam Berinski, a professor of political science at MIT, tracked the number of people who believed the rumors that Obama wasn't born in the United States. In April 2011, shortly before Obama released his complete birth certificate, 45 percent of the American public said they had some doubts about his credentials (despite the efforts he had already made to clear up the rumor). Shortly after he released the certificate, the number fell to 33 percent. Admittedly, that's still a lot of people questioning the president's right to be president, but at least the evidence seemed to have made a dent, right? Unfortunately, the effect was short-lived. Within a few months, the Birthers had bounced back. By January 2012, 41 percent of people doubted Obama's citizenship—only a few percent less than before Obama had gone to the trouble of releasing the certificate. (Among Republicans, it's worth noting, there were slightly *more* Birthers than before; 72 percent had doubts about Obama's particulars, up from 70 percent before he put out the certificate—but we'll talk more about which side of the political divide is more conspiracy-minded in a moment.)

Misinformation followed Obama into the White House. One of the centerpieces of his first term as president was the Affordable Care Act, affectionately—or disparagingly, depending on how you assimilate it—known as Obamacare. One vocal opponent of Obamacare was Sarah Palin, the former governor of Alaska. In August 2009, Palin sparked fears that Obamacare was a secret plot to kill off old people. Sick people, she claimed in a Facebook post, would have to "stand in front of Obama's 'death panel' so his bureaucrats can decide . . . whether they are worthy of health care." Doctors, Palin implied, would be encouraged to euthanize Grandma rather than giving her expensive life-extending medicine.

It was a troubling idea, and it proved to be catchy. Just one week after Palin's Facebook post, almost nine out of ten Americans had heard the "death panels" claim, and three out of ten said they believed it. But it wasn't true. The Obamacare legislation made no mention of bureaucratic death panels (nor did Palin cite any such wording to back up her claim). Again, it ought to be easy to set the record straight. The Obama administration made repeated efforts to debunk the rumor, and it was widely refuted in the mainstream media. Yet the misconception was frustratingly resistant to correction. By August 2012 the number of people concerned about death panels had grown to around four in ten.

How is it that after Obama presented his birth certificate to the world, the number of people who believed he was an impostor was virtually unchanged (and in some circles increased)? How come after three years of pointing out the lack of facts behind the death panel myth (and the panels failing to materialize), *more* people believed the panels might be on the horizon? Brendan Nyhan, assistant professor of political science at Dartmouth

College, specializes in studying these kinds of political misconceptions. His research shows that correcting incorrect beliefs can be surprisingly difficult. Sometimes, showing somebody the facts that ought to set them straight can make them even *more* confident in their misguided belief. Nyhan dubbed this the *backfire effect*.

Over the course of several studies, Nyhan and his colleagues have found that explaining to people why Obamacare doesn't entail government-mandated death panels can make them more certain that the death panels are a coming reality; showing people a video of President Obama saying he is a Christian can make them more suspicious that he is a secret Muslim (another rumor that arose during his presidential campaign and has lingered ever since); telling people vaccines don't cause autism can make them less willing to vaccinate their children; and warning people of the potentially dire consequences of global warming can make them more resistant to policies designed to curtail climate change.

The backfire effect is perhaps the ultimate demonstration of the power of confirmation bias. Even when the facts are incontrovertible, some people will find a way to controvert them.

And if you're looking to rationalize away an inconvenient fact, nothing beats a conspiracy theory. When you assert that nobody can be trusted, seemingly incontestable facts can simply be written off as part of the cover-up. Thus, when President Obama posted his birth certificate online, conspiracy-minded Birthers were quick to assert that it was a Photoshopped forgery. Bloggers analyzed every pixel in minute detail, pointing out supposed irregularities with the design and hue, and the apparent absence of a crease from being folded and mailed. One even pointed out what could be a subtle smiley face in the signature of the official who signed the certificate—presumably a sly clue left by the forger. (Why a master forger would leave clues remains a mystery.) Rather than convincing the Birthers of their mistake, Obama's certificate merely provided them with more ammunition.

Likewise, the "death panels" rumor remained stubbornly popular in part because of conspiracist claims that the Obama administration was implementing its death panels through more covert means. For anti-vaccinationists, the lack of evidence linking vaccines to autism is proof of a Big Pharma cover-up. For climate-change deniers, the overwhelming consensus among scientists that the Earth is heating up is easily written off as a conspiracy among scientists to mislead the public.

A common refrain among conspiracy theorists is that just one conclusive piece of evidence that the conspiracy theory is wrong would set their mind at ease. While that may be true for some, the backfire effect ensures that once a belief is deeply entrenched in our brain, that one piece of conclusive evidence can paradoxically push us even farther into our belief. Confirmation bias coupled with a predilection for conspiracy thinking makes for an impenetrable shield, which can protect a belief from just about any challenge.

Partisan Paranoia

At this point, it's worth taking a moment to tackle a question that often comes up when talking about conspiracy theories. Are conspiracy theories more popular among the political left or the right, liberals or conservatives, Democrats or Republicans?

My singling out of conspiracy theories about President Obama might give the impression that conspiracy theories are more common among Republicans. And as far as many left-wing pundits are concerned there's no question about it. Jonathan Chait, formerly a senior editor of the left-leaning *New Republic* magazine, argued that the political right "evinces a kind of paranoid thinking that . . . cannot be found in the mainstream left." Arthur Goldwag, writing for the progressive website Salon.com, proposed that conspiracy theories naturally "resonate within the Republican mainstream."

But not so fast. If you listen to *right-wing* pundits, conservatives are unfairly maligned for pointing out simple facts; it's the *left* that gets swept up in fanciful conspiracy theories. A 2008 article in the conservative *Washington Times*, for example, laments that in "liberal Hollywood . . . to express skepticism about man-made global warming is to be labeled—with all its obvious connotations—a 'denier,'" while the "insinuation that the U.S. government was complicit . . . in the destruction of the Twin Towers and the murder of 3,000 people has elicited nary a peep in condemnation."

In short, which side of the aisle is home to more conspiracy theorists depends on who you ask. As Joe Uscinski and Joseph Parent put it, each side seems convinced that the other "routinely spawns conspiracy theories in a febrile delirium while its own conspiracy theories are reasonable and factual, if not self-evidently true. The other side, they say, dangerously welcomes conspiracy theories into the mainstream while their own side safely relegates them to the lunatic fringe." Does this sound like a familiar state of affairs? The fact that each side sees the other as more conspiracy-prone is another example of the confirmation bias in action.

Whichever side of the fence you are on, it might surprise you to learn that, on the whole, people to the left and right of the political spectrum are just as conspiracy-minded as each other. Neither is conspiracism appreciably stronger the farther somebody rates themselves from the middle of the spectrum. The difference between liberals and conservatives is not in how much they like conspiracy theories in general, but in *which* particular conspiracy theories they are likely to latch on to. Uscinski and Parent collected a mass of data on people's political preferences, and on the type of conspiracy theories that they buy into. They found, perhaps unsurprisingly, that people on the political right are more likely to suspect liberals and socialists of conspiring against them; their allegations of conspiracy are typically thrown at the Obama administration, the liberal media, and ivory-tower elites. People on the left are more likely to see conspiracies of conservatives and corporations; they throw allegations of conspiracy at groups like the Bush administration and Monsanto. Conspiracy thinking is a product of psychological quirks that are built into *everyone's* brain, independent of political ideology. While they might throw accusations in different directions, there's no reason to suspect liberals and conservatives would be differently predisposed to conspiracism in general—and, according to the data, they aren't. The number of Birthers on the political right (around four in ten) is a near mirror image of the number of Truthers on the left (around four in ten).

A person's political affiliation can determine whether he or she clings to an idea in the face of contradictory evidence, too. When Brendan Nyhan studied the backfire effect in the context of Sarah Palin's death panels, he found that the people who were the biggest fans of Palin were the most resistant to information debunking the rumor. People farther to the left of the aisle were much more likely to admit their mistake and update their beliefs. In another study, psychologist John Bullock showed people a news story about mistreatment of prisoners at Guantanamo Bay. At the end, there was a correction stating that the mistreatment hadn't actually taken place. Republican readers were happy to incorporate the correction into their beliefs; they came to disapprove less of U.S. treatment of detainees than they had to begin with. Democrats, however, seemed to take the false mistreatment allegation on board and entirely neglect the disclaimer that it wasn't true; they came to disapprove much more strongly of the detainees' treatment.

It is interesting to note that the first people to question Obama's place of birth weren't, as you might have assumed, Republicans. The Birther rumor was first floated in spring 2008 by Democrats supporting Hillary Clinton's presidential bid. Yet after Obama won the presidential nomination and the competition with Clinton was over, the rumor was almost entirely abandoned by Democrats. Only then did it take on a new life among Republicans. In his 2006 book *The Audacity of Hope*, Obama wrote, "in distilled form, the explanations of both the right and the left have become mirror images of each other. They are stories of conspiracy, of America being hijacked by an evil cabal." Little did Obama know how right the coming years would prove him.

Reasonable Creatures

In the previous few chapters, we talked about how a handful of mental quirks and shortcuts can give us a gut feeling that a conspiracy is afoot. Those processes sow the seeds of conspiracy thinking. Confirmation bias helps the seeds take root. Our brain sifts through the mounds of available data, hoarding any morsels that appear to fit a conspiracy and ignoring or dismissing the rest. Confirmation bias wraps a vague suspicion in a cocoon of seemingly positive evidence, where it can blossom into a confidently held conspiracy theory.

It bears repeating that conspiracy theorists are not alone in their susceptibility to confirmation bias. We all do it. Recall that in John McHoskey's study of JFK conspiracy beliefs, an inconclusive pool of evidence made conspiracy theorists more convinced of the conspiracy, but it also made lone-gunman theorists more confident that Oswald acted alone. Or recall Steve Regan's predicament from the beginning of the chapter. For the police officer who came into the investigation anticipating a cover-up, Steve's protestations, the lack of evidence, and the overly convenient flare were all signs that he was right. For the officer who came in doubting UFO stories, the same signs pointed to a more mundane explanation. Just because you're right doesn't mean you aren't biased.

To be fair, the positive test strategy isn't necessarily a bad way to test a hunch—after all, just looking for something you expect to find doesn't mean you'll find it. Likewise, some resistance to unwelcome information is often a good idea. We're constantly being pelted with conflicting factual claims, and it can be hard to know which ones are worth listening to. If we did fairly assess—or worse, uncritically accept—every new fact that came our way, we might well become frozen by indecision, paralyzed by the bewilderment of constantly questioning our entire worldview.

The problem is that confirmation bias at its worst can help misguided beliefs linger on in our minds long after their best-before date. In a 1998 review of the literature, psychologist Raymond Nickerson had some harsh words for the bias. Of all the quirks, foibles, and biases in our thinking, confirmation bias might be one of the most pernicious, he suggested. Our other biases—connecting dots, seeking intentions, and looking for big causes to explain big events, for instance—might not be much of a problem if we were in the habit of questioning our intuition, after all. Confirmation bias can lock our gut reaction in place. "One is led to wonder whether the bias, by itself, might account for a significant fraction of the disputes, altercations, and misunderstandings that occur among individuals, groups, and nations," Nickerson concluded. Think about the last time you had a difference of opinion with someone. Did you manage to change his or her mind? Did you change *your* mind? Did you consider the possibility that the confirmation bias was pushing both ways?

Why do we have such a hard time changing our minds? It's not because we're stupid. Studies have found no relationship between intelligence and susceptibility to confirmation bias. Neither is it because we're simply ill-informed. You might expect that the biggest differences of opinion would be found among people who know the least about the topic in question, but in fact, it's people who are the most scientifically and politically knowledgeable who tend to be the most polarized on topics like the reality of climate change and death panels. Our beliefs come first; we make up reasons for them as we go along. Being smarter or having access to more information doesn't necessarily make us less susceptible to faulty beliefs. Sometimes it just makes us better able to explain away unpalatable facts.

As Benjamin Franklin wryly observed, "so convenient a thing is it to be a reasonable creature, since it enables us to find or make a reason for everything one has a mind to."

Epilogue: Only Human

At the Bilderberg Fringe Festival I got talking with a born-again Christian. He was standing discreetly off to the side of the field, next to a sign urging people to accept Jesus into their lives. When he quoted Bible verses his tone of voice became animated and resolute. Otherwise, he was quiet and contemplative and a little wistful. He struck me as an outsider in a field full of outsiders.

It is his Christian duty to hold leaders accountable, and to spread the word of God while he's at it, he told me. In terms of believing the Bilderbergers are secretly controlling world affairs, though, he was one of the most reserved people I spoke to. When I asked what he thought the delegates were up to, he said, "I wouldn't really like to comment. I just don't know enough basically. I'd be speculating. I'm not here to speculate really, I'm here to preach absolute truth from the word of God, so I leave that to others." The allegations against Bilderberg are certainly grave, he said, but he just wanted the truth to be known one way or the other.

I asked how he came to be born again. "I had a religious upbringing in the Anglo-Catholic Church of England. But I never found Christ there," he said. "Then I went off into the world, thirty years going down the road of hedonism. I was doing quite well in my career as a graphic designer and I ended up working in the States for a short while, and all my friends thought, Wow, he's doing well." But the work was unfulfilling, he told me. And he had a drinking problem. "I'd never been so miserable in my life. Earning all this money in this prestigious place in California in this top agency. Never been so miserable in my entire life."

Then he said something that I think rings true for us all. "The world made no sense. I was out of control, and thoroughly lacking any reason *why*—where have I come from, what am I doing here, and what's my destiny? Those are very fundamental questions that we all need to have answers to. If you don't have the answer to those questions, any certain truth on those questions, your life is without any foundation. Yes, you can obscure that for a while with parties and whatever else you get up to. Even with *this* movement"—he surveyed the field full of Bilderberg Fringe Festival attendees, with their strongly worded placards and meditation circles and ironic T-shirts. "They get busy with things, they can busy themselves to hide that. But it's still there underneath, the gnawing emptiness."

Most of the time it's not so dramatic. It doesn't take a full-blown existential crisis to get us looking for meaning and answers and certainty. But even on our most mundane days, we're all looking for answers, in one way or another. Some people find solace in the Bible. Some try to convert their PC-using friends to Mac. Some gather in a field to shout at a hotel they think is hosting the secret rulers of the world. Some read books about why those other people are probably wrong.

Conspiracy theories resonate with our brain's foibles. But that doesn't make conspiracy theories psychologically aberrant or unique. Just the opposite. As we've seen, the same biases and quirks that can lead us to buy into a conspiracy theory shape our thinking in all sorts of ways, from how we roll a die to how we interpret a barroom altercation to which side we favor in a far-flung conflict between nations.

Now and again, there are even uncanny echoes of conspiracism in the thinking of conspiracy debunkers. In Chapter 7 we saw that conspiracy theories tap into archetypal narratives about good versus evil. But conspiracy theorists don't have a monopoly on apocalyptic alarmism. In the eyes of some fervent debunkers, as Peter Knight has pointed out, conspiracism itself becomes "a demonized and reified entity on which most of the ills of history can be blamed." David Aaronovitch, for instance, warns readers of *Voodoo Histories* that "the Internet has created shadow armies" of conspiracy theorists "whose size and power are unknowable." Daniel Pipes paints conspiracism as a contagious disease, which "manages to insinuate itself in the most alert and intelligent minds, so excluding it amounts to a perpetual struggle." Jonathan Kay worries that the Age of Reason is in imminent peril of succumbing to the irrationality of 9/11 Truthers. Francis Wheen lamented that "mumbo-jumbo" has already "conquered the world." Even among people endeavoring to rid the world of faulty beliefs, the lure of painting in black and white, casting the world in terms of "us versus them," is apparently hard to resist.

My aim with this book was to break down this false division. There is no "us versus them." *They* are us. We are *them*. By painting conspiracism as some bizarre psychological tick that blights the minds of a handful of paranoid kooks, we smugly absolve ourselves of the faulty thinking we see so readily in others. But we're doing the same thing as conspiracists who blame all of society's ills on some small shadowy cabal. And we're wrong. Conspiracy-thinking is ubiquitous, because it's a product, in part, of how all of our minds are working all the time. If three people were stranded on a desert island, it wouldn't be long before each found him–or herself wondering if the other two were up to something behind their back.

I'm not saying that conspiracy theories ought to be ignored or embraced across the board. As we saw in Chapter 2, some conspiracy theories can lead to devastating consequences. Some can have more subtle, insidious effects. We should be wary of conspiracy theories that scapegoat vulnerable people and incite violence, and that foster mistaken ideas about issues that can have grave consequences for us all, such as vaccines and climate change. But I don't think conspiracy-thinking in general is an affliction in need of eradication, either. Most people don't base important life decisions on conspiracy theories. And sometimes it might turn out the conspiracists were on to something. Sometimes people really do get up to no good behind closed doors. Leaders need to be held accountable. Sometimes paranoia is prudent.

By shining a light on how our biases can shape our beliefs, my hope isn't to debunk any particular theory, much less to castigate conspiracy-thinking across the board. My hope is that we might scrutinize our intuition, ask ourselves why we think what we think. Are we being prudently paranoid? Or are our biases getting the best of us?

Not that our brain's biases and quirks and shortcuts are all bad, of course. Without them, we would constantly be taking to our beds in a Victorian swoon, unsure of anything, unable to make the simplest decision, constantly having to reevaluate our entire worldview. Our brain works this way for a reason: to help us muddle our way through life in an uncertain—and sometimes treacherous—world. Our biases make us what we are: human. Astoundingly, confoundingly, imperfectly, brilliantly, human.

Except those of us who are intergalactic shape-shifting aliens.

References and Notes

Introduction: Down the Rabbit Hole

Page

10 **women are just as conspiracy-minded as men:** Numerous studies have analyzed gender differences in conspiracism and found none, e.g. Uscinski, J. E., & Parent, J. M. (2014). *American Conspiracy Theories*. Oxford University Press. pp. 82–83.

10 **slightly more high school dropouts than college graduates:** Some studies have found no reliable relationship between education and conspiracism. Some, however, have found a slight negative correlation, e.g., Ibid. pp. 86–87.

10 **Senior citizens . . . Millennials:** Most studies have found no reliable association between endorsement of conspiracy theories and age. Ibid.

10 **Louis Tomlinson and Harry Styles . . . are secretly an item:** At the time of writing, this YouTube video, titled "Top 30 Iconic Larry Stylinson Moments," has more than a million and a half views: https://www.youtube.com/watch?v=EGQZk9F6Dxs

10 **around half of Americans . . . the 9/11 attacks:** According to various polls conducted in 2004, 2006, and 2007 by Zogby, Scripps Howard/Ohio University, and CBS/*New York Times*. See http://www.aei.org/files/2013/11/06/-public-opinion-on-conspiracy-theories_181649218739.pdf

10 **Almost four in ten . . . climate change is a scientific fraud:** http://www.publicpolicypolling.com/pdf/2011/PPP_Release_National_ConspiracyTheories_040213.pdf

10 **Something like a third . . . hiding evidence of aliens:** According to 2006 and 2007 polls by Scripps Howard/Ohio University. See http://www.aei.org/files/2013/11/06/-public-opinion-on-conspiracy-theories_181649218739.pdf

10   **More than a quarter . . . the New World Order:**
      http://www.publicpolicypolling.com/pdf/2011/PPP_
      Release_National_ConspiracyTheories_040213.pdf

10   **In a 2013 survey:** Ibid.

11   **According to a 2011 Pew Research Center survey . . .
      people in various Middle Eastern countries:** http://
      www.pewglobal.org/2011/07/21/muslim-western-tensions-
      persist/

11   **Four out of ten Russians:** http://translate.google.com/
      translate?hl=en&sl=ru&tl=en&u=http%3A%2F%2Fwww.
      rbcdaily.ru%2Fpolitics%2F562949980129006&sandbox=1

11   **"the assassination of Indira Gandhi is the doing of a
      vast conspiracy":** Moscovici, S. (1987). The conspiracy
      mentality. In Graumann, C. F., & Moscovici, S. (Eds.).
      Changing Conceptions of Conspiracy. Springer. p. 151.

11   **in Brazil, a popular conspiracy theory . . . invade the
      Amazon rain forest:** Mitchell, S. T. (2010). Paranoid
      styles of nationalism after the Cold War. In Kelly, J. D.,
      Jauregui, B., Mitchell, S. T., & Walton, J. (Eds.). *Anthropology
      and Global Counterinsurgency.* University of Chicago Press.
      pp. 89–104.

12   **In a recent experiment . . . something that they felt
      ambivalent about:** Van Harreveld, F., Rutjens, B. T.,
      Schneider, I. K., Nohlen, H. U., & Keskinis, K. (2014). In
      doubt and disorderly: Ambivalence promotes compensatory
      perceptions of order. *Journal of Experimental Psychology:
      General, 143*(4), 1666–1676.

14   **In another experiment . . . students were asked to
      imagine they had been passed over for a promotion:**
      Ibid.

14   **In another recent study . . . rate how plausible they
      found a handful of popular conspiracy theories:**
      Swami, V., Voracek, M., Stieger, S., Tran, U. S., & Furnham,
      A. (2014). Analytic thinking reduces belief in conspiracy
      theories. *Cognition, 133*(3), 572–585.

15   **As David Eagleman points out . . . there is a
      complicated network of machinery hidden just
      beneath your skin:** Eagleman, D. (2011). *Incognito.*
      Pantheon. p. 1.

15   **made up of billions of specialized cells:** Ibid.

16   "your consciousness is like a tiny stowaway on a transatlantic steamship": Ibid. p. 4.

16   Jonathan Haidt likened consciousness to a rider on the back of an elephant: Haidt, J. (2006). *The Happiness Hypothesis*. Basic Books. p. 4.

16   consciousness "would be a supporting character who believes herself to be the hero": Kahneman, D. (2011). *Thinking, Fast and Slow*. Farrar, Straus and Giroux. p. 31.

17   Michael Billig . . . ; warned that, when it comes to conspiracism, "it is easy to overemphasise its eccentricities": Billig, M. (1978). *Fascists*. Academic Press. p. 314.

Chapter 1: The Age of Conspiracy

Page

19   "This is the age of conspiracy . . . the age of connections, links, secret relationships": DeLillo, D. (1989). *Running Dog*. Vintage. p. 111.

19   "other centuries have only dabbled in conspiracy": Moscovici, S. (1987). The conspiracy mentality. In Graumann, C. F., & Moscovici, S. (Eds.). *Changing Conceptions of Conspiracy*. Springer. p. 153.

19   Political scientist Jodi Dean began . . . by asserting: http://muse.jhu.edu/journals/theory_and_event/v004/4.3r_dean.html

19   a 2015 study . . . dubbed this the "Age of Misinformation": Bessi, A., Coletto, M., Davidescu, G. A., Scala, A., Caldarelli, G., & Quattrociocchi, W. (2015). Science vs conspiracy: Collective narratives in the age of misinformation. *PLOS ONE*, 10(2). e0118093

19   For journalist Jonathan Kay . . . "a wide range of political paranoiacs": Kay, J. (2011). *Among the Truthers*. HarperCollins. p. xix.

20   letters to the editor are a good barometer of public opinion: Sigelman, L., & Walkosz, B. J. (1992). Letters to the editor as a public opinion thermometer: The Martin Luther King holiday vote in Arizona. *Social Science Quarterly*, 73(4), 938–946.

20   **Uscinski and Parent set about analyzing . . . letters
      to the editor:** Uscinski, J. E., & Parent, J. M. (2014).
      American Conspiracy Theories. Oxford University Press.
      pp. 110-129.

22   **July 19, C.E. 64 . . . reduced to rubble and ash:**
      Dando-Collins, S. (2010). *The Great Fire of Rome*. Da Capo
      Press. pp. 86–98.

22   **According to the Roman historian Tacitus . . .
      "nobody dared fight the flames":** http://www.
      eyewitnesstohistory.com/rome.htm

22   **"Pretending to be disgusted":** quoted in Dando-
      Collins, S. (2010). *The Great Fire of Rome*. Da Capo Press.
      pp. 3–4.

23   **"Nero set his heart . . . the Capture of Rome":**
      http://penelope.uchicago.edu/Thayer/E/Roman/Texts/
      Cassius_Dio/62*.html

23   **According to Tacitus, "Nero fastened the guilt":** quoted
      in Dando-Collins, S. (2010). *The Great Fire of Rome*. Da
      Capo Press. p. 8.

24   **Cassius Dio described the deed . . . "rent him limb
      from limb":** http://penelope.uchicago.edu/Thayer/E/
      Roman/Texts/Cassius_Dio/1*.html

24   **Joseph Roisman points out . . . ancient Athens was
      riddled with "tales of plotting":** Roisman, J. (2006).
      The Rhetoric of Conspiracy in Ancient Athens. University of
      California Press. p. 1.

25   **Famine-struck peasants often saw their plight . . .
      "the politics of their own day":** Coward, B., & Swann, J.
      (2004). *Conspiracies and Conspiracy Theory in Early Modern
      Europe*. Ashgate. p. 2.

25   **Samuel Pepys noted . . . "that there is a plot in it":**
      http://www.pepys.info/1666/1666sep.html

25   **some even drew "an odious parallel between his
      Majesty and Nero":** quoted in Hanson, N. (2001). *The
      Dreadful Judgement*. Doubleday. p. 257.

25   **A Frenchman, Robert Hubert, was soon arrested . . .
      delighted spectators:** Ibid. pp. 271–302.

26   **Illuminati panic:** Except where otherwise noted,
      historical details and quotes about Adam Weishaupt, the
      Illuminati, the French Revolution, and Augustin de Barruel

are from Roberts, J. M. (1972). *The Mythology of the Secret Societies*. Secker & Warburg. pp. 118–202.

29   **"Even the most horrid deeds . . . were the offspring of deep-thought villainy":** quoted in Byford, J. (2011). *Conspiracy Theories*. Palgrave Macmillan. p. 1.

29   **According to Robison, the Illuminati leaders "disbelieved *every word* that they uttered":** Robison, J. (1798). *Proofs of a Conspiracy* (3rd Edition). Dobson & Corbett. p. 13.

30   **"Illuminati puppets . . . traumatic mind-control performances":** http://www.pakalertpress.com/2013/10/28/top-10-illuminati-puppets-and-masters-of-entertainment/

30   **"I know who the real Illuminati are":** http://www.theguardian.com/music/2014/dec/21/madonna-album-hack-living-state-terror

30   **Seymour Lipset and Earl Raab speculated . . . two elements:** Lipset, S. M., & Raab, E. (1973). *The Politics of Unreason*. Harper & Row. p. 221.

31   **The *Protocols of the Learned Elders of Zion*:** https://archive.org/details/TheProtocolsOfTheLearnedEldersOfZion

32   **As Richard Levy put it . . . "veritable Rosetta stone of history":** Segel, B. W. (1995). *A Lie and a Libel*. University of Nebraska Press. p. 7.

32   **Observant readers needed only to fill in the blanks:** Segel, B. W. (1995). *A Lie and a Libel*. University of Nebraska Press. p. 12.

32   **"the abandoned sensuousness of sliding notes" and . . . "indecent dancing":** https://archive.org/details/TheInternationalJew_655

33   **distributing chewing gum:** Ben-Itto, H. (2005). *The Lie that Wouldn't Die*. Vallentine Mitchell. p. 371.

33   **encouraging prostitution . . . dog exhibitions:** Wistrich, R. (1985). *Hitler's Apocalypse*. Weidenfeld & Nicolson. p. 181

33   **One scholar estimated in 1939 that . . . the *Protocols* was second only the Bible:** cited in Partridge, C., & Geaves, R. (2007). Antisemitism, conspiracy culture, christianity, and Islam. In Lewis, J. R., & Hammer, O. (Eds.). *The Invention of Sacred Tradition*. Cambridge University Press. p. 75.

33   **"atrociously written piece of reactionary
        balderdash":** Cohn, N. (2005). *Warrant for Genocide.* Serif.
        p. 81.

33   **Saint John Chrysostom . . . denounced Jews as
        baby-killing devil worshipers:** http://legacy.fordham.
        edu/halsall/source/chrysostom-jews6.asp

33-4   **In 1215, Pope Innocent III . . . mass burnings of
        their holy books:** Rader, J. (1999). *The Jew in the Medieval
        World.* Hebrew Union College Press. pp. 153–158.

34   **the Jewish Talmud was . . . a testament to the
        truth of Christian teaching:** Woolf, J. (2011). The
        Devil's hoofs. In Landes, R., & Katz, S. (Eds.). *The
        Paranoid Apocalypse.* NYU Press. p. 52.

34   **The worst of the pogroms was in Strasbourg:**
        Rader, J. (1999). *The Jew in the Medieval World.* Hebrew
        Union College Press. pp. 149–158.

35   **the "blood libel":** Ibid. pp. 135–141.

35   **Jews were no longer enemies of God, but enemies
        of man:** Heil, J. (2011). Thomas of Monmouth and the
        Protocols of the Sages of Narbonne. In Landes, R., &
        Katz, S. (Eds.). *The Paranoid Apocalypse.* NYU Press. p. 69.

35   **a new word, antisemitism, was coined:** Segel, B. W.
        (1995). *A Lie and a Libel.* University of Nebraska Press. p.
        7. Note: Except when quoting the writing of others, I
        refer to "antisemitism," rather than the more common
        formulation, "anti-Semitism." In his preface to *A Lie and
        a Libel* (p. x), Richard S. Levy explains that *anti-Semitism*
        is a pernicious misnomer. For one thing, "it does not
        apply to the majority of Semites, that is, the Arab peoples."
        Moreover, the hyphen, upper-case "S," and exclusive
        application to Jewish people give rise to a myth.
        "'Semitism,' a collection of exclusively negative traits
        comprising a monolithic Jewish essence, existed only in
        the minds of the enemies of Jews. Jews and their allies
        who opposed the antisemites were defending not this
        imaginary 'Semitism' but their human rights."

35   **It was first published . . . in the Russian newspaper
        Znamia:** Cohn, N. (2005). *Warrant for Genocide.* Serif. p. 118.

35   **"I cannot get the public to treat the *Protocols*
        seriously":** Ibid. p. 124.

36   The London *Times* prevaricated, "Are they a
        forgery?": Ibid. p. 168.

36   a German scholar, Joseph Stanjek, had pointed
        out: cited in Aaronovitch, D. (2009). *Voodoo Histories*.
        Jonathan Cape. p. 31.

36   a "scandal-mongering writer of trashy novels":
        Segel, B. W. (1995). *A Lie and a Libel*. University of
        Nebraska Press. p. 66.

36   "a clumsy piece of blood-curdling fiction of the
        dime-novel variety": Bernstein, H. (1921). *The History
        of a Lie*. Ogilvie Publishing Company. p. 18.

36   "Every substantive statement contained in the
        Protocols": Ibid. p. 17.

36-7   Philip Graves, correspondent for the London
        Times in Istanbul, began his exposé: http://
        emperors-clothes.com/antisem/graves-text.htm

38   Princess Katerina Radziwill . . . provided more
        pieces of the puzzle: Ben-Itto, H. (2005). *The Lie that
        Wouldn't Die*. Vallentine Mitchell. pp. 74–83.

38   An editorial . . . might "be allowed to pass into
        oblivion": http://gfisher.org/protocols.htm

Chapter 2: What's the Harm?

Page

39   Shortly before eleven o'clock on a sunny
        Saturday morning in June 1922: Evans, R. J. (2012).
        Prophet in a Tuxedo. *London Review of Books, 34*(22),
        20-22.

39   on the witness stand . . . Rathenau was an Elder of
        Zion: Cohn, N. (2005). *Warrant for Genocide*. Serif.
        pp. 160–161.

40   Adolf Hitler . . . had a monument to Rathenau's
        killers erected: http://www.spiegel.de/international/
        germany/memorial-to-far-right-killers-of-jewish-
        minister-walter-rathenau-a-846604.html

40   leading Nazis offered heartfelt eulogies:
        Loewenberg, P. (1995). *Fantasy and Reality in History*.
        Oxford University Press. p. 114.

40   mass book burnings . . . "the era of extreme Jewish
      intellectualism": http://www.historyplace.com/worldwar2/
      triumph/tr-bookburn.htm

41   "though I came from a fairly cosmopolitan family":
      Master, W. (1974). *Hitler's Letters and Notes*. Harper & Row.
      p. 107.

41   "Hitler heard the call of a kindred spirit": Cohn, N.
      (2005). *Warrant for Genocide*. Serif. p. 213.

41   He began citing the *Protocols* in speeches as early as
      1921: Kellogg, M. (2005). *The Russian Roots of Nazism*.
      Cambridge University Press. p. 75.

41   Hitler kept a large photograph of Henry Ford . . .
      "heroic American, Heinrich Ford": Segel, B. W.
      (1995). *A Lie and a Libel*. University of Nebraska Press. p. 27.

41   Hitler's 1924 manifesto, *Mein Kampf* . . . lavishes
      praise on the *Protocols*: Cohn, N. (2005). *Warrant for
      Genocide*. Serif. pp. 200–201.

41   they soon added the *Protocols* to the national school
      curriculum: Ibid. p. 45.

41   "it is the duty of every German": Ibid. p. 221.

42   "to restore Germany to freedom and power":
      Frymier, J. R., & Roaden, A. L. (2003). *Cultures of States*.
      Scarecrow Press. p. 88.

42   "reduced to the status of outlaws": Wistrich, R.
      (1985). *Hitler's Apocalypse*. Weidenfeld & Nicolson. p. 87.

42   "Has it not struck you how the Jew is the exact
      opposite of the German": Rauschning, H. (1940). *The
      Voice of Destruction*. Pelican. p. 238.

42   "There are two possibilities": quoted in Redles, D.
      (2011). The turning point. In Landes, R., & Katz, S. (Eds.).
      The Paranoid Apocalypse. NYU Press. p. 125.

42   "In the course of my life I have very often been a
      prophet": https://archive.org/details/SpeechOfJan.301939

43   "It is untrue that I or anyone else in Germany
      wanted the war in 1939": http://www.historylearning
      site.co.uk/adolf_hitler_political_testament.htm

43   "a preposterous fabrication": Cohn, N. (2005). *Warrant
      for Genocide*. Serif. p 213.

43   "appeal to all the paranoid and destructive
      potentialities in human beings": Ibid. p. xiv.

43   **Anders Breivik ... conspiracy to destroy Western civilization:** http://www.irr.org.uk/pdf2/ERA_Briefing Paper5.pdf

44   **Tamerlan Tsarnaev . . . "this is a good book":** http://www.bostonglobe.com/metro/2013/08/07/unlikely-friendship/xQao9NHjkUvtvhTcKIuwCL/story.html

44   **"the government is implying mind control":** http://www.newyorker.com/books/page-turner/the-language-and-literature-of-jared-loughner

44   **James Wenneker von Brunn . . . "the Holocaust is a lie":** http://www.cbsnews.com/news/von-brunn-obama-was-created-by-jews/

44   **On the morning of April 19, 1995, McVeigh:** Michel, L., & Herbeck, D. (2001). *American Terrorist*. ReganBooks. pp. 223–246.

44   **McVeigh was wearing a T-shirt with a picture of Abraham Lincoln:** Ibid. p. 3.

45   **"planning a massive raid on gun owners":** Ibid. p. 161.

45   **"declared war on a government that he felt had declared war on its own people":** http://www.vanityfair.com/news/2001/09/mcveigh200109

45   **imagining that a religious sect called the Branch Davidians was stockpiling illegal weapons:** As Malcolm Gladwell notes in an article for the *New Yorker*, the Bureau of Alcohol, Tobacco, and Firearms sent an undercover agent into the compound to look for evidence that the Branch Davidians were illegally converting firearms from semiautomatic to automatic. He found no evidence. Gladwell, M. "Sacred and Profane," *The New Yorker*, 31 March 2014.

45   **and abusing children:** According to a Department of Justice investigation after the events at Waco, "historical evidence suggested that Koresh had engaged in child physical and sexual abuse over a long period of time prior to the ATF shootout on February 28. This evidence was insufficient to establish probable cause to indict or proof beyond a reasonable doubt to convict, but it was sufficient to be relevant to the decision making process involving the proposed tear gas plan . . . There was no direct evidence

indicating that Koresh engaged in any physical or sexual abuse of children during the standoff." http://www.justice. gov/publications/waco/report-deputy-attorney-general-events-waco-texas-child-abuse

45   Jamie Bartlett and Carl Miller . . . more than fifty extremist groups: http://www.demos.co.uk/publications/ thepowerofunreason

46   a survey designed to reveal . . . potentially violent tendencies: Uscinski, J. E., & Parent, J. M. (2014). *American Conspiracy Theories*. Oxford University Press. pp. 97–100.

46   as journalist Chip Berlet pointed out: http://www. publiceye.org/conspire/toxic2democracy/

46   "if only 1 percent of the population agreed with the statement": Uscinski, J. E., & Parent, J. M. (2014). *American Conspiracy Theories*. Oxford University Press. p. 99.

47   "takes children on a journey": http://www. barnesandnoble.com/w/melanies-marvelous-measles-stephanie-messenger/1113910333?ean=9781466938892&it m=1&usri=melanie%27s+marvelous+measles

47   "vested interests" in selling "some potion or vaccine": http://www.theguardian.com/books/2015/ feb/10/melanies-marvelous-measles-anti-vaccination-bad-amazon-reviews-us-outbreak

47   Dahl's own feelings about measles vaccination, which he wrote about in 1986: http://www.roalddahl. com/roald-dahl/timeline/1960s/november-1962

47   In 1962 . . . practically everyone caught the measles: Orenstein, W. A., Papania, M. J., & Wharton, M. E. (2004). Measles elimination in the United States. *Journal of Infectious Diseases, 189*(Supplement 1), S1–S3.

47   When a vaccine was . . . plummeted by 98 percent: http://www.cdc.gov/vaccines/pubs/pinkbook/meas. html

48   The World Health Organization estimates . . . saved more than fifteen million lives around the world: http://www.who.int/mediacentre/factsheets/fs286/en/

48   In the first year, a million children were vaccinated: Boyce, T. (2007). *Health, Risk and News: The MMR Vaccine and the Media*. Peter Lang Publishing. p. 2.

48   Andrew Wakefield, along with a team of colleagues,
        published a study: Wakefield, A. J., Murch, S. H., Anthony,
        A., Linnell, J., Casson, D. M., Malik, M., . . . Walker-Smith, J.
        A. (1998). Ileal-lymphoid–nodular hyperplasia, non-specific
        colitis, and pervasive developmental disorder in children.
        The Lancet, 351(9103), 637–41.

48-9   the panic that followed Wakefield's alarming
        announcement . . . drastically lower vaccination
        rates: Boyce, T. (2007). *Health, Risk and News: The MMR
        Vaccine and the Media.* Peter Lang Publishing. pp. 3–6.

49   in Dublin . . . three died: McBrien, J., Murphy, J.,
        Gill, D., Cronin, M., O'Donovan, C., & Cafferkey, M.
        T. (2003). Measles outbreak in Dublin, 2000. *Pediatric
        Infectious Disease Journal, 22*(7), 580–584.

49   A thirteen-year-old boy died in England in 2006:
        http://news.bbc.co.uk/2/hi/uk_news/england/
        4871728.stm

49   In 2008, measles was declared endemic in the
        United Kingdom: http://www.eurosurveillance.org/
        viewarticle.aspx?articleid=18919

49   In 2012 there were more than two thousand cases:
        http://www.theguardian.com/society/2013/feb/08/
        measles-outbreak-hits-18-year-high

49   In 2013, another outbreak in Wales infected more
        than a thousand people: http://www.wales.nhs.uk/
        sitesplus/888/news/29688

49   Investigative journalist Brian Deer uncovered
        evidence: http://briandeer.com/mmr/lancet-summary.
        htm

50   studies . . . found no association whatsoever
        between the MMR vaccine and autism: Gerber, J. S.,
        & Offit, P. A. (2009). Vaccines and autism: A tale of shifting
        hypotheses. *Clinical Infectious Diseases, 48*(4), 456–461.

50   thimerosal . . . Studies have shown this claim to
        be mistaken: Ibid.

50   According to a 2009 survey, more than one in ten
        American parents: cited in Largent, M. A. (2012).
        Vaccine: The Debate in America. Johns Hopkins University
        Press. p. 32

50   **"father of the anti-vaccine movement"**: http://www.
      newsweek.com/2015/02/20/andrew-wakefield-father-
      anti-vaccine-movement-sticks-his-story-305836.html

51   **The World Health Organization estimates . . . die
      each year from whooping cough**: http://www.who.
      int/immunization/topics/pertussis/en/

51   **In 1973, a British doctor called John Wilson . . . six
      hundred children died in the outbreak**: Offit, P. (2011).
      Deadly Choices. Basic Books. pp. 13–17.

52   **a "pre-emptive strike"**: http://www.thelancet.com/
      journals/lancet/article/PIIS0140-6736%2805%2979088-7/
      fulltext

52   **Common symptoms of smallpox**: Tucker, J. B. (2002).
      Scourge. Grove Press.

53   **The vaccine was discovered by Edward Jenner**:
      Riedel, S. (2005). Edward Jenner and the history of
      smallpox and vaccination. *Baylor University Medical Center
      Proceedings, 18*(1), 21–25.

53   **He dabbled in things like fossil collecting, hot air
      ballooning, and growing oversized vegetables**: Allen, A.
      (2007). *Vaccine*. W. W. Norton & Company. pp. 47–48.

53   **sporadic opposition to the vaccine**: Ibid. pp. 56–57.

54   **Compulsory Vaccination Acts**: Wolfe, R. M., & Sharp,
      L. K. (2002). Anti-vaccinationists past and present. *British
      Medical Journal, 325*(7361), 430–432.

54   **how little the arguments have changed over the
      centuries**: Offit, P. (2011). *Deadly Choices*. Basic Books.
      pp. 111–125.

54   **"Doctors want power to kill disabled babies"**: http://
      vaccineawakening.blogspot.com/2006/11/colleges-royal-
      college-of-obstetricians.html

55   **"poison of adders, the blood, entrails, and excretion
      of bats, toads and suckling whelps"**: quoted in Offit,
      P. (2011). *Deadly Choices*. Basic Books. p. 182.

55   **"green our vaccines" . . . "toxins"**: https://www.
      sciencebasedmedicine.org/toxic-myths-about-vaccines/

55   **as Paul Offit has pointed out, the current concerns
      about MMR . . . are about as plausible**: Offit, P. (2011).
      Deadly Choices. Basic Books. p. 115.

56   **"this infection scare is a sham"**: Ibid. p. 118.

56   **"one of the biggest money making schemes"**: http://
        vaccineawakening.blogspot.com/2006_08_01_archive.html
        In parts of Pakistan . . . ploy to sterilize Muslims:
        http://wwwnc.cdc.gov/eid/article/15/6/09-0087_article

56   **more than sixty polio workers . . . since 2012**:
        http://www.bbc.com/news/world-asia-30200222

56   **The CIA . . . fake vaccination program**: www.
        theguardian.com/world/2011/jul/11/cia-fake-
        vaccinations-osama-bin-ladens-dna

57   **reading anti-vaccine conspiracy theories can
        reduce parents' willingness to have their children
        vaccinated**: Jolley, D., & Douglas, K. M. (2014). The
        effects of anti-vaccine conspiracy theories on vaccination
        intentions. *PLOS ONE*, *9*(2), e89177.

57   **people walking out of the showing said they were
        less likely to vote**: Butler, L. D., Koopman, C., &
        Zimbardo, P. G. (1995). The psychological impact of
        viewing the film J.F.K.: Emotions, beliefs, and political
        behavioral intentions. *Political Psychology, 16*(2), 237–257.

58   **surveyed Americans shortly after the 2012
        presidential election**: Uscinski, J. E., & Parent, J. M.
        (2014). *American Conspiracy Theories*. Oxford University
        Press. pp. 94–97.

59   **an agent ... repeatedly emailed his superiors**: Wright,
        L. (2006). *The Looming Tower*. Knopf Doubleday. p. 311.

59   **"Conspiracy theorists are correct about one thing"**:
        http://www.publiceye.org/conspire/toxic2democracy/

Chapter 3: What is a Conspiracy Theory?

Page

62   **defining the term** *conspiracy theory* **has been likened
        to attempting to define pornography**: Byford.
        J. (2011). *Conspiracy Theories*. Palgrave Macmillan. p. 31.

62–3   **Richard Hofstadter . . . talked about conspiracy
        theories as a "style" of explanation**: Hofstadter, R.
        (1964). The paranoid style in American politics. *Harper's
        Magazine, 229*(1374), 77–86.

63   **"If you're down at a bar in the slums"**: http://
        www.chomsky.info/interviews/20040217.htm

63   **George W. Bush . . . urged his fellow Americans never to "tolerate outrageous conspiracy theories":** http://www.un.org/webcast/ga/56/statements/011110usaE.htm

64   **"To be sure, wacko conspiracy theories do exist":** Parenti, M. (1996). *Dirty Truths.* City Lights Books. p. 172.

64   **"I am not a conspiracy theorist. Spare me the ravers. Spare me the plots":** http://www.independent.co.uk/voices/commentators/fisk/robert-fisk-even-i-question-the-truth-about-911-462904.html

64   **As Jovan Byford points out:** Byford. J. (2011). *Conspiracy Theories.* Palgrave Macmillan. pp. 26–29.

64   **According to historian Daniel Pipes's definition:** Pipes, D. (1997). *Conspiracy.* The Free Press. pp. 21–22.

64   **Cass Sunstein and Adrian Vermeule made the same point:** Sunstein, C. R., & Vermeule, A. (2009). Conspiracy theories: Causes and cures. *The Journal of Political Philosophy, 17*(2), 202–227.

64   **an "intuitive understanding of how things do not happen":** Aaronovitch, D. (2010). *Voodoo Histories.* Jonathan Cape. p. 7.

65   **"a conspiracy theory is a proposal about a conspiracy that may or may not be true":** Olmsted, K. S. (2011). *Real Enemies.* Oxford University Press. p. 3.

65   **According to another account . . . Nixon wasn't behind the Watergate conspiracy at all:** http://www.reformation.org/rockefeller-file.html

66   **conspiracy theories . . . purport to** *reveal* **hitherto undiscovered plots:** Fenster, M. (2008). *Conspiracy Theories.* University of Minnesota Press. pp. 93–117.

66   **The term originally referred to ships literally hoisting a flag:** deHaven-Smith, L. (2013). *Conspiracy Theory in America.* University of Texas Press. pp. 225–226.

66–7   **"We could blow up a U.S. ship in Guantanamo Bay":** Bamford, J. (2001). *Body of Secrets.* Doubleday. p. 84.

68   **As Jesse Walker points out:** Walker, J. (2013). *United States of Paranoia.* Harper. p. 111.

68   **"there are two worlds":** Wood, M. J., & Douglas, K. M. (2013). "What about building 7?" A social psychological study of online discussion of 9/11

conspiracy theories. *Frontiers in Personality Science and Individual Differences,* 4(409).

69   **"A virtuoso conspiracy theorist turns black into white and white into black":** Pipes, D. (1996). *The Hidden Hand.* St. Martin's Press. p. 279.

69   **"Just look at us":** quoted in Icke, D. (2007). *The David Icke Guide to the Global Conspiracy (and How to End It).* David Icke Books.

69   **"Ladies and Gentlemen: Here the captain":** National Commission on Terrorist Attacks. (2011). *The 9/11 Commission Report.* W. W. Norton & Company. p. 12.

69   **"don't worry, we're going to do something":** http://www.tomburnettfoundation.org/transcript.html

70   **In fact, United 93 didn't crash at all:** http://911research. wtc7.net/reviews/loose_change/flight93.html

70   **failures "in imagination, policy, capabilities, and management":** National Commission on Terrorist Attacks. (2011). *The 9/11 Commission Report.* W. W. Norton & Company. p. 339.

70   **conspiracy theorists seem to have "startling faith in the capabilities of their enemies":** Pipes, D. (1997). *Conspiracy.* The Free Press. p. 44.

70   **Richard Hofstadter captured this element of the conspiracist style:** Hofstadter, R. (1964). The paranoid style in American politics. *Harper's Magazine,* 229(1374), 77–86.

71   **the conspiracy always seems to be "exactly as competent and powerful":** Collins, L. (2012). *Bullspotting.* Prometheus Books. p. 76.

71   **"It is already possible to know" ... David Ray Griffin told audiences:** Powell, M. "The Disbelievers," *The Washington Post,* 8 September 2006.

71–2 **Jones told passersby, "the government is carrying out terrorist attacks":** https://www.youtube.com/watch?v=YzCoIEn5n-Q

72   **"AN ASSOCIATION HAS BEEN FORMED for the express purpose":** Robison, J. (1798). *Proofs of a Conspiracy* (3rd Edition). Dobson & Corbett. p. 12.

72   **"As far as we are aware . . . hardly worth theorizing them":** Jane, E. A., & Fleming, C. (2014). *Modern Conspiracy.* Bloomsbury Academic. pp. 104–105.

72 They "have a prize worth cheating for": Uscinski, J. E., & Parent, J. M. (2014). *American Conspiracy Theories*. Oxford University Press. p. 45.

73 "all-encompassing expressions of organized evil": Jane, E. A., & Fleming, C. (2014). *Modern Conspiracy*. Bloomsbury Academic. p. 130.

73 "One could ironically say that [conspiracy theories] brought the Devil back": Zawadzki, P. (2011). "Jewish World Conspiracy" and the Question of Secular Religions: An Interpretative Perspective. In Landes, R., & Katz, S. (Eds.). *The Paranoid Apocalypse*. NYU Press. p. 107.

73 "We have become entranced by demonic power": Powell, M. "The Disbelievers," *The Washington Post*, 8 September 2006.

73 Richard Hofstadter noted the "heroic strivings": Hofstadter, R. (1964). The paranoid style in American politics. *Harper's Magazine, 229*(1374), 77–86.

73 "Conspiracy theorists do not see themselves as raconteurs of alluring stories": Byford, J. (2011). *Conspiracy Theories*. Palgrave Macmillan. p. 88.

74 At 4:54 Eastern Time: http://whatreallyhappened.com/WRHARTICLES/bbc_wtc7_videos.html

74 Conspiracy theories "*always* explain more than competing theories": Keeley, B. L. (1999). Of conspiracy theories. *Journal of Philosophy, 96*(3), p. 119.

75 only five percent of witnesses reported hearing four or more shots: http://www.skeptic.com/reading_room/jfk-conspiracy-theories-at-50-how-the-skeptics-got-it-wrong-and-why-it-matters/

76 "military areas" from which "any or all persons may be excluded": http://www.ourdocuments.gov/doc.php?flash=true&doc=74&page=transcript

76 "Unfortunately ... many of our people and some of our authorities": https://archive.org/stream/nationaldefensem29unit/nationaldefensem29unit_djvu.txt

76 illustrated by radio host Charles Goyette: http://forums.sherdog.com/forums/f54/popular-mechanics-9-11-author-grilled-talk-radio-422492

77 A 1967 CIA memo on the topic of Kennedy conspiracy theories: deHaven-Smith, L. (2013).

Conspiracy Theory in America. University of Texas Press. pp. 197–203.

77   **The assassination "actually had the hallmarks of true expertise":** Ibid. p. 113.

78   **what Peter Knight refers to as the "How-to-tell-if-your-neighbor-is-a-Communist" approach:** Knight, P. (2013). *Conspiracy Culture*. Routledge. p. 7.

78   **as Emma Jane and Chris Fleming point out, "conspiracies and conspiracy theories vary so dramatically":** Jane, E. A., & Fleming, C. (2014). *Modern Conspiracy*. Bloomsbury Academic. pp. 20–21.

78   **This tactic, according to psychologist Mike Wood, seems to have gained in popularity with the rise of the Internet:** Wood, M. J. (2013). Has the internet been good for conspiracy theorising? *PsyPAG Quarterly, 88*(3), 31–34.

78   **16 Questions on the Assassination:**   http://22november 1963.org.uk/bertrand-russell-16-questions-on-the-assassination

79   **"Imagine if neutrinos were not simply hard to detect, but actively sought to avoid detection!":** Keeley, B. L. (1999). Of conspiracy theories. *Journal of Philosophy, 96*(3). p. 120.

Chapter 4: Conspiracy Minded

Page

81   **On the Internet message board … suspicion was mounting:** Unfortunately the forum was taken offline when the TV channel went defunct in 2013. The two unattributed quotes are preserved on the conference organizer's blog: http://stephenlaw.blogspot.com/2011/09/just-to-remind-you-of-this-upcoming.html. I included the quote from Angryhead in the talk I gave at the conference, which is available on YouTube: https://www.youtube.com/watch?v=V6s_Jw3RU9g

81   **Ian R. Crane, according to his website:** http://www.ianrcrane.com/

82   **you can't stop a speeding train just by standing in
        its way:** Vallée, J. (1991). *Revelations*. Ballantine Books.
        p. 81.

83   **"was planned and orchestrated by the government
        itself":** deHaven-Smith, L. (2013). *Conspiracy Theory in
        America*. University of Texas Press. p. 21.

83   **According to Bob Blaskiewicz ... idea has been
        around since the late 1990s:** Also counting against
        deHaven-Smith's theory that the CIA pushed the term
        "conspiracy theory" as a smear, Blaskiewicz points to
        examples of the phrase being used to dismiss claims as
        outlandish dating back as far as 1870—long before the
        CIA came into being. http://www.csicop.org/
        specialarticles/show/nope_it_was_always_already_
        wrong

84   **passing around unconfirmed rumors:** http://www.
        businessinsider.com/sandy-hook-shooting-media-
        inaccuracies-2012-12

84   **the distraught parents of murdered children were
        "crisis actors":** http://www.snopes.com/politics/
        guns/newtown.asp

84   **President Obama faked tears during a press
        conference:** http://www.infowars.com/obama-wipes-
        away-fake-tears/

84   **One theorist eventually sent a letter to Adam
        Lanza's father:** Solomon, A. "The Reckoning," *The
        New Yorker*, 17 March 2014.

84–5   **Alex Jones tweeted, "Our hearts go out":** http://
        www.thewire.com/national/2013/04/what-is-false-
        flag-attack-boston-bombing/64260/

85   **Online, thousands of people . . . looking for
        anomalies:** http://www.snopes.com/politics/conspiracy/
        boston.asp

85   **Writing for *The Wire*, Philip Bump reported:**
        http://www.thewire.com/national/2013/04/
        what-is-false-flag-attack-boston-bombing/64260/

85   **what they considered to be an insufficient amount
        of blood:** http://www.huffingtonpost.co.uk/2013/
        05/23/woolwich-attack-bizarre-conspiracy-theories-
        claim-incident-hoax-video_n_3324962.html

86   "Official narratives are inherently suspect": http://www.globalresearch.ca/what-the-charlie-hebdo-execution-video-really-shows/5424505

86   the hurricane was conjured up out of thin air: http://montalk.net/conspiracy/142/haarp-earthquakes-and-hurricanes

86   "by sheer weight of numbers, there are bound to be some apparent inconsistencies": Wood, M. J. (2013). Has the internet been good for conspiracy theorising? *PsyPAG Quarterly, 88*(3), 31–34.

87   "these are conclusions lying in wait for friendly 'facts'": Jane, E. A., & Fleming, C. (2014). *Modern Conspiracy*. Bloomsbury Academic. p. 96.

88   "several YouTube videos purport to point out": Wood, M. J. (2013). Has the internet been good for conspiracy theorising? *PsyPAG Quarterly, 88*(3), 31–34.

88   "Scratch the surface of a middle-aged 9/11 Truther": Kay, J. (2011). *Among the Truthers*. Harper. p. 51.

88   "People say I see conspiracies everywhere," Icke said: http://www.newstatesman.com/lifestyle/2014/11/psycho-lizards-saturn-godlike-genius-david-icke

91   Americans . . . more likely to think vaccines are unsafe: Lewandowsky, S., Oberauer, K., & Gignac, G. E. (2013). NASA faked the moon landing—therefore, (climate) science is a hoax: An anatomy of the motivated rejection of science. *Psychological Science, 24*(5), 622–633.

91   Londoners ... assassination of Martin Luther King Jr. was the result of conspiracy: Swami, V., Coles, R., Stieger, S., Pietschnig, J., Furnham, A., Rehim, S., & Voracek, M. (2011). Conspiracist ideation in Britain and Austria: Evidence of a monological belief system and associations between individual psychological differences and real-world and fictitious conspiracy theories. *British Journal of Psychology, 102*, 443–463.

91   Austrians . . . more likely to believe that AIDS was manufactured: Stieger, S., Gumhalter, N., Tran, U. S., Voracek, M., & Swami, V. (2013). Girl in the cellar: A repeated cross-sectional investigation of belief in conspiracy theories about the kidnapping of Natascha Kampusch. *Frontiers in Personality Science and Individual Differences, 4*(297).

91   **Germans . . . more likely to believe that the New
        World Order is planning to take over:** Swami, V.,
        Pietschnig, J., Tran, U. S., Nader, I. W., Stieger, S., &
        Voracek, M. (2013). Lunar lies: The impact of
        informational framing and individual differences in
        shaping conspiracist beliefs about the moon landings.
        Applied Cognitive Psychology, 27(1), 71–80.

91   **visitors of climate science blogs . . . Princess
        Diana got whacked by the British royal family:**
        Lewandowsky, S., Oberauer, K., & Gignac, G. E. (2013).
        NASA faked the moon landing—therefore, (climate)
        science is a hoax: An anatomy of the motivated rejection
        of science. *Psychological Science, 24*(5), 622–633.

91   **concocted a theory about the popular energy
        drink Red Bull:** Swami, V., Coles, R., Stieger, S.,
        Pietschnig, J., Furnham, A., Rehim, S., & Voracek, M.
        (2011). Conspiracist ideation in Britain and Austria:
        Evidence of a monological belief system and associations
        between individual psychological differences and real-
        world and fictitious conspiracy theories. *British Journal of
        Psychology, 102,* 443–463.

92   **One possible answer, suggested by sociologist
        Ted Goertzel:** Goertzel, T. (1994). Belief in conspiracy
        theories. *Political Psychology, 15*(4), 731–742.

93   **presenting the Diana conspiracy theory as
        plausible . . . opened the door:** Jolley, D., & Douglas,
        K. M. (2014). The social consequences of conspiracism:
        Exposure to conspiracy theories decreases intentions to
        engage in politics and to reduce one's carbon footprint.
        British Journal of Psychology, 105(1), 35–56.

93   **take al-Qaeda mastermind Osama Bin Laden
        "dead or alive":** http://abcnews.go.com/US/
        story?id=92483

93   **"After a firefight," the President later announced:**
        http://www.whitehouse.gov/blog/2011/05/02/osama-bin-
        laden-dead

93–4   **some people think Bin Laden may have had
        Marfan syndrome:** http://www.infowars.com/top-
        doctor-confirms-bin-laden-had-marfan-syndrome/

94 **Glenn Beck ... suggested that Bin Laden may have actually been captured alive:** http://archives.politicusa.com/2011/05/03/glenn-beck-bin-laden.html

94 **Mahmoud Ahmadinejad ... Bin Laden was living safe and sound in Washington, D.C.:** http://www.theguardian.com/world/richard-adams-blog/2010/may/05/osama-bin-laden-mahmoud-ahmadinejad-washington

94 **a paper by psychologists Mike Wood and Karen Douglas:** Wood, M. J., Douglas, K. M., & Sutton, R. M. (2012). Dead and alive: Beliefs in contradictory conspiracy theories. *Social Psychological and Personality Science, 3*(6), 767–773.

95 **Wood and Douglas ran another study looking at belief in ... theories about Princess Diana:** Ibid.

95 **the U.S. government had advanced knowledge . . . actively planned the whole thing:** Swami, V., Chamorro-Premuzic, T., & Furnham, A. (2010). Unanswered questions: A preliminary investigation of personality and individual difference predictors of 9/11 conspiracist beliefs. *Applied Cognitive Psychology, 24*, 749–761.

95 **Thabo Mbeki . . . or that it doesn't even exist:** Nattrass, N. (2012). *The AIDS Conspiracy.* Columbia University Press. p. 105.

95 **"when Washington and Baghdad get along, Tehran sees a conspiracy":** Pipes, D. (1996). *The Hidden Hand.* St. Martin's Press. p. 228.

97 **Joe Uscinski and Joseph Parent point to the restaurant chain Godfather's Pizza:** Uscinski, J. E., & Parent, J. M. (2014). *American Conspiracy Theories.* Oxford University Press. p. 75.

Chapter 5: The Paranoid Fringe

Page

99 **a 1927 short story by the lesser-known Huxley:** Huxley, J. (1927). *The Tissue-Culture King.* http://www.revolutionsf.com/fiction/tissue/

100   **Missouri taxpayers became unwitting accomplices in a foil-based jibe:** http://www.columbiatribune.com/blogs/between_party_lines/state-to-buy-tinfoil-hats-to-combat-common-core/article_3ad6e6c8-998e-11e3-b353-001a4bcf6878.html

100   **The Common Core opponents ... got payback:** http://www.missourinet.com/2014/02/20/tin-foil-hats-line-item-leads-to-tin-foil-covered-desk-for-representative/

101   **"almost nondescript" ... "the odd, the warped, the zanies":** Wakeman, J. (1975). *World Authors: 1950–1970.* Wilson. p. 659.

101   **Hofstadter published an essay in** *Harper's Magazine*: Hofstadter, R. (1964). The paranoid style in American politics. *Harper's Magazine, 229*(1374), 77–86.

102   **Goertzel and a team of researchers telephoned hundreds of Jerseyites:** Goertzel, T. (1994). Belief in conspiracy theories. *Political Psychology, 15*(4), 731–742.

103   **Other scientists have . . . found the same trend:** Darwin, H., Neave, N., & Holmes, J. (2011). Belief in conspiracy theories. The role of paranormal belief, paranoid ideation and schizotypy. *Personality and Individual Differences, 50*(8), 1289–1293.

103   **hostile:** Abalakina-Paap, M., Stephan, W. G., Craig, T., & Gregory, W. L. (1999). Beliefs in conspiracies. *Political Psychology, 20*(3), 637–647.

103   **cynical:** Parsons, S., Simmons, W., Shinhoster, F., & Kilburn, J. (1999). A test of the grapevine: An empirical examination of conspiracy theories among African Americans. *Sociological Spectrum, 19*(2), 201–222.

103   **defiant of authority:** Swami, V., Chamorro-Premuzic, T., & Furnham, A. (2010). Unanswered questions: A preliminary investigation of personality and individual difference predictors of 9/11 conspiracist beliefs. *Applied Cognitive Psychology, 24,* 749–761.

103   **anxious:** Swami, V., Pietschnig, J., Tran, U. S., Nader, I. W., Stieger, S., & Voracek, M. (2013). Lunar lies: The impact of informational framing and individual differences in shaping conspiracist beliefs about the moon landings. *Applied Cognitive Psychology, 27*(1), 71–80.

103 **disagreeable:** Bruder, M., Haffke, P., Neave, N., Nouripanah, N., & Imhoff, R. (2013). Measuring individual differences in generic beliefs in conspiracy theories across cultures: Conspiracy Mentality Questionnaire. *Frontiers in Personality Science and Individual Differences, 4, 225.*

103 **people ... debunking conspiracy theories were sometimes more hostile:** Wood, M. J., & Douglas, K. M. (2013). "What about building 7?" A social psychological study of online discussion of 9/11 conspiracy theories. *Frontiers in Personality Science and Individual Differences, 4*(409).

104 **a team of researchers at New Mexico State University found the same trend:** Abalakina-Paap, M., Stephan, W. G., Craig, T., & Gregory, W. L. (1999). Beliefs in conspiracies. *Political Psychology, 20*(3), 637–647.

104 **In 2006, another team of researchers:** Stempel, C., Hargrove, T., & Stempel, G. H. (2007). Media use, social structure, and belief in 9/11 conspiracy theories. *Journalism & Mass Communication Quarterly, 84*(2), 353–372.

104 **recent opinion polls show similar demographic differences:** http://www.aei.org/files/2013/11/06/-public-opinion-on-conspiracy-theories_181649218739.pdf

104 **The establishment ... "has conspiracy theories of its own":** http://www.slate.com/articles/technology/future_tense/2014/05/conspiracy_theory_research_can_t_be_believed.html

105 **"on the contrary, no one is more truly satisfied of this fact than I am":** quoted in Jane, E. A., & Fleming, C. (2014). *Modern Conspiracy.* Bloomsbury Academic. p. 98.

105 **presidents Theodore Roosevelt and Woodrow Wilson both felt there was a hidden hand behind government:** Ibid. pp. 98–99.

105 **"U.S. officials asserted":** deHaven-Smith, L. (2013). *Conspiracy Theory in America.* University of Texas Press. p. 8.

105 **President Obama . . . accused "secretive oil billionaires" of distorting his record:** http://www.politico.com/politico44/2012/04/obama-campaign-secretive-oil-billionaires-funding-121757.html

105 **While slaves in antebellum America . . . manipulated into violent revolt by Northern abolitionists:** Walker, J. (2013). *The United States of Paranoia.* Harper. p. 8.

105 "cunningly devised and powerfully organized cabal": Ibid. p. 12.

105 a vast, insidious conspiracy to kidnap innocent young white women: http://reason.com/archives/2008/03/13/the-white-slavery-panic

106 a wave of "satanic panic" swept Britain and the United States: Walker, J. (2013). *The United States of Paranoia*. Harper. pp. 213–216.

106 he later upgraded his estimate to a "considerable" minority: Hofstadter, R. (2008). *The Paranoid Style in American Politics and Other Essays*. Vintage. p. 39.

107 "any one conspiracy theory is an accurate bellwether": Uscinski, J. E., & Parent, J. M. (2014). *American Conspiracy Theories*. Oxford University Press. p. 56.

107 63 percent of the American public believed at least one political conspiracy theory: http://www.scribd.com/doc/120815791/Fairleigh-Dickinson-poll-on-conspiracy-theories

107 half of Americans believed at least one medical conspiracy theory: Oliver, J. E., & Wood, T. (2014). Medical conspiracy theories and health behaviors in the United States. *JAMA Internal Medicine, 174*(5), 817.

108 debilitating paranoia is only ever experienced by a tiny fraction of the population: Freeman, D. (2007). Suspicious minds: The psychology of persecutory delusions. *Clinical Psychology Review, 27*(4), 425–457.

109 Freeman and a team of colleagues asked more than a thousand perfectly ordinary college students: Freeman, D., Garety, P. A., Bebbington, P. E., Smith, B., Rollinson, R., Fowler, D., ... Dunn, G. (2005). Psychological investigation of the structure of paranoia in a non-clinical population. *The British Journal of Psychiatry, 186*(5), 427–435.

110 Psychologists call this *compensatory control*: Kay, A. C., Whitson, J. A., Gaucher, D., & Galinsky, A. D. (2009). Compensatory control: Achieving order through the mind, our institutions, and the heavens. *Current Directions in Psychological Science, 18*(5), 264–268.

111 threats to our sense of control spur our brain into action: Kramer, R. M. (1998). Paranoid cognition in social

systems: Thinking and acting in the shadow of doubt. *Personality and Social Psychology Review, 2*(4), 251–75.

111 **Daniel Sullivan and colleagues . . . designed a series of experiments:** Sullivan, D., Landau, M. J., & Rothschild, Z. K. (2010). An existential function of enemyship: Evidence that people attribute influence to personal and political enemies to compensate for threats to control. *Journal of Personality and Social Psychology, 98*(3), 434–449.

111 **Jennifer Whitson and Adam Galinsky came up with another approach:** Whitson, J. A., & Galinsky, A. D. (2008). Lacking control increases illusory pattern perception. *Science, 322*(5898), 115–117.

112 **Monika Grzesiak-Feldman had students answer questions ... fifteen minutes before an important exam:** Grzesiak-Feldman, M. (2013). The effect of high-anxiety situations on conspiracy thinking. *Current Psychology, 32*(1), 100–118.

112 **people who are new somewhere, are under intense scrutiny, or are in a relatively lowly position:** Kramer, R. M. (1998). Paranoid cognition in social systems: Thinking and acting in the shadow of doubt. *Personality and Social Psychology Review, 2*(4), 251–75.

112 **"walking down certain streets can feel threatening":** Freeman, D. (2007). Suspicious minds: The psychology of persecutory delusions. *Clinical Psychology Review, 27*(4), 425–457.

112 **Roderick Kramer calls this "prudent paranoia":** Kramer, R. M. (2002). When paranoia makes sense. *Harvard Business Review, 80*(7), 62–69.

113 **psychologist Kelley Main and her colleagues put shoppers in this situation:** Main, K. J., Dahl, D. W., & Darke, P. R. (2007). Deliberative and Automatic Bases of Suspicion: Empirical Evidence of the Sinister Attribution Error. *Journal of Consumer Psychology, 17*(1), 59–69.

114 **a study carried out in the Deep South state of Louisiana:** Parsons, S., Simmons, W., Shinhoster, F., & Kilburn, J. (1999). A test of the grapevine: An empirical examination of conspiracy theories among African Americans. *Sociological Spectrum, 19*(2), 201–222.

114 **"the life blood of the African-American community"**: quoted in Pipes, D. (1997). *Conspiracy.* The Free Press. p. 2.

115 **"bizarre as it may seem to most people"**: http://www.nytimes.com/1992/05/12/opinion/the-aids-plot-against-blacks.html

115 **white slave owners controlled their slaves' reproductive rights:** http://nationalhumanitiescenter.org/pds/maai/enslavement/text6/masterslavesexualabuse.pdf

115 **slaves and "free persons of color" were disproportionately used for medical experiments:** Savitt, T. L. (1982). The Use of Blacks for Medical Experimentation and Demonstration in the Old South. *The Journal of Southern History, 48*(3), 331–348.

115 **lynchings were a form of public entertainment:** Lightweis-Goff, J. (2011). *Blood at the Root.* SUNY Press. p. 164.

115 **"expose, disrupt, misdirect, discredit, or otherwise neutralize"**: Cunningham, D. (2003). The patterning of repression: FBI counterintelligence and the new left. *Social Forces, 82*(1), 209–240.

115 **a Department of Justice investigation found evidence of deliberate racial discrimination:** http://www.justice.gov/opa/pr/justice-department-announces-findings-two-civil-rights-investigations-ferguson-missouri

115 **the Tuskegee Study of Untreated Syphilis in the Negro Male:** Thomas, S. B., & Quinn, S. C. (1991). The Tuskegee syphilis study, 1932 to 1972. *American Journal of Public Health, 81*(11), 1498–1505.

117 **Black people who know about the Tuskegee study are more likely to believe AIDS conspiracy theories:** Mays, V. M., Coles, C. N., & Cochran, S. D. (2012). Is there a legacy of the U.S. public health syphilis study at Tuskegee in HIV/AIDS-related beliefs among heterosexual African Americans and Latinos? *Ethics & Behavior, 22*(6), 461–471.

117 **African Americans are more likely . . . to feel that they could be used as guinea pigs:** Ibid.

117 **"Labeling a view paranoid has now become an empty circular description"**: Knight, P. (2013). *Conspiracy Culture.* Routledge. p. 15.

118 **scientists at the Massachusetts Institute of Technology finally put the idea to the test:** http://web.archive.org/web/20100708230258/http://people.csail.mit.edu/rahimi/helmet

Chapter 6: I Want to Believe

Page

119 **The group, it has been pointed out, always meets in a five-star hotel:** Ronson, J. (2001). *Them.* Simon & Schuster. p. 112.

119 **"a forum for informal discussions about . . . major issues facing the world":** http://www.bilderberg-meetings.org/index.php

121 **"Conspiracy theories are easy ways of telling complicated stories":** Olmsted, K. S. (2011). *Real Enemies.* Oxford University Press. p. 6.

121 **"the most serious problems of a nation's existence could be definitively solved":** Segel, B. W. (1995) *A Lie and a Libel.* University of Nebraska Press. pp. 52–53.

121 **"in essence . . . [conspiracy theories] are simple":** Billig, M. (1978). *Fascists.* Academic Press. p. 315.

121 **"myriad troublemakers become a single hostile force":** Pipes, D. (1996). *The Hidden Hand.* St. Martin's Press. p. 229.

121 **"to causes extremely complicated":** Mounier, J. (1801). *On the Influence Attributed to Philosophers, Freemasons, and to the Illuminati.* W. & C. Spilsbury. p. v.

121 **"This ridiculously simplistic philosophy of history":** Segel, B. W. (1995) *A Lie and a Libel.* University of Nebraska Press. p. 52.

122 **psychologists . . . gave students a stack of questionnaires designed to assess their thinking style:** Abalakina-Paap, M., Stephan, W. G., Craig, T., & Gregory, W. L. (1999). Beliefs in conspiracies. *Political Psychology, 20*(3), 637–647.

122 **"at the same time, conspiracy theorists find solace in complexity":** Pipes, D. (1996). *The Hidden Hand.* St. Martin's Press. p. 229.

123 'the higher someone scores in openness: e.g. Swami, V., Pietschnig, J., Tran, U. S., Nader, I. W., Stieger, S., & Voracek, M. (2013). Lunar lies: The impact of informational framing and individual differences in shaping conspiracist beliefs about the moon landings. *Applied Cognitive Psychology, 27*(1), 71–80.

123 a few other studies have failed to reproduce it: e.g. Imhoff, R., & Bruder, M. (2014). Speaking (un-)truth to power. *European Journal of Personality, 28*(1), 25–43.

123 Lobato and colleagues barraged college students with claims representing three varieties of weirdness: Lobato, E., Mendoza, J., Sims, V., & Chin, M. (2014). Examining the relationship between conspiracy theories, paranormal beliefs, and pseudoscience acceptance among a university population. *Applied Cognitive Psychology, 28*(5), 617–625.

124 conspiracy theorists tend to be a relatively superstitious bunch: e.g. Stieger, S., Gumhalter, N., Tran, U. S., Voracek, M., & Swami, V. (2013). Girl in the cellar: A repeated cross-sectional investigation of belief in conspiracy theories about the kidnapping of Natascha Kampusch. *Frontiers in Personality Science and Individual Differences, 4*(297).

124 more likely to suspect that there's a grain of truth to urban legends: Drinkwater, K., Dagnall, N., & Parker, A. (2012). Reality testing, conspiracy theories and paranormal beliefs. *Journal of Parapsychology, 76*(1), 57–77.

124 they're more likely to reject mainstream science and its products: Lewandowsky, S., Gignac, G. E., & Oberauer, K. (2013). The Role of Conspiracist Ideation and Worldviews in Predicting Rejection of Science. *PLOS ONE, 8*(10), e75637.

124 Someone who believes conspiracy theories is more likely to be into New Age spiritualism: e.g. Swami, V., Pietschnig, J., Tran, U. S., Nader, I. W., Stieger, S., & Voracek, M. (2013). Lunar lies: The impact of informational framing and individual differences in shaping conspiracist beliefs about the moon landings. *Applied Cognitive Psychology, 27*(1), 71–80.

125 sociologist Colin Campbell wrote about . . . the *cultic milieu*: Campbell, C. (2002). The cult, the cultic milieu and secularization. In Kaplan, J., & Lööw, H. (Eds.). *The Cultic Milieu*. Rowman & Littlefield. pp. 12–25.

126 As Nicoli Nattrass notes, a brief foray into the world of conspiracy theories: Nattrass, N. (2012). *The AIDS Conspiracy*. Columbia University Press. p. 108.

126 conspiracist logic ... *requires* the believer to dive ever deeper into the cultic milieu: Barkun, M. (1997). *Religion and the Racist Right*. UNC Press. p. 258.

127 "the values of the Enlightenment have been abandoned": Wheen, F. (2005). *How Mumbo-Jumbo Conquered the World*. PublicAffairs. p. 8.

127 "irrationalists": Ibid. p. 118.

127 Jonathan Kay declares 9/11 Truthers "enemies" of the Enlightenment: Kay, J. (2011). *Among the Truthers*. HarperCollins. p. xxiii.

127 "portrays conspiracists and their mumbo-jumbo-ing ilk": Jane, E. A., & Fleming, C. (2014). *Modern Conspiracy*. Bloomsbury Academic. p. 60.

127 British philosopher John Locke wrote, "we should make greater progress": http://metaphors.iath.virginia.edu/metaphors/24309

127 Immanuel Kant ... suggested as a motto, "*Sapere aude!*": http://www.columbia.edu/acis/ets/CCREAD/etscc/kant.html

128 "Far from representing a rupture from rationalism," Jane and Fleming write: Jane, E. A., & Fleming, C. (2014). *Modern Conspiracy*. Bloomsbury Academic. p. 132.

128 Jane and Fleming point out that the great Enlightenment thinkers . . . relatively slim encyclopedia: Ibid. pp. 53–70.

129 There is fun to be had cracking codes . . . Susan Harding and Kathleen Stewart point out: quoted in Nattrass, N. (2012). *The AIDS Conspiracy*. Columbia University Press. p. 107.

129 "a member of the avant-garde": Hofstadter, R. (1964). The paranoid style in American politics. *Harper's Magazine*, 229(1374), 77–86.

129 "a passport to a thrilling alternative universe": Thompson, D. (2008). *Counterknowledge*. Atlantic Books. p. 10.

130 When psychologist Rebecca Lawson set people this challenge: Lawson, R. (2006). The science of cycology:

Failures to understand how everyday objects work. *Memory & Cognition, 34*(8), 1667–1675.

131 **Leon Rozenblit and his adviser Frank Keil asked people how well they thought they understood devices:** Rozenblit, L., & Keil, F. (2002). The misunderstood limits of folk science: an illusion of explanatory depth. *Cognitive Science, 26*(5), 521–562.

132 **People overrate their understanding of simple physics problems:** http://www.psmag.com/health-and-behavior/confident-idiots-92793

132 **and more complex natural phenomena:** Rozenblit, L., & Keil, F. (2002). The misunderstood limits of folk science: an illusion of explanatory depth. *Cognitive Science, 26*(5), 521–562.

132 **People think they understand the law:** Kim, P. T. (1997). Bargaining with imperfect information: A study of worker perceptions of legal protection in an at-will world. *Cornell Law Review, 83*, 105–160.

132 **and political policies better than they really do:** Fernbach, P. M., Rogers, T., Fox, C. R., & Sloman, S. A. (2013). Political extremism is supported by an illusion of understanding. *Psychological Science, 24*(6), 939–946.

132 **As Dan Simons and Chris Chabris note:** Chabris, C., & Simons, D. (2011). *The Invisible Gorilla.* Broadway Paperbacks. pp. 123–127.

132 **Offering people cold hard cash . . . forcing them to justify their assessment:** Ehrlinger, J., Johnson, K., Banner, M., Dunning, D., & Kruger, J. (2008). Why the unskilled are unaware. *Organizational Behavior and Human Decision Processes, 105*, 98–121.

132 **"As we know, there are known knowns":** http://www.defense.gov/transcripts/transcript.aspx?transcriptid=2636

133 **"An ignorant mind is precisely not a spotless, empty vessel":** http://www.psmag.com/navigation/health-and-behavior/confident-idiots-92793/

134 **"vivid, blueprint-like" sense of how things work:** Rozenblit, L., & Keil, F. (2002). The misunderstood limits

of folk science: an illusion of explanatory depth. *Cognitive Science*, *26*(5), 522.

134   **to paraphrase Chris Chabris and Dan Simons:** Chabris, C., & Simons, D. (2011). *The Invisible Gorilla.* Broadway Paperbacks. p. 122.

135   **"One might think that opinions about an esoteric technology":** http://www.psmag.com/navigation/health-and-behavior/confident-idiots-92793/

135   **the majority of people . . . little or nothing about nanotech:** http://www.nanotechproject.org/file_download/files/HartReport.pdf

135   **In another study . . . entirely nonjudgmental description of the technology:** Kahan, D. M., Braman, D., Slovic, P., Gastil, J., & Cohen, G. L. (2008). The future of nanotechnology risk perceptions. Harvard Law School Program on Risk Regulation Research Paper, (08–24). http://papers.ssrn.com/sol3/papers.cfm?abstract_id=1089230

136   **On September 18, 2007, Jenny McCarthy appeared on the *Oprah Winfrey Show*:** http://blogs.plos.org/thepanicvirus/2013/07/15/a-jenny-mccarthy-reader-pt-2-jenny-brings-her-anti-vaccine-views-to-oprah/

136   **Christine Maggiore was a businesswoman from Chicago:** Nattrass, N. (2012). *The AIDS Conspiracy.* Columbia University Press. pp. 118–127.

138   **In the words of one festival-goer, "Well it's basically exposing the truth":** This interview was conducted by my colleague Mike Wood. Full recordings of all the interviews Mike and I recorded at the Bilderberg Fringe Festival are available at http://conspiracypsychology.com/2013/06/14/a-trip-to-the-bilderberg-fringe-festival/

138   **"To admit that we know less than we think we do":** Jane, E. A., & Fleming, C. (2014). *Modern Conspiracy.* Bloomsbury Academic. p. 138.

Chapter 7: (Official) Stories

Page

139   **"Well, I like daydreaming more than listening to *you*":** Icke, D. "Remember Who You Are," live at Wembley Arena, 28 October 2012.

139   **he felt increasingly dissatisfied with life:** Icke, D.
      (1993). *In the Light of Experience.* Warner. p. 106.

139   **Here's the story of reality as David Icke tells it:** My
      understanding was gleaned mainly from attending a
      day-long lecture of Icke's; Icke, D. "Remember Who You
      Are," live at Wembley Arena, 28 October 2012.

140   **"have become the poster child for the fringiest of
      fringe thought":** Collins, L. (2012). *Bullspotting.*
      Prometheus Books. p. 38.

141   **Once Upon a Time . . . :** This section, and the synopses
      of *The Epic of Gilgamesh*, *Beowulf,* and *Jaws*, were informed
      primarily by Booker, C. (2004). *The Seven Basic Plots.*
      Continuum. pp. 1–2, 21–50.

143   **"the ancient river beds along which our psychic
      current naturally flows":** Ibid. p. 12.

143   **Even children as young as three understand story
      structure:** Mancuso, J. C. (1986). The acquisition and use
      of narrative grammar structure. In Sarbin, T. R. (Ed.).
      Narrative psychology. Praeger. pp. 91–110.

143   **According to author Ronald B. Tobias, there are
      twenty:** Tobias, R. B. (2012). *20 Master Plots.* Writer's
      Digest Books.

143   **Screenwriter Blake Snyder ... ten essential genres:**
      Snyder, B. (2005). *Save the Cat.* Michael Wiese
      Productions.

143   **Joseph Campbell . . . there is but a single grand
      "monomyth":** Campbell, J. (1968). *The Hero with A
      Thousand Faces.* Princeton University Press.

143   **"you can package plot any number of ways":**
      Tobias, R. B. (2012). *20 Master Plots.* Writer's Digest
      Books. p. 11.

143   **In a classic 1973 study, a team of researchers led by
      Robert Cialdini:** Cialdini, R. B., Borden, R. J.,
      Thorne, A., Walker, M. R., Freeman, S., & Sloan, L. R.
      (1976). Basking in reflected glory: Three (football) field
      studies. *Journal of Personality and Social Psychology, 34*(3),
      366–375.

145   **J. K. Rowling . . . gave him glasses as a constant
      reminder of his vulnerability:** http://www.accio-
      quote.org/articles/2000/1200-readersdigest-boquet.htm

145 A month before the 2004 Summer Olympics, Vandello and colleagues: Vandello, J. A., Goldschmied, N. P., & Richards, D. A. R. (2007). The Appeal of the Underdog. *Personality and Social Psychology Bulletin, 33*(12), 1603–1616.

145–6 "from swimmer Michael Phelps's single mother": Paharia, N., Keinan, A., Avery, J., & Schor, J. B. (2011). The Underdog Effect. *Journal of Consumer Research, 37*(5), 775–790.

146 "brewery Samuel Adams reminds us how small it is": Keinan, A., Avery, J., & Paharia, N. (2010). Capitalizing on the Underdog Effect. *Harvard Business Review, 88*(11), 32–32.

146 political candidates often clamor to play down their credentials: Paharia, N., Keinan, A., Avery, J., & Schor, J. B. (2011). The Underdog Effect. *Journal of Consumer Research, 37*(5), 775–790.

146 "When your name is Barack Obama": quoted in Goldschmied, N., & Vandello, J. A. (2009). The advantage of disadvantage: Underdogs in the political arena. *Basic and Applied Social Psychology, 31*(1), 24–31.

146 "Absolutely . . . I'm used to being an underdog.": http://abcnews.go.com/Politics/president-obama-calls-underdog-2012-race-white-house/story?id=14656286

146 "It's always a good thing to be seen as the underdog": http://abcnews.go.com/blogs/politics/2012/02/romney-says-hes-fine-being-the-underdog/

146 we see a political candidate as more likable: Goldschmied, N., & Vandello, J. A. (2009). The advantage of disadvantage: Underdogs in the political arena. *Basic and Applied Social Psychology, 31*(1), 24–31.

146 Vandello asked students how they felt about Israel and Palestine: Vandello, J. A., Goldschmied, N. P., & Richards, D. A. R. (2007). The appeal of the underdog. *Personality and Social Psychology Bulletin, 33*(12), 1603–1616.

147 we even see an underdog applicant as more physically attractive: Michniewicz, K. S., & Vandello, J. A. (2013). The attractive underdog. *Journal of Social and Personal Relationships, 30*(7), 942–952.

147   **Scott Allison and colleagues demonstrated just how deeply ingrained it is:** Kim, J., Allison, S. T., Eylon, D., Goethals, G. R., Markus, M. J., Hindle, S. M., & McGuire, H. A. (2008). Rooting for (and then abandoning) the underdog. *Journal of Applied Social Psychology, 38*(10), 2550–2573.

147–8   **Viewers were "visibly agitated":** Allison, S. T., & Goethals, G. R. (2011). *Heroes.* Oxford University Press. p. 130.

148   **"If it is not clear to you this far, let me be frank about it":** http://adventuresinautism.blogspot.com/2011/01/our-book-vaccine-epidemic-how-corporate.html

148   **"Dr. Wakefield did something I wish all doctors would do":** http://www.huffingtonpost.com/jenny-mccarthy/vaccine-autism-debate_b_806857.html

149   **two awards for "Courage in Science":** One was from Barbara Loe Fisher's National Vaccine Information Center, presented in 2000. The other was from the group AutismOne, presented in 2009.

149   **AIDS denialists have a renegade scientist in Peter Duesberg:** Nattrass, N. (2012). *The AIDS Conspiracy.* Columbia University Press. pp. 110–115.

149   **"mainly the ones that are used by the gays":** http://www.duesberg.com/articles/bginterview.html

149   **A biography on Duesberg's website:** http://www.duesberg.com/index.html

149   **"Bush administration had its dirty hand in forcing BYU to 'shut up' its professor":** http://www.rense.com/general69/discred.htm

150   **"Telling the truth can be a scary thing sometimes":** Extract from *JFK* movie screenplay, by Oliver Stone and Zachary Sklar; directed by Oliver Stone screenplay © 1991 Warner Bros. Inc., Regency Enterprises V.O.F. & Le Studio Canal+.

150   **Christopher Booker notes that archetypal heroes act not to further their own interests:** Booker, C. (2004). *The Seven Basic Plots.* Continuum. p. 245.

151   **"shaped by inspirational archetypal stories of odds overcome":** Goldschmied, N. P., & Vandello,

J. A. (2012). The future is bright. *Basic and Applied Social Psychology, 34*(1), 34–43.

152   **archetypal monsters represent . . . the very worst elements of the human psyche:** Booker, C. (2004). *The Seven Basic Plots*. Continuum. pp. 555–556.

152   **Comic book villains, Baumeister points out:** Pizarro, D. A., & Baumeister, R. (2013). Superhero comics as moral pornography. In Rosenberg, R. (Ed.). *Our Superheroes, Ourselves*. Oxford University Press. pp. 19–36.

152   **Around half of players reject an offer that strays too far from an even split:** Sanfey, A. G., Rilling, J. K., Aronson, J. A., Nystrom, L. E., & Cohen, J. D. (2003). The neural basis of economic decision-making in the ultimatum game. *Science, 300*(5626), 1755–1758.

152   **When people play the game inside brain imaging scanners:** Ibid.

152   **constantly monitoring their behavior, even their fleeting facial expressions:** Ames, D. R., & Johar, G. V. (2009). I'll know what you're like when I see how you feel. *Psychological Science, 20*(5), 586–593.

152   **According to psychologist Robin Dunbar, a primary function of gossip:** Dunbar, R. I. M. (2004). Gossip in evolutionary perspective. *Review of General Psychology, 8*(2), 100–110.

153   **the quality we value above all else is a person's trustworthiness:** Fiske, S. T., Cuddy, A. J. C., & Glick, P. (2007). Universal dimensions of social cognition: Warmth and competence. *Trends in Cognitive Sciences, 11*(2), 77–83.

153   **"It became established doctrine," Trilling explains:** Trilling, L. (1972). *Sincerity and Authenticity*. Harvard University Press. p. 14.

153   **Every one of the ten top-grossing films of 2014 had a villain of some form; five were comic book adaptations:** http://www.boxofficemojo.com/yearly/chart/?view2=worldwide&yr=2014&p=.htm

154   **what Baumeister calls "the myth of pure evil":** Baumeister, R. F. (1996). *Evil*. W. H. Freeman and Company. pp. 60–96.

154   **the monsters next door:** http://newsfeed.time.com/
        2013/01/16/a-history-of-violence-gun-control-in-the-
        pages-of-time/slide/may-3-1999-the-monsters-
        next-door/

154   **hatred of "our freedoms":** http://www.
        washingtonpost.com/wp-srv/nation/specials/attacked/
        transcripts/bushaddress_092001.html

154   **"The myth of pure evil depicts malicious, alien
        forces":** Baumeister, R. F. (1996). *Evil.* W. H. Freeman
        and Company. p. 89.

154   **"The world often breaks down in us against them":**
        Ibid. p. 62.

154-5   **psychologists Eric Oliver and Thomas Wood
        surveyed one thousand Americans:** Oliver, J. E., &
        Wood, T. J. (2014). Conspiracy Theories and the
        Paranoid Style(s) of Mass Opinion. *American Journal of
        Political Science, 58*(4), 952–966.

155   **"Where regular politicians highlight problems":**
        Uscinski, J. E., & Parent, J. M. (2014). *American Conspiracy
        Theories.* Oxford University Press. p. 146.

155   **compared the world as portrayed in conspiracy
        theories to a theatrical performance:** Moscovici, S.
        (1987). The conspiracy mentality. In Graumann, C. F.,
        & Moscovici, S. (Eds.). *Changing Conceptions of Conspiracy.*
        Springer. pp. 154–155.

156   **"If you go see something like *Captain America*, it's
        almost like I co-wrote the thing":** *The Alex Jones
        Show,* 13 February 2015. http://www.infowars.com/listen-
        to-the-radio-show-archive/

156   **"He explained to me that he considered all those
        people . . . guilty by association":** http://law2.
        umkc.edu/faculty/projects/ftrials/mcveigh/mcveigh
        account.html

156   **"We are all tellers of tales":** McAdams, D. (1993).
        The Stories We Live By. Guilford Press. p. 11.

156   **"No history is without an implicit sense of
        protagonists and antagonists":** Patterson, M., &
        Monroe, K. R. (1998). Narrative in political science.
        Annual Review of Political Science, 1(1), 315.

157   **stories lure us in, bypassing our critical faculties:**
        Green, M. C., & Brock, T. C. (2000). The role of
        transportation in the persuasiveness of public narratives.
        Journal of Personality and Social Psychology, 79(5), 701–721.

157   **the story . . . of Christopher Columbus's discovery
        of the Americas:** Brock, T. C., Strange, J. J., & Green,
        M. C. (2002). Power beyond reckoning. In Green, M.
        C., Strange, J. J., & Brock, T. C. (Eds.). *Narrative Impact.*
        Lawrence Erlbaum Associates. pp. 1–16.

158   **"They told me twenty-five years ago":** http://www.
        newstatesman.com/lifestyle/2014/11/psycho-lizards-
        saturn-godlike-genius-david-icke

Chapter 8: Connect the Dots

Page

159   **Abraham Zapruder almost didn't make the film
        at all:** Bugliosi, V. (2007). *Reclaiming History.* W. W.
        Norton & Company. pp. 452–454.

159   **Zapruder never looked through the lens of a
        camera   again:**   http://www.theguardian.com/
        film/2013/nov/14/abraham-zapruder-film-kennedy-
        killing-parkland

160   **Richard Sprague and Robert Cutler published a
        detailed   diagram:**   http://www.ratical.org/ratville/
        JFK/TUM.html

162   **the Kanizsa triangle:** Kanizsa, G. (1976). Subjective
        contours. *Scientific American,* 234(4), 48–52.

163   **roughly the size of our thumbnail at arm's length:**
        Storr, W. (2014). *The Unpersuadables.* The Overlook Press.
        p. 79.

163   **around a third of our cortex is devoted to vision:**
        Eagleman, D. (2011). *Incognito.* Pantheon. pp. 22–23.

164   **Schiaparelli persuaded the Italian government to
        invest in a cutting-edge telescope:** Bernagozzi, A.,
        Testa, A., & Tucci, P. (2004). Observing Mars with
        Schiaparelli's telescope. *Third European Workshop on
        Exo-Astrobiology,* 545, 157–158.

164–5   **an intricate network of long, dark, straight lines
        crisscrossing the Martian surface:** Maria Lane,

K. D. (2006). Mapping the Mars canal mania. *Imago Mundi, 58*(2), 198–211.

165   **Vincenzo Cerulli ... first suggested the lines might be an illusion:** http://www.mbennardo.com/blog/2012/01/setting-the-record-straight-on-the-canals-of-mars/

165   **As Carl Sagan noted, the canals were undoubtedly of intelligent origin:** Sagan, C. (1985). *Cosmos.* Ballantine Books. p. 90.

165   **eagle-eyed anomaly hunters have spotted . . . and a petrified iguana:** http://www.huffingtonpost.com/2013/11/19/aliens-on-mars-photos_n_4303447.html

166   **Hill called out "Hey, we want to take your picture!":** Bugliosi, V. (2007). *Reclaiming History.* W. W. Norton & Company. p. 41.

166   **"There, visible on the printed page":** Lifton, D. S. (1980). *Best Evidence.* Macmillan. p. 9.

167   **As far as forensic analysts can tell:** http://www.skeptic.com/reading_room/jfk-conspiracy-theories-at-50-how-the-skeptics-got-it-wrong-and-why-it-matters/

167   **"It became evident that those who were already in disagreement":** Lifton, D. S. (1980). *Best Evidence.* Macmillan. p. 11.

168   **around eight out of ten people confidently answer "two":** Park, H., & Reder, L. M. (2004). Moses illusion. In Pohl, R. F. (Ed.). *Cognitive Illusions.* Psychology Press. pp. 275–292.

169   **journalist Sarah Koenig tells a story from her early days as a reporter:** http://www.thisamericanlife.org/radio-archives/episode/489/transcript

170   **A coincidence by itself . . . an unfinished tax return:** Beitman, B. D. (2009). Brains seek patterns in coincidences. *Psychiatric Annals, 39*(5), 255–264.

172   **as Michael Luo explained:** Luo, M. (2004). "For Exercise in New York Futility, Push Button," *The New York Times,* 27 February 2004.

172   **"In most elevators":** Paumgarten, N., "Up and then Down," *The New Yorker,* 21 April 2008.

172 **throw the whole rhythm off kilter:** This explanation was offered by a guest on an episode of the podcast *Radiolab*. http://www.radiolab.org/story/buttons-not-buttons/

172 **the button simply broke or was never wired up in the first place:** http://www.straightdope.com/columns/read/595/do-close-door-buttons-on-elevators-ever-actually-work

173 **"As a young mother":** Messenger, S. (2008). Jason's journey. In Dorey, M., Lindberg, S., & Messenger, S. (Eds.). *Vaccination Roulette*. Australian Vaccination Network. pp. 85–88.

174 **Messenger wrote an essay describing her first-born son:** Ibid.

174 **"I trusted without questioning . . . no longer smiled":** Fisher, B. (2004). "In the wake of vaccines," *Mothering*, September/October 2004.

175 **Chris "was diagnosed with minimal brain damage":** http://www.nvic.org/nvic-vaccine-news/november-2014/vaccination--defending-your-right-to-know-and-free.aspx

175 **more than half of American parents:** Freed, G. L., Clark, S. J., Butchart, A. T., Singer, D. C., & Davis, M. M. (2010). Parental vaccine safety concerns in 2009. *Pediatrics, 125*(4), 654–659.

175 **The Internet is an important source of information for many parents:** Jones, A. M., Omer, S. B., Bednarczyk, R. A., Halsey, N. A., Moulton, L. H., & Salmon, D. A. (2012). Parents' source of vaccine information and impact on vaccine attitudes, beliefs, and nonmedical exemptions. *Advances in Preventive Medicine, 2012,* e932741.

176 **Anna Kata undertook a comprehensive survey:** Kata, A. (2010). A postmodern Pandora's box. *Vaccine, 28*(7), 1709–1716.

176 **one fifth of American adults:** Oliver, J. E., & Wood, T. (2014). Medical Conspiracy Theories and Health Behaviors in the United States. *JAMA Internal Medicine, 174*(5), 817.

176 **Emma Jane and Chris Fleming trawled through Icke's opus:** Jane, E. A., & Fleming, C. (2014). *Modern Conspiracy*. Bloomsbury Academic. p. 116.

177 **"anomalous and ominous. He dangles around history's neck like a fetish":** Updike, J., "Notes and Comments," *The New Yorker*, 9 December 1967.

177 "Did the umbrella ... contain a gun or a weapon of any sort?": http://history-matters.com/archive/jfk/hsca/reportvols/vol4/pdf/HSCA_Vol4_0925_7_Witt.pdf

Chapter 9: Intention Seekers

Page

181 More than half of a thousand Americans: http://www.cnn.com/2014/05/06/world/asia/malaysia-airlines-plane-poll/

181 "Airplanes don't just disappear": http://chedet.cc/?p=1361

181 On July 2, 1937, Amelia Earhart departed Lae, New Guinea: Gillespie, R. (2011). *Finding Amelia*. Naval Institute Press.

182 In a 2012 survey: Swami, V., & Furnham, A. (2012). Examining conspiracist beliefs about the disappearance of Amelia Earhart. *The Journal of General Psychology, 139*(4), 244–259.

182 On April 10, 2010, a Polish Air Force jet crashed: http://www.thedailybeast.com/articles/2014/04/11/did-putin-blow-up-the-whole-polish-government-in-2010-a-second-look.html

183 Dorothy Hunt ... was among the passengers killed onboard: http://listverse.com/2014/07/23/10-controversial-air-crash-conspiracy-theories/

183 the NTSB rebutted the evidence and declined to reopen the investigation: http://www.forbes.com/sites/johngoglia/2014/07/02/ntsb-denies-twa-800-conspiracy-theory-petition/

184 Daniel Kahneman offers this as an example: Kahneman, D. (2011). *Thinking, Fast and Slow*. Farrar, Straus and Giroux. pp. 19–20.

185 imagine if I could ... turn your intention detector off: Baldwin, D. A., & Baird, J. A. (2001). Discerning intentions in dynamic human action. *Trends in Cognitive Sciences, 5*(4), 171–178.

186 there might be no society at all: Bering, J. M. (2002). The existential theory of mind. *Review of General Psychology, 6*(1), 3–24.

187 **Fritz Heider and ... Marianne Simmel:** Heider, F., & Simmel, M. (1944). An experimental study of apparent behavior. *American Journal of Psychology, 57,* 243–259.

188 **If you ask a four-year-old why somebody yawned or sneezed:** Smith, M. C. (1978). Cognizing the Behavior Stream. *Child Development, 49*(3), 736–743.

188–9 **children even sometimes make up intentions for their own involuntary actions:** Montgomery, D. E., & Lightner, M. (2004). Children's developing understanding of differences between their own intentional action and passive movement. *British Journal of Developmental Psychology, 22*(3), 417–438.

189 **Children see the natural world as having some underlying purpose:** Kelemen, D. (1999). Why are rocks pointy? Children's preference for teleological explanations of the natural world. *Developmental Psychology, 35*(6), 1440–1452.

189 **According to psychologist Evelyn Rosset:** Rosset, E. (2008). It's no accident: Our bias for intentional explanations. *Cognition, 108*(3), 771–780.

190 **it's up and running within the first few months of life:** Luo, Y. (2011). Three-month-old infants attribute goals to a non-human agent. *Developmental Science, 14*(2), 453–460.

190 **In one study, she found that all it takes is a few drinks:** Bègue, L., Bushman, B. J., Giancola, P. R., Subra, B., & Rosset, E. (2010). "There is no such thing as an accident," especially when people are drunk. *Personality and Social Psychology Bulletin, 36*(10), 1301–1304.

190 **"hundreds of duels in the hard-drinking eighteenth century":** Landale, J. (2005). *The Last Duel.* Canongate. p. 250.

190 **"intoxication is not a full excuse for insult, but it will greatly palliate":** Holland, B. (2004). *Gentlemen's Blood.* Bloomsbury. p. 151.

190 **questions like whether "the sun radiates heat because warmth nurtures life":** Kelemen, D., & Rosset, E. (2009). The human function compunction: Teleological explanation in adults. *Cognition, 111*(1), 138–143.

190   **even science professors at Ivy League universities:** Kelemen, D., Rottman, J., & Seston, R. (2013). Professional physical scientists display tenacious teleological tendencies: Purpose-based reasoning as a cognitive default. *Journal of Experimental Psychology: General, 142*(4), 1074–1083.

191   **The findings demonstrate, Rosset argues:** Rosset, E., & Rottman, J. (2014). The big "whoops!" in the study of intentional behavior: An appeal for a new framework in understanding human actions. *Journal of Cognition and Culture, 14,* 27–39.

191   **even people who don't believe in God can't help wondering what the meaning of life is:** Bering, J. (2011). *The Belief Instinct.* W. W. Norton. p. 46.

192   **the way you interpret innocuous sentences:** Brotherton, R., & French, C. C. (2015). Intention seekers: Conspiracy theories and biased attributions of intentionality. *PLOS ONE. 10*(5). e0124125.

193   **Karen Douglas . . . had more than five hundred people watch the little shapes dance around their computer screens:** Email to the author from Professor Karen Douglas. Douglas, K., Sutton, R. M., Callan, M. J., Dawtry, R. J., & Harvey, A. J. (2016). Someone is pulling the strings: Hypersensitive agency detection and belief in conspiracy theories. *Thinking And Reasoning.* (In press.)

195   **Any time you see someone do something, your brain runs a quick simulation:** Blakemore, S. J., & Decety, J. (2001). From the perception of action to the understanding of intention. *Nature Reviews Neuroscience, 2*(8), 561–567.

196   **Daniel Katz and Floyd Allport provided one of the first demonstrations:** Katz, D., & Allport, F. H. (1931). Students' Attitudes. Craftsman Press.

196   **If you think of yourself as outgoing you'll probably guess there are a lot more fellow extroverts:** Ross, L., Greene, D., & House, P. (1977). The "false consensus effect": An egocentric bias in social perception and attribution processes. *Journal of Experimental Social Psychology, 13*(3), 279–301.

196   **if you support federal funding for space exploration . . . long distance phone calls:** Ibid.

196 **When you're cold you think other people are bothered by the cold:** O'Brien, E., & Ellsworth, P. C. (2012). More than skin deep visceral states aare not projected onto dissimilar others. *Psychological Science, 23*(4), 391–396.

196 **researchers tried to persuade students to walk around campus wearing a large advertising sandwich board:** Ross, L., Greene, D., & House, P. (1977). The "false consensus effect": An egocentric bias in social perception and attribution processes. *Journal of Experimental Social Psychology, 13*(3), 279–301.

197 **Karen Douglas and Robbie Sutton asked . . . would you have faked the moon landing:** Douglas, K. M., & Sutton, R. M. (2011). Does it take one to know one? Endorsement of conspiracy theories is influenced by personal willingness to conspire. *British Journal of Social Psychology, 50*(3), 544–552.

198 **The pope, they feared, was planning to declare war on Protestants:** Wade, W. C. (1998). *The Fiery Cross.* Oxford University Press. p. 226.

198 **as Richard Hofstadter pointed out, the Klan increasingly became a parody of its enemy:** Hofstadter, R. (1964). The paranoid style in American politics. *Harper's Magazine, 229*(1374), 77–86.

198 **"not only did the Klan oppose a resolution condemning secret societies":** http://www.danielpipes. org/220/plotters

198 **when individual conspiracy theorists find themselves in positions of power, their actions are often conspiratorial:** Popper, K. R. (2006). The conspiracy theory of society. In Coady, D. (Ed.). *Conspiracy Theories: The Philosophical Debate* (pp. 13–15). Burlington, VT: Ashgate.

198 **Nixon was concerned with "Jews, the intellectual elite":** Uscinski, J. E., & Parent, J. M. (2014). *American Conspiracy Theories.* Oxford University Press. p. 15.

198 **"we're up against an enemy, a conspiracy. They're using any means":** Kutler, S. (1999). *Abuse of Power.* Simon and Schuster. p. 8.

199 **Daniel Pipes notes that many Middle Eastern heads of state suffer chronic paranoia:** Pipes, D. (1996). *The Hidden Hand.* St. Martin's Press. p. 25.

199 "I have read the Protocols of the Elders of Zion,"
     Hitler is reported to have said: Rauschning, H. (1940).
     The Voice of Destruction. Pelican. p. 238.

199 "what begins as a search for subversives ends in
     subversion": http://www.danielpipes.org/220/plotters

199 As Douglas and Sutton put it . . . *it takes one to know
     one*: Douglas, K. M., & Sutton, R. M. (2011). Does it take
     one to know one? Endorsement of conspiracy theories is
     influenced by personal willingness to conspire. *British
     Journal of Social Psychology, 50*(3), 544–552.

199 Preston Bost and Stephen Prunier presented
     participants: Bost, P. R., Prunier, S. G., & Piper, A. J. (2010).
     Relations of familiarity with reasoning strategies in
     conspiracy beliefs. *Psychological Reports, 107*(2), 593–602.

200 the world we live in is "not really one made of
     rocks, trees and physical objects": Haidt, J. (2006).
     The Happiness Hypothesis. Basic Books. p. 76.

200 "a tree branch that another person drops on you":
     Waytz, A., Gray, K., Epley, N., & Wegner, D. M. (2010).
     Causes and consequences of mind perception. *Trends in
     Cognitive Sciences, 14*(8), 383–388.

Chapter 10: Proportion Distortion

Page

203 eighty-two *specific* individuals: http://www.dallasnews.
     com/news/jfk50/explore/20131116-jfk-conspiracy-
     theories-abound-despite-a-lack-of-evidence.ece

203 surveys over the years: http://www.gallup.com/poll/
     165893/majority-believe-jfk-killed-conspiracy.aspx

204 a sizable minority elsewhere: https://yougov.co.uk/
     news/2012/07/04/we-ask-conspiracy-theories/

204 Unusual Suspects: Except where otherwise noted, the
     information in this section is from Bugliosi, V. (2007).
     Reclaiming History. W. W. Norton & Company.

205 "in the final analysis, it is their [the South
     Vietnamese's] war": http://www.presidency.ucsb.edu/
     ws/?pid=9388

207 according to one theory, the killer was . . . Jacqueline
     Bouvier Kennedy: http://jackieiskillerqueen.blogspot.com/

207 **"two federal investigations of breathtaking scope":** Melley, T. (2000). *Empire of Conspiracy*. Cornell University Press. p. 134.

208 **"Jodie, I would abandon this idea of getting Reagan in a second":** http://www.theatlantic.com/politics/archive/2011/03/picture-of-the-day-john-hinckleys-letter-to-jodie-foster/73223/

209 **the Manhattan Project:** http://energy.gov/management/office-management/operational-management/history/manhattan-project

210 **In 1967, sociologist James Henslin:** Henslin, J. M. (1967). Craps and magic. *American Journal of Sociology, 73*(3), 316–330.

211 **When big things happen to us, we look for big causes:** Lupfer, M. B., & Layman, E. (1996). Invoking naturalistic and religious attributions: A case of applying the availability heuristic? The representativeness heuristic? *Social Cognition, 14*(1), 55–76.

212 **According to studies by political scientist Richard Lebow:** Tetlock, P. E., & Lebow, R. N. (2001). Poking counterfactual holes in covering laws: Cognitive styles and historical reasoning. *American Political Science Review, 95*(4), 829–844.

212 **Linguists point out that saying words like** *little*: Ramachandran, V. S., & Hubbard, E. M. (2001). Synaesthesia: A window into perception, thought and language. *Journal of Consciousness Studies, 8*(12), 3–34.

213 **A 2010 study . . . involved stories about an explosion in an airplane's cargo hold:** Ebel-Lam, A. P., Fabrigar, L. R., MacDonald, T. K., & Jones, S. (2010). Balancing causes and consequences: The magnitude-matching principle in explanations for complex social events. *Basic & Applied Social Psychology, 32*(4), 348–359.

214 **stories in which a disease outbreak swept through an accounting office:** Ibid.

214 **a story about an outbreak of an unusual disease among the animals at a zoo:** LeBoeuf, R. A., & Norton, M. I. (2012). Consequence-cause matching: Looking to the consequences of events to infer their causes. *Journal of Consumer Research, 39*(1), 128–141.

214 **people prefer extreme causes for extreme crimes:** McClure, J., Lalljee, M., & Jaspars, J. (1991). Explanations of extreme and moderate events. *Journal of Research in Personality, 25*(2), 146–166.

214 **for particularly destructive natural disasters:** Spina, R. R., Ji, L.-J., Guo, T., Zhang, Z., Li, Y., & Fabrigar, L. R. (2010). Cultural differences in the representativeness heuristic: Expecting a correspondence in magnitude between cause and effect. *Personality and Social Psychology Bulletin, 36*(5), 583–597.

214 **and for devastating accidents:** Ebel-Lam, A. P., Fabrigar, L. R., MacDonald, T. K., & Jones, S. (2010). Balancing causes and consequences: The magnitude-matching principle in explanations for complex social events. *Basic & Applied Social Psychology, 32*(4), 348–359.

215 **a 1979 study by psychologists Clark McCauley and Susan Jacques:** McCauley, C., & Jacques, S. (1979). Popularity of conspiracy theories of presidential assassination: A Bayesian analysis. *Journal of Personality and Social Psychology, 37*(5), 637–644.

215 **Patrick Leman and Marco Cinnirella repeated the experiment:** Leman, P. J., & Cinnirella, M. (2007). A major event has a major cause: Evidence for the role of heuristics in reasoning about conspiracy theories. *Social Psychological Review, 9,* 18–28.

216 **assassination scenarios in which the causal chain ... was even further removed:** LeBoeuf, R. A., & Norton, M. I. (2012). Consequence-cause matching: Looking to the consequences of events to infer their causes. *Journal of Consumer Research, 39*(1), 128–141.

217 **One more experiment . . . explicitly mentioned JFK.:** Ibid.

217 **The most extensive investigation . . . by Dutch researchers Jan-Willem van Prooijen and Eric van Dijk:** Van Prooijen, J.-W., & van Dijk, E. (2014). When consequence size predicts belief in conspiracy theories: The moderating role of perspective taking. *Journal of Experimental Social Psychology, 55,* 63–73.

219 **Tom Bethell captured the incongruity of President Kennedy's death:** Bethell, T. "The Quote Circuit," *The Washington Monthly*, December 1975, pp. 34–39.

219   **Assassination buff Kenneth Rahn put it similarly:** quoted in Bugliosi, V. (2007). *Reclaiming History*. W. W. Norton & Company. p. xxvii.

Chapter 11: I *Knew* It

Page

221   **Steve Regan sets the scene:** Interview with the author, 7 March 2014.

224   **In the 1960s, psychologist Peter Wason invented a game:** Wason, P. C. (1960). On the failure to eliminate hypotheses in a conceptual task. *Quarterly Journal of Experimental Psychology, 12*(3), 129–140.

225   **The news sources we read:** Adamic, L. A., & Glance, N. (2005). The political blogosphere and the 2004 US election: divided they blog. In *Proceedings of the 3rd international workshop on Link discovery*. ACM. pp. 36–43.

225   **the links we click:** Schweiger, S., Oeberst, A., & Cress, U. (2014). Confirmation bias in web-based search: A randomized online study on the effects of expert information and social tags on information search and evaluation. *Journal of Medical Internet Research*, 16(3), 369–382.

225   **the views of people we surround ourselves with:** Lazarsfeld, P. F., & Merton, R. K. (1954). Friendship as social process: A substantive and methodological analysis. In Berger, M., Abel, T., & Page, C. H. (Eds.). *Freedom and control in modern society*. Octagon Books. pp. 18–66. Park, J., Konana, P., Gu, B., Kumar, A., & Raghunathan, R. (2013). Information Valuation and Confirmation Bias in Virtual Communities: Evidence from Stock Message Boards. *Information Systems Research*, 24(4), 1050–1067.

225   **political scientists Charles Taber and Milton Lodge gave people a choice of essays:** Taber, C. S., & Lodge, M. (2006). Motivated Skepticism in the Evaluation of Political Beliefs. *American Journal of Political Science, 50*(3), 755–769.

226   **MacDougall came up with a game he called "The Paranoid Style":** http://www.robmacdougall.org/blog/2010/05/pastplay/

226   **"conspiracy of vampires that has pulled the strings behind the world":** Ibid.

226   **they quickly spun a yarn ... get humans used to living in the dark:** Email to the author from Professor Rob MacDougall.

226   **MacDougall notes that people got hung up on the 'rules' of vampirism, like avoiding sunlight:** Ibid.

226–7 **"People are creative, and good at finding patterns . . . a powerful and even uncanny feeling":** Ibid.

227   **"The evidence starts to line up all too well with the fantasy you have just concocted":** http://www. robmacdougall.org/blog/2010/05/pastplay/

227   **Here are just a few of the things Icke looks for:** Icke, D. "Remember Who You Are," live at Wembley Arena, 28 October 2012.

228   **At 3 a.m. on November 9, 1979 . . . a dreaded phone call:** http://nsarchive.gwu.edu/nukevault/ebb371/

229   **Plous designed a . . . set of studies:** Plous, S. (1991). Biases in the assimilation of technological breakdowns: Do accidents make us safer? *Journal of Applied Social Psychology, 21*(13), 1058–1082.

229   **a real 1981 government inquiry into nuclear warning system malfunctions:** *Failures of the North American Aerospace Defense Command's (NORAD) attack warning system: hearings before a subcommittee of the Committee on Government Operations, May 19 and 20, 1981.* pp. 131–133.

230   **"the only thing that stops a bad guy with a gun":** http://www.nytimes.com/2012/12/22/us/nra-calls-for-armed-guards-at-schools.html

230   **people on opposite sides of the political aisle:** Sigelman, L., & Sigelman, C. K. (1984). Judgments of the Carter-Reagan debate: The eyes of the beholders. *Public Opinion Quarterly, 48*(3), 624–628.

230   **For football fans . . . which team a penalty call favors:** Hastorf, A. H., & Cantril, H. (1954). They saw a game: A case study. *The Journal of Abnormal and Social Psychology, 49*(1), 129–134.

230   **psychologists looked at students' opinions about . . . the death penalty:** Lord, C. G., Ross, L., & Lepper, M. R. (1979). Biased assimilation and attitude polarization: The effects of prior theories on subsequently considered evidence. *Journal of Personality and Social Psychology, 37,* 2098–2109.

230 **studies have focused on peoples' prejudices about homosexuality:** Munro, G. D., & Ditto, P. H. (1997). Biased assimilation, attitude polarization, and affect in reactions to stereotype-relevant scientific information. *Personality and Social Psychology Bulletin, 23*(6), 636–653.

230 **Affirmative action:** Miller, A. G., McHoskey, J. W., Bane, C. M., & Dowd, T. G. (1993). The attitude polarization phenomenon: Role of response measure, attitude extremity, and behavioral consequences of reported attitude change. *Journal of Personality and Social Psychology, 64*(4), 561–574.

230 **tax policies:** Kosnik, L.-R. D. (2008). Refusing to budge: A confirmatory bias in decision making? *Mind and Society, 7*(2), 193–214.

230 **abortion:** Baron, J. (1995). Myside bias in thinking about abortion. *Thinking & Reasoning, 1*(3), 221–235.

230 **gun control laws:** Taber, C. S., & Lodge, M. (2006). Motivated skepticism in the evaluation of political beliefs. *American Journal of Political Science, 50*(3), 755–769.

230 **secondhand smoke:** Stanovich, K. E., & West, R. F. (2007). Natural myside bias is independent of cognitive ability. *Thinking & Reasoning, 13*(3), 225–247.

230 **belief in psychic powers:** Jones, W. H., & Russell, D. (1980). The selective processing of belief disconfirming information. *European Journal of Social Psychology, 10*(3), 309–312.

230 **McHoskey wanted to know:** McHoskey, J. W. (1995). Case closed? On the John F. Kennedy assassination: Biased assimilation of evidence and attitude polarization. *Basic and Applied Social Psychology, 17*(3), 395–409.

232 **Adam Berinski . . . tracked the number of people who believed the rumors:** https://today.yougov.com/news/2012/02/03/birthers-are-back/

233 **In August 2009, Palin sparked fears:** https://www.facebook.com/notes/sarah-palin/statementon-the-current-health-care-debate/113851103434

233 **one week after Palin's Facebook post, almost nine out of ten Americans:** http://www.people-press.org/2009/08/20/health-care-reform-closely-followed-much-discussed/

233   **By August 2012:** http://ap-gfkpoll.com/uncategorized/our-latest-poll-findings-12

233   **more certain that the death panels are a coming reality:** Nyhan, B., Reifler, J., & Ubel, P. A. (2013). The hazards of correcting myths about health care reform. *Medical Care, 51*(2), 127–132.

234   **more suspicious that he is a secret Muslim:** http://www.dartmouth.edu/~nyhan/obama-muslim.pdf

234   **less willing to vaccinate their children:** Nyhan, B., Reifler, J., Richey, S., & Freed, G. L. (2014). Effective messages in vaccine promotion: A randomized trial. *Pediatrics, 133*(4), e835–e842.

234   **more resistant to policies designed to curtail climate change:** Hart, P. S., & Nisbet, E. C. (2012). Boomerang effects in science communication: How motivated reasoning and identity cues amplify opinion polarization about climate mitigation policies. *Communication Research, 39*(6), 701–723.

234   **a subtle smiley face in the signature of the official who signed the certificate:** http://www.wnd.com/2011/05/301329/

235   **Jonathan Chait . . . argued that the political right:** Chait, J. (2008). *The Big Con.* Houghton Mifflin Harcourt. p. 242.

235   **Arthur Goldwag, writing for the progressive website Salon.com:** http://www.salon.com/2013/10/20/conspiracy_theories_explain_the_right/

235   **A 2008 article in the conservative *Washington Times*:** http://www.washingtontimes.com/news/2008/mar/06/celebrity-911-conspiracy-club-still-growing/

236   **"routinely spawns conspiracy theories in a febrile delirium":** Uscinski, J. E., & Parent, J. M. (2014). *American Conspiracy Theories.* Oxford University Press. p. 87.

236   **people to the left and right . . . are just as conspiracy-minded as each other:** Ibid. pp. 87–94.

237   **people who were the biggest fans of Palin were the most resistant:** Nyhan, B., Reifler, J., & Ubel, P. A. (2013). The hazards of correcting myths about health care reform. *Medical Care, 51*(2), 127–132.

237   **psychologist John Bullock showed people a news story:** http://www.nyu.edu/gsas/dept/politics/seminars/bullock_f06.pdf

237 **The Birther rumor was first floated in spring 2008 by Democrats:** http://www.politico.com/news/stories/0411/53563.html

237 **Obama wrote, "in distilled form":** Obama, B. (2006). *The Audacity of Hope.* Three Rivers Press. p. 24.

238 **Nickerson had some harsh words for the bias:** Nickerson, R. S. (1998). Confirmation bias: A ubiquitous phenomenon in many guises. *Review of General Psychology, 2*(2), 175–220.

239 **no relationship between intelligence and . . . confirmation bias:** Toplak, M. E., & Stanovich, K. E. (2003). Associations between myside bias on an informal reasoning task and amount of post-secondary education. *Applied Cognitive Psychology, 17*(7), 851–860.

239 **the most scientifically and politically knowledgeable . . . most polarized:** Nyhan, B., Reifler, J., & Ubel, P. A. (2013). The hazards of correcting myths about health care reform. *Medical Care, 51*(2), 127–132.

239 **"so convenient a thing is it to be a reasonable creature":** http://www.ushistory.org/franklin/autobiography/page18.htm

Epilogue: Only Human

242 **echoes of conspiracism in the thinking of conspiracy theory debunkers:** Jane, E. A., & Fleming, C. (2014). *Modern Conspiracy.* Bloomsbury Academic. pp. 78–79.

242 **"a demonized and reified entity":** Knight, P. (2013). *Conspiracy Culture.* Routledge. p. 7.

242 **"the Internet has created shadow armies":** Aaronovitch, D. (2010). *Voodoo Histories.* Riverhead. p. 232.

242 **"manages to insinuate itself in the most alert and intelligent minds":** Pipes, D. (1997). *Conspiracy.* The Free Press. p. 49.

242 **Jonathan Kay worries that the Age of Reason is in imminent peril:** Kay, J. (2011). *Among the Truthers.* HarperCollins. p. xxiii.

242 **"mumbo-jumbo" . . . "conquered the world":** Wheen, F. (2005). *How Mumbo-Jumbo Conquered the World.* PublicAffairs.

Permissions

Figures from "Lacking Control Increases Illusory Pattern Perception" (2008), Supporting Online Material, by Jennifer A. Whitson and Adam D. Galinsky used by permission of the authors

Excerpt from *Measles—A Dangerous Illness* (1986) by Roald Dahl used by permission of David Higham Associates

Ann Davis, a woman with smallpox and horns growing out of her head. Stipple engraving by T. Woolnoth, 1806. Wellcome Library, London

Figure from "Rooting for (and Then Abandoning) the Underdog" (2008) by JongHan Kim, Scott T. Allison, Dafna Eylon, George R. Goethals, Michael J. Markus, Sheila M. Hindle, and Heather A. McGuire used by permission of the authors

Robert Cutler's Diagram, "The Piece" (1975) used by permission of R.B. Cutler Collection, Baylor Collections of Political Materials, W.R. Poage Legislative Library, Baylor University, Waco Texas

Kanizsa triangle, Wikimedia Commons

Offended girl used by permission of Radharani/Shutterstock.com

Acknowledgments

For giving up their time to talk or email with me about various topics covered in the book, thanks to Professor Rob MacDougall, Professor Roderick Kramer, Professor Brendan Nyhan, Dr. Chris Street, Dr. Sean Mitchell, Dr. Frenk van Harreveld, Professor Jennifer Whitson, and Professor Charles Taber. Special thanks to Steve Regan for telling me his story, which provides the introduction to Chapter 11, not once but twice. For reading early drafts, thanks to Laurence, Lindsay, Rob, and Chris. For my career in conspiracy psychology, thanks to Professor Karen Douglas, and to Professor Chris French, who guided me through a master's and a doctorate. I couldn't have had a better mentor and friend.

Thanks to everyone at Bloomsbury who worked to make this book what it is, particularly my editor, Jacqueline Johnson. And finally, this book would not have happened if not for Jim Martin, the contagiously enthusiastic commissioning editor at Bloomsbury Sigma, who contacted me out of the blue and suggested I write a book. Given the slightly mysterious circumstances, I thought it best to check whether I was becoming a pawn in some conspiracy. Just before submitting this manuscript, I shot off an email: "Are you some kind of government disinformation agent, Illuminati spy, and/or shape-shifting lizard?" I signed my name in green type—an old "freemen on the land" trick to make the email legally binding. Jim's reply came almost immediately. I opened it with bated breath. "I'm away from the office until the 28th of April. I'll get back to you then." (He has since denied the allegations.)

Index